Whole-Scale Change Toolkit

Whole-Scale Change Toolkit

Tools for Unleashing the Magic in Organizations

Dannemiller Tyson Associates

BERRETT-KOEHLER PUBLISHERS, INC.
San Francisco

Berrett-Koehler Publishers, Inc.
450 Sansome Street, Suite 1200
San Francisco, CA 94111-3320
Tel: (415) 288-0260   Fax: (415) 362-2512   www.bkconnection.com

ORDERING INFORMATION

Quantity sales. Special discounts are available on quantity purchases by corporations, associations, and others. For details, contact the "Special Sales Department" at the Berrett-Koehler address above.

Individual sales. Berrett-Koehler publications are available through most bookstores. They can also be ordered direct from Berrett-Koehler: Tel: (800) 929-2929; Fax: (802) 864-7626; www.bkconnection.com

Orders for college textbook/course adoption use. Please contact Berrett-Koehler: Tel: (800) 929-2929; Fax: (802) 864-7626.

Orders by U.S. trade bookstores and wholesalers. Please contact Publishers Group West, 1700 Fourth Street, Berkeley, CA 94710. Tel: (510) 528-1444; Fax: (510) 528-3444.

Printed in the United States of America
Printed on acid-free and recycled paper that is composed of 85% recovered fiber, including 15% post consumer waste.

Library of Congress Cataloging-in-Publication Data

Whole-scale change toolkit : tools for unleashing the magic
in organizations / by Dannemiller Tyson Associates
        p. cm.
    ISBN 1-57675-089-2
    1. Organizational change. I. Dannemiller Tyson Associates.
II. Whole-scale change. III. Title.
    HD58.8 .W496 2000
    658.4'06 — dc21

First Edition
    05   04   03   02   01   00   10 9 8 7 6 5 4 3 2 1

The authors of this book are fifteen consultants,
all partners of Dannemiller Tyson Associates in 1999
when we wrote this book together.
Using our own Whole-Scale processes,
we worked as a community,
one-brain and one-heart,
to bring our best wisdom to
the content of this book.

Kathleen D. Dannemiller, Paul D. Tolchinsky, Ronald Loup, Sylvia James,
Jeff Belanger, Albert B. Blixt, Kathryn Church, Mary Eggers, Allen B. Gates,
Leigh M. Hennen, Henry Johnson, Lorri E. Johnson,
Stas Kazmierski, Ron Koller, Jim McNeil

Special thanks to Christine Valenza for her creative graphic contributions.

WHOLE-SCALE CHANGE TOOLKIT:

CONTENTS

PREFACE   vii.

OVERVIEW   WHAT IS WHOLE SCALE?   1

CHAPTER 1   DISCOVERING THE MAGIC OF WHOLE SCALE   3

CHAPTER 2   DESIGNING A WHOLE SCALE MEETING   13

CHAPTER 3   FACILITING: WHOLE SCALE STYLE   49

CHAPTER 4   LOGISTICS: FREEING PARTICIPANTS TO BE CREATIVE   61

CHAPTER 5   DESIGN POSSIBILITY: A GENERIC THREE DAY EVENT PLAN   89

CHAPTER 6   ALTERNATIVE DESIGNS: POSSIBILITIES FOR SPECIFIC WHOLE-SCALE
INTERVENTIONS   161

CHAPTER 7   THE REAL SECRETS OF WHOLE SCALE   281

ABOUT DANNEMILLER TYSON ASSOCIATES   290

ABOUT THE AUTHORS   291

PREFACE

A number of years ago I was in the change business at Ford Motor Company, and I was in trouble. I had been working for two years at the manufacturing plant level--all 80 of them, in fact--as part of the team that had helped bring the turnaround in the company's approach to building a quality car once more. I was in trouble because I had been handed a big challenge by a very far-seeing Executive Vice President: what was the breakthrough in managing whole businesses which would match the breakthrough in managing the quality efforts?

The executive, Tom Page, and I had agreed that his ten businesses--good size businesses, with revenues (in 1981 dollars) of between $1 and $3 billion, would take part in a very large change effort over the next year. One business at a time would be challenged with changing the way it was managed. Despite the staggering losses still being registered in the car industry, Tom agreed to the (then) audacious notion that one to two hundred managers at a time would turn over their headquarters and field operations to third level subordinates, so that the entire intact management structure of the business could go off-site for a week and re-think their world.

He had given me, as a change agent, an incredible opportunity. And I had blown it.

I was in trouble for two reasons. First, although I had seen with my own eyes the fact that managing people differently lay at the heart of the quality story (by then a story told over and over in the national press), I wasn't seeing the simple parallel with managing executives differently if you wanted a better business outcome.

Second, although I knew that nobody had TRAINED quality into anyone at Ford, I was just dumb enough to have spent a fair amount of time and money with a group of well-meaning but patronizing college professors whose aim and approach it was to TRAIN fully adult executives into being better business managers. Oh, they could talk about business cases, and ROI, and the elements of strategy, but what it boiled down to was that the professors had the answers and the "students" were going to be taught them.

I knew I was in trouble when, halfway through the second day of a pilot of this business seminar, the room (made up of change agent colleagues from all over Ford) was awash in pity--pity for me, pity for the professors, and most of all, pity for any poor fool who might actually have to sit through a whole week of this approach. (By then, of course, the grapevine at Ford being what it was at all companies, the word was out: this seminar STUNK.)

What all of us (except the professors) in that room were suddenly seeing was that Ford had been taught on the plant floor--by its employees--what the zestful pursuit of new learning looked like. And it certainly wasn't done this way. We were used to a far messier, but more potent, way. We were used to debate, and challenge, identifying what we could improve first, and what would have the highest leverage and pay-off. We were used to teams calling for specialists if they thought their expertise was needed. Nobody thought they were being trained; they thought they were calling for briefings as they pursued a significant competitive advantage.
Why had I thought that executives had lower standards?

My insight about what I should have done, or at least what I should have looked for when it came to the right approach for these ten business teams, arrived before the second day of the pilot was over. But it was a little late. I had a calendar that said we were to go live in 4 weeks with the first 130-person management team, with the nine other businesses following in a brisk line-up. I hadn't endured Day 3 of my own pilot, but I already knew I had no program.

I also realized that I didn't have a model for what I was doing with these executives, as I had on the plant level. And I didn't have the right professors. In fact, I now knew I didn't want professors. In my Ford network, I knew a few people who had worked with groups larger than 20, but they were used to working on the plant floor and they thought I was crazy to be working with an intact power structure. I knew consultants who had helped in the Quality movement, but they only operated with small groups.

I didn't know who I needed-- I just knew they needed to help me design something for a whole business at a time, something that would startle and delight and compel executives the way the manufacturing world of Ford had come to embrace the pursuit of quality. I needed lion tamers with a sense of humor. And heart.

Enter the team who got me out of trouble: Kathie Dannemiller, Chuck Tyson, Alan Davenport, and Bruce Gibb. They hadn't worked together as a group before, but they came together as if in answer to a prayer…(actually, in answer to me describing to a friend my need for lion tamers as opposed to professors!)

Over the next three weeks, they designed an event, which went on to become memorable in the lives of the participating executives, and ultimately changed the Ford Motor Company. Business after business went through the five day session, and whether it was the Plastics group, or Electronics, or Casting, or Land Development, or Aerospace, the executives came to understand each other, the competition, and the market for the first time as a coherent, energized, focused and aligned whole. They created strategic plans that they all owned, and they amended management structures and decision-making practices to support their goals.

This is not the place to recount the next twenty years of Ford Motor Company history; nor mine, even though we had a glorious time improving ourselves. But I will say that the seminar became famous internally; the President of Ford, Donald Petersen, decided to use its principles extensively when the company embarked on its global strategy. He continued doing so after becoming Chairman of Ford, as did his successors. Much of the publicity given to Ford's turnaround centered on the people issues which began to be understood and practiced in these sessions.

The book that you are reading contains the principles and practices which those marvelous consultants designed for Ford, and then took so successfully to many other companies, I continued to use them throughout my career at Ford, and now find them invaluable wherever I consult. What I like about Dannemiller-Tyson as a firm is their passion to pass on what has been discovered to work; sharing breakthroughs generously has always been their hallmark. May your experience with these methods bring you the success and satisfaction that it has brought me.

Nancy Lloyd Badore
Executive Director
Ford Motor Company (ret.)
Dearborn, Michigan
November, 1999

OVERVIEW: WHAT IS WHOLE-SCALE?

For the last two decades, we at Dannemiller Tyson Associates (DTA) have dedicated our lives to "thinking globally and acting locally" in an organizational sense. We have based our work with both public and private organizations—large and small—on our beliefs about thinking "whole system" as we help organizations change.

What our clients and we have learned in the last two decades is that no single person can know the answers that will lead an organization to success. The best answer comes when all the people speak and thus develop their own wisdom about what they need to do together. When an organization is able to combine its multiple voices, it discovers THE answer and ensures that its people will unite around a lasting system-wide commitment. It unleashes the magic within.

One of the best descriptions of whole system change in action is a story taken from *The Renewal Factor* by Robert Waterman_(Bantam Books, 1987), where Waterman illustrates the process through a change story of Sanwa Bank:

> ...In 1969, I was part of a team working with the Sanwa Bank in Japan, now one of the largest banks in the world. It's unusual for anyone from the outside, let alone a foreign consulting firm, to be working with a Japanese company. Fortunately, the problem–a substantial market share loss–was fairly easy to solve intellectually. After a few months we were ready to go to the board to present our analysis and recommendations.
>
> But a couple of strange things were going on at Sanwa. At the beginning of the project we had asked for a full-time Sanwa team to complement our own team. Joint consultant and client task forces are more effective than solo consultant teams. The client members know their way around the organization and where the facts are buried; and, too, they are there after the outside consultants have left. After a long negotiation in which we thought Sanwa management had agreed with us, we figured that two or three of their people would join forces with us the next day. Twenty showed up.
>
> "What's this?" we wanted to know. "Your study team," they explained. We protested that what we had meant by a team was smaller–certainly not twenty people. They said we had done such a good job of explaining the need for a client team that they thought they would do it right. We couldn't understand why this otherwise bright group of executives insisted on such a large team when it was obvious that the problem-solving would have been more efficient with a smaller one. But they were paying the bills, so we lurched forward with our unwieldy gang of twenty.
>
> After two months we presented our results. The team of twenty reacted with horror. They explained that before we talked to the *jomus*, we should discuss our findings with a fairly large group of people around the bank. They started a list that grew to several hundred people. We told them that would take a few months, reminded them of the project's cost, and suggested again that we simply report our solution to the board and get on with restoring market share. They reminded us that they were paying the bills and suggested we do it their way.

Several months later we finally made the presentation to the *jomu-kai*. It lasted only an hour and was mainly ceremonial. By then all of the *jomus* were well acquainted with what we were going to say.

Then something amazing happened. About two days after the presentation their market share started to rise! We had never seen results that fast. (In fact, as anyone who has consulted will tell you, getting results at all is sometimes a surprise.)

Involving twenty people on the team had nothing to do with problem-solving "efficiency." Our talking to hundreds more after we had the "answer" to the market share problem had nothing to do with crisp decision-making. Both processes had everything to do with getting something done.

By the time we made the final presentation to the *jomus*, a significant part of the entire Sanwa organization had already been involved in the project. All those study-team members, all their friends in the bank, and all the people we talked to subsequently understood that market share was of prime concern to top management. They knew what the study team thought was the root of the problem. But most important, they had the chance to engage in the problem themselves. They could, and did, vigorously express their own views on the cause of the problem and solutions to it. They could, and did, contribute to the team's thinking. There was deep wisdom in Sanwa's insistence that we conduct the project in a way that at the time appeared to me to be inefficient, burdensome, and more than a little foolish.

When Andy Pearson was still President of Pepsi Co, he said, "We have 120,000 employees stashed in various places around the world, and I frankly have no idea what the hell they're doing." Throughout the Sanwa project, with hundreds of people involved, we had no idea what they were all doing. In any sense of the word control, the project seemed out of control. But in a broader sense the thing was under control. The market share went up. Give up control, in the narrow sense, to get control, in a broader sense.

Later, one of the members of the team of twenty commented about presenting the results to the board early. "Good show business, bad consulting," he said. It says a lot about why "implementation is a bitch" for so many American and European managers. We are so busy grandstanding with "crisp decision" that we don't take time to involve those who have to make the decisions work.

We at Dannemiller Tyson Associates, as practitioners of this type of change described by Waterman in this book, want to share with you the tools, theories and underlying principles we have used in this type of system-wide work over the years. We hope that our ideas and learnings can enable you to do truly amazing work with your own clients.

We want to share with you because we believe that many of us are on the same path…And we believe it is an important one for the future of the human race: to help people and the organizations they live within to be as good as they can be as they proceed into the chaotic future.

OVERVIEW: WHAT IS WHOLE-SCALE?

Chapter 1
Discovering the Magic of Whole-Scale

Introduction

Large group approaches to organizational change have become increasingly popular in the last few years because many leaders have learned that the style of management often referred to as "command and control" no longer works. Leaders are learning that they need to get real buy-in on strategy from their people. They need to find new ways to align and engage large numbers of people around a common, effective strategic focus. And they have come to realize that top management may not have all the answers.

The organizations we at Dannemiller Tyson Associates (DTA) work with are typically being challenged by a quickly changing environment and experiencing a sense of urgency about operating in that environment. It is our goal to help leaders and organizations understand and believe in the change processes we call *Whole-Scale* as a viable way of responding to that urgency.

Living In a New World

In this first stage of the new millennium, organizations find themselves looking for ways to survive and thrive in a new age. Our world now engages us in a truly global community. Governments, corporations, institutions and organizations of all sizes and forms must redefine who they are, the functions they serve and the new roles they must fill. The problems organizations now face no longer respond to solutions rooted in older 20th century—or even 19th century—problem-solving models.

Most astonishing in this "information age" is the speed at which the activities in our world function:
- We transmit information in a millisecond from one corner of the world to the other
- We observe nations fighting a war "live" on television
- Civic groups demand "time delays" in reporting news as it happens to protect children from the harsher realities of life and death
- We broadcast new technologies and processes in an instant across the entire planet

Our world—smaller than ever—seems upside down. People in China, Great Britain, Brazil and Romania build parts for an automobile designed in Japan; people in Mexico assemble the vehicle, and someone in Detroit or another American city sells it to a customer.

Organizations slow to accept and adopt these changes and new technological marvels seem to fall farther and farther behind.

Why Use Whole-Scale?

This new and ever changing environment moving at the speed of light has placed unparalleled demands and expectations on today's organizations. Leaders must help their organizations harness the tumult, speed, and complexity of the new environment. Whole-Scale enables an organization to quickly and effectively assess its environment, map a system-wide strategy to be successful within it, implement that strategy and achieve the success they desire. For these reasons, we believe that Whole-Scale methodology makes important sense today.

We at Dannemiller Tyson Associates (DTA) believe that organizations overwhelmingly need to change from old structural organizational methods to new, dynamic methods. We believe they can best determine such methods by tapping into and unleashing the wisdom of the entire workforce. We have found that Whole-Scale processes work well to release and combine the organization's inherent knowledge. Thus, we want to "open our hands" and pass on ideas, designs, and processes that we have used and found to be robust in creating change. When you finish this book, we want you to be excited to try these processes and truly able to be successful.

What Is Whole-Scale?

Whole-Scale consists of several key processes to help an organization change in order to meet the challenges of its environment: taking an action-learning journey, unleashing the power of the microcosm, uniting multiple realities, and creating a paradigm shift...a change in the way the organization sees its future actions... that enables it to change real-time. As you help clients do these things using Whole-Scale methods, two models and a formula will guide you: the Converge/Diverge Model, the Action Learning Model, and the DVF formula.

Whole-Scale processes also consist of a series of events, typically alternating small and large group interactions, that enable the organization to undergo the necessary paradigm shift. The whole process is an action-learning approach that uses Whole-Scale events as accelerators and works with microcosms of the organization.

If you want to shift the whole system at one time, you must be able to think the way the whole system thinks. Using microcosms—real subsets of the larger group that represent all the "voices" of the organization—in the overall change process is one of the features of the Whole-Scale approach that allows you—and the organization—to think and see "whole system." The microcosm contains the essential "DNA" of the whole organization. Working with groups that mirror the "whole" allows you to work with the "whole system" at a different level. The best way to change a system is to engage the *whole* system. Microcosms are the best windows through which to view the whole system in *real time*. They provide access to the whole system quickly and effectively. Having a critical mass of microcosms experiencing a paradigm shift helps the whole organization shift.

The underlying assumption in the use of microcosms is that the wisdom necessary for success is in *all the people* of the organization. The most effective change efforts include the voices of all key stakeholders, not just the voices of the top or the bottom or the middle. A*ll* of the people in the organization—plus those who are depending on the organization, like customers, owners or suppliers—must be able to speak and be heard.

Why is this is so important?

The traditional consulting approach has been to pull together the "experts" on a particular issue—often people who thought alike or had the same background or had the "right" status in the organization. This view is necessarily limited, often focusing on data of high-ranking, influential views. It's necessary to include those views, and, by themselves, they are not sufficient. Using the holistic view from a microcosm (or many microcosms) will illuminate the fact that people can contribute powerfully when they have enough information and when they are invited to do so.

In Whole-Scale, using microcosms means tapping into the wisdom of *every* area and *every* level of the organization—*all the way* throughout the process, not just the night before implementation. In Whole-Scale, involving people means engaging each person in a deep and meaningful way.

Whole-Scale processes evoke the system's wisdom without needing to direct or control the results. Thus, when the system is ready, the answers come. Your job as a consultant is to help the system get ready. The microcosm will have all of the knowledge it needs, once the organization has uncovered and combined the knowledge. Through the power of the microcosm, it is possible to create identity in the moment and to form new identities, without having to define every aspect of the system or get inside each person's head.

Some examples of microcosms that make the difference in Whole-Scale are research teams, cross-functional task teams, and event-planning teams. In Whole-Scale events, you can use microcosms in several ways. One of the most useful techniques is to use "max-mix" seating, which is simply a group of eight people at a table, representing basically the same mix of knowledge and yearnings that will be in the larger group. Each table in a Whole-Scale event is thus a microcosm of the room, and all those in the room together are a microcosm of the system.

Uniting Multiple Realities

You must keep a continual focus on the simultaneous and often conflicting realities that exist in the internal and external environments of the organization. During events the real needs of participants in their back-home work shape the content. Do not use simulations or role-plays. Rather, encourage participants to discuss real issues in real face-to-face dialogue.

Many organizations base their improvement efforts on the assumptions of problem solving. In fact, assuming that there is one "right" answer dis-empowers employees. If there is a "right" solution, it follows that there must also be a "wrong" solution. The right/wrong paradigm is a limiting and ineffective way to help organizations change.

You will have greater success if you operate under the belief that there is no " right" or "wrong" answer. An individual's answer is his or her "truth." "Each person's truth is truth" is the phrase we use to help individuals listen to each other's perspectives. Helping people realize that all of the truths matter is equally important.

The following formula helps us think about multiple realities:

| Each Person's + | All Truths | = | The Whole Truth |
| Truth Is Truth | Matter | | |

Going Whole

The Converge-Diverge Model

An important model to use is the **Converge/Diverge Model,** depicted in Figure 1 below. The model shows a process in which an organization moves, over time, through a series of activities that create and sustain change in the organization. It represents a connected flow that integrates the individual, small group, and large group work that the organization's people go through to expand their database (diverge), combine their multiple realities (converge), explore possibilities (diverge), and make system-wide decisions (converge). The large ovals depict opportunities for a critical mass to "get whole" (converge). In the flow of convergence/divergence, large group events accelerate the change journey. They bring together a critical mass that combine everything people have been learning from their individual and small group efforts into a whole picture. In the larger group, they will make the decisions that will move them forward faster and deeper. The wisdom for the consultant is knowing when to "go whole" and when to go smaller and deeper.

Converge-Diverge Model

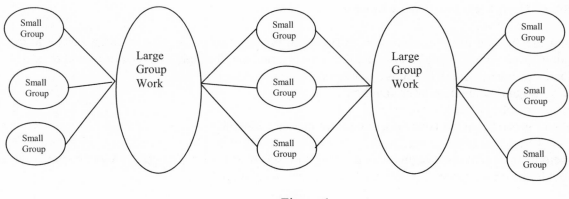

Figure 1

Dannemiller Tyson's process for thinking about when to "go whole" comes from the work of Lawrence & Lorsch, in their book *Organization and Environment (Organization and Environment: Managing Differentiation and Integration by Paul R. Lawrence and J. W. Lorsch*). In this book the authors talk about the need for an organization to have both differentiation and integration. They define differentiation as "differences in attitudes and behaviors among functional organizations resulting from organizational segmentation with consequent development of specialized knowledge and mental processes." They see integration as "the quality of the state of collaboration that exists among departments that are required to achieve unity of effort by the demands of the environment." They also use the term integration as a process of achieving a state of integration.

In the Whole-Scale approach, the Converge-Diverge diagram depicts how we seek to help an organization unleash and combine its wisdom and magic by ensuring that productive differentiation is brought "whole" by productive integration.

Taking an Action-Learning Journey

Another model that describes Whole-Scale processes is the **Action Learning Model** found in Figure 2 at the end of this chapter. The Action Learning model is a picture of wholeness emerging—generating, releasing and focusing individual and organizational energy. It provides a continual "plan-do-check-act " set of action learning processes. Following the Action Learning path can facilitate a systems approach to engage all of the key stakeholders in the change journey. Based on Kurt Lewin's Action Research theories and Ron Lippitt's experiential learning and change theories, the model is an application of systems thinking and action learning, aimed at keeping the system whole at every step of the way.

The Action Learning Roadmap is a common sense way to look at how organizations get on the path to change. The Roadmap describes a powerful way to help a client system stay "whole" throughout the learning cycle. Organizations must continually reexamine the results they achieve at different points throughout a change process in order to inform the next step. This axiom is true for the next agenda items in a meeting, the next day of an event, and for the next step in the whole organization's journey.

Whether you are focusing on an event as an accelerator or the change journey as a whole, as a process consultant your best approach is to help the client get the right people (a few or thousands) to have the right conversations that will enable them to achieve their purpose. Your interventions must be intentional at each step in the cycle. Design your work to engage the organization to provide its own answers to the questions noted beside each step in the model.

Throughout the flow of change, each oval carries a different set of tasks and outcomes on the journey. The questions between the ovals ensure that the right people have the right conversations and thus ensure the wholeness of the system in the subsequent oval:
- What's next and who needs to be involved?
- What conversations need to take place?
- What will be different because these conversations take place?

The answers to these three questions will tell the team whether or not you need a large group or small group to achieve your purpose: do you need to converge or diverge?

Converge - Diverge

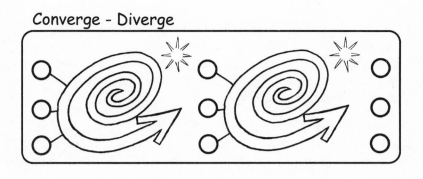

A key design issue at each oval and throughout the learning cycle is when the organization is answering the question "Who needs to be involved?" Is this the moment when the organization needs to engage a critical mass of the system to reunite around head and heart—to get a critical mass of the system whole again around its own collective wisdom? Or is it time to get small, focussed and deep?

Within each oval, the "who" is a microcosm or multiple microcosms (i.e., 20 people or 500 people). One of the initial activities of the microcosm is to build its own common database to inform its conversation and its work. Then, within each oval, the common database that the microcosm builds helps the organization uncover the right issues to address at that point. Once the issues are visible, the microcosm can address those issues and move the system towards the next level of the change process.

Shared information is the common thread that connects all the ovals in the learning cycle. The content of the information shifts as the system moves through that cycle. The focus is to create "wholeness" every step of the way.

In different parts of this model, different microcosms are involved. When a critical mass of the microcosms has gone through the action learning model on the right issues, the whole system will change because it has in fact become an organization with a new paradigm…an organization that has a whole new picture of what it wants to be. Dannemiller Tyson Associates refer to this magical moment when the paradigm shift occurs as becoming "one-brain and one-heart." Everyone in the organization sees the same things and cares passionately about creating this new picture.

The Action Learning model serves as a general architecture for an over-all Whole-Scale change process. Within a change process, the organization may go through many iterations of the learning cycle. For example, when designing and conducting a critical mass/Whole-Scale meeting and follow-up, the organization goes through the whole action-learning cycle. Each cycle takes the organizational learning deeper and helps the organization re-energize itself to sustain the change process and embed the new paradigm in its day-to-day workings.

Creating Paradigm Shifts With DVF

The **DVF formula** depicted in Figure 3 is a cornerstone of Whole-Scale work. Dannemiller Tyson Associates first developed this concept from the work of Richard Beckhard (*Organizational Transitions: Managing Complex Change*, Richard Beckhard and Reuben T. Harris, Addison-Wesley Publishing Company, 1987) at the National Training Laboratories. DTA's version of the model explains what it takes to bring about real change, in an organization or in an individual.

Figure 3: $D \times V \times F > R$
A MODEL THAT DESCRIBES CONDITIONS
NECESSARY FOR CHANGE

$$D \times V \times F > R$$

D = Dissatisfaction with the current situation
V = Vision of a positive possibility, more than the absence of pain of the present situation
F = First steps in the direction of the vision
R = Resistance to change

Change will occur and sustain itself when there is a common database of D, V, and F in an individual and/or the microcosm of the system or the system as a whole. If any of these bases is zero, change will not occur. The product will be 0 which will not be greater than R. It is appropriate for members of an organization to resist when they can't see the larger picture.

The first step in lasting organizational change is for each individual and the organization as a whole to share a common database of dissatisfaction (D) with things as they are right now. Everyone must be able to see and understand the view that others hold, and to understand that "each person's truth is truth." Everyone needs to see and value others' views and combine those views with their own perspective to create a common database from which the entire organization can move forward. They need to articulate their own yearnings for the future of the organization and combine with others' a common vision (V) of what they all yearn to be in the future; and they also need agreement on significant system-wide first steps (F) to take that they believe will begin to move them toward the vision. If any of these three elements is zero, the drive for change cannot overcome the natural forces of resistance (R) that exist within any individual or organization.

The $D \times V \times F > R$ model is a great deal more than simply a model for change. It is, in fact, an important model that enables the necessary paradigm shift to occur. When you help an organization to combine D, V, and F, each member of the organization sees the multiple realities that connect them. When this happens, the system as a whole shifts, and so do they as individuals. When the shift occurs, you can feel it in terms of higher level of excitement and energy in the room. The paradigm shift lasts beyond the initial euphoria. It is literally impossible, once an organization has made a real shift, for it to go back to seeing the world in the old ways.

Now people (individually and as a whole) are seeing the world differently, seeing their organization differently, and seeing themselves differently. They have connected with each other around a common picture of their future and the actions they will take to get there. After the paradigm shift experience, participants are clamoring to use their newly uncovered wisdom to build toward the yearnings they have uncovered together.

In Conclusion

Pulling together a microcosm and/or a series of microcosms creates a critical mass of an organization—"one-brain and one-heart"—capable of building and living a new culture *in the moment*. As this same critical mass proceeds to model what the organization can be and how it will work, it becomes the vehicle by which powerful change occurs in the whole system.

Whole-Scale includes robust processes capable of quickly changing client systems and preparing them for further substantive change by:

- Clarifying and connecting multiple current realities
- Uniting multiple yearnings around a common picture of the future
- Reaching agreement on the action plans that move them toward that future
- Building the processes, structures and relationships that keep the organization moving forward
- Aligning the organization leaders and employees so that they can implement the changes together

When the microcosm has gone through this series of processes, it will produce a paradigm shift—a new way of seeing the world. Once the organization experiences the paradigm shift, people see the world differently. They are ready to take the actions that will begin to transform their shared vision into their shared reality. Probably the most exciting thing we at DTA have learned through the years is that the processes we have used with a client, that have led to a paradigm shift, become new "common sense" ways of holding meetings and leading change. They believe…as do we …that those processes are simply good organizational change processes.

Equation for Change

Figure 2   The Action Learning Roadmap pictures how we see incremental emergence of wholeness, generating, releasing and focusing individual and organizational energy using the Whole-Scale approach:

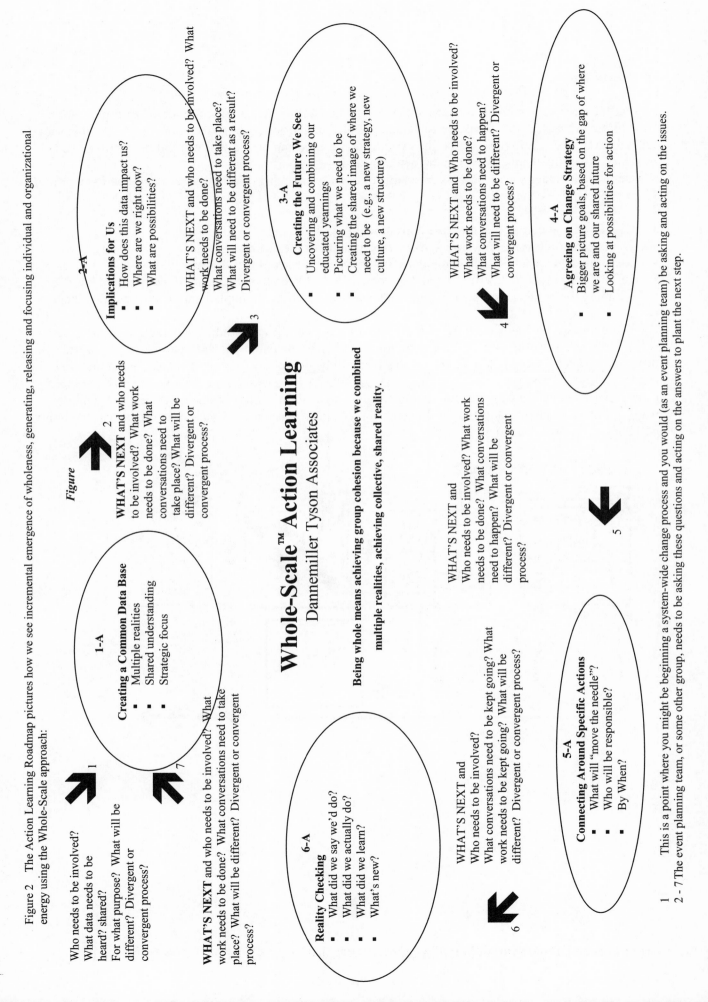

Who needs to be involved?
What data needs to be heard?
For what purpose? Divergent or convergent process?

WHAT'S NEXT and who needs to be involved? What work needs to be done? What conversations need to take place? What will be different? Divergent or convergent process?

Figure

WHAT'S NEXT and who needs to be involved? What work needs to be done? What conversations need to take place? What will be different? Divergent or convergent process?

1-A
Creating a Common Data Base
- Multiple realities
- Shared understanding
- Strategic focus

2-A
Implications for Us
- How does this data impact us?
- Where are we right now?
- What are possibilities?

WHAT'S NEXT and who needs to be involved? What work needs to be done? What conversations need to take place? What will need to be different as a result? Divergent or convergent process?

3-A
Creating the Future We See
- Uncovering and combining our educated yearnings
- Picturing what we need to be
- Creating the shared image of where we need to be (e.g., a new strategy, new culture, a new structure)

WHAT'S NEXT and Who needs to be involved? What work needs to be done? What conversations need to happen? What will need to be different? Divergent or convergent process?

4-A
Agreeing on Change Strategy
- Bigger picture goals, based on the gap of where we are and our shared future
- Looking at possibilities for action

Whole-Scale™ Action Learning
Dannemiller Tyson Associates

Being whole means achieving group cohesion because we combined multiple realities, achieving collective, shared reality.

WHAT'S NEXT and Who needs to be involved? What work needs to be done? What conversations need to happen? What will be different? Divergent or convergent process?

WHAT'S NEXT and Who needs to be involved? What work needs to be done? What conversations need to be kept going? What will be different? Divergent or convergent process?

6-A
Reality Checking
- What did we say we'd do?
- What did we actually do?
- What did we learn?
- What's new?

5-A
Connecting Around Specific Actions
- What will "move the needle"?
- Who will be responsible?
- By When?

WHAT'S NEXT and who needs to be involved? What work needs to be done? What conversations need to take place? What will be different? Divergent or convergent process?

1   This is a point where you might be beginning a system-wide change process and you would (as an event planning team) be asking and acting on the issues.

2 - 7 The event planning team, or some other group, needs to be asking these questions and acting on the answers to plant the next step.

CHAPTER 1:   DISCOVERING THE MAGIC OF WHOLE-SCALE

Chapter 2
Designing a Whole-Scale Meeting
Planning an Event as an Accelerator of System-wide Change

Event Planning Teams: Overview

This chapter describes the planning and designing process leading up to Whole-Scale events that accelerate total system change. The term "event" describes a meeting of any size, whether it is for a purpose that involves a small group (e.g., leadership alignment), a larger group (e.g., multiple task teams coming together to integrate their work), or a critical mass of the system (if not the entire system). It is, of course, important to keep in mind that each client is unique, and therefore you should adjust this planning and designing process to meet specific client requirements.

Use a microcosm of the whole organization to form an Event Planning Team (EPT). The EPT thus brings together the levels, functions, viewpoints, cultures and diversities of the whole organization. The size of an EPT can vary from six to 25, as long as it's a good microcosm. The makeup of each EPT is different *because* it is a microcosm of the whole group that will participate in the event itself. The use of the microcosm and how you engage it is a distinguishing characteristic of the Whole-Scale change methodology.

STRATEGY DEVELOPMENT/IMPLEMENTATION ROADMAP (Whole-Scale Change for Strategy Development)

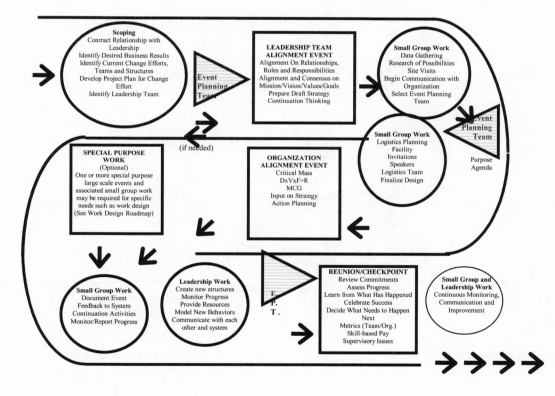

STAR OF SUCCESS
Framing the key questions critical
to a successful whole system journey

Strategic Direction—*True North*
- What's going on in our environment—now and in the future?
- What business are we in?
- Who are our stakeholders?
- What value do we choose to create for our stakeholders?
- How do we intend to create and deliver our value?
- What does success look like and how do we measure our performance?

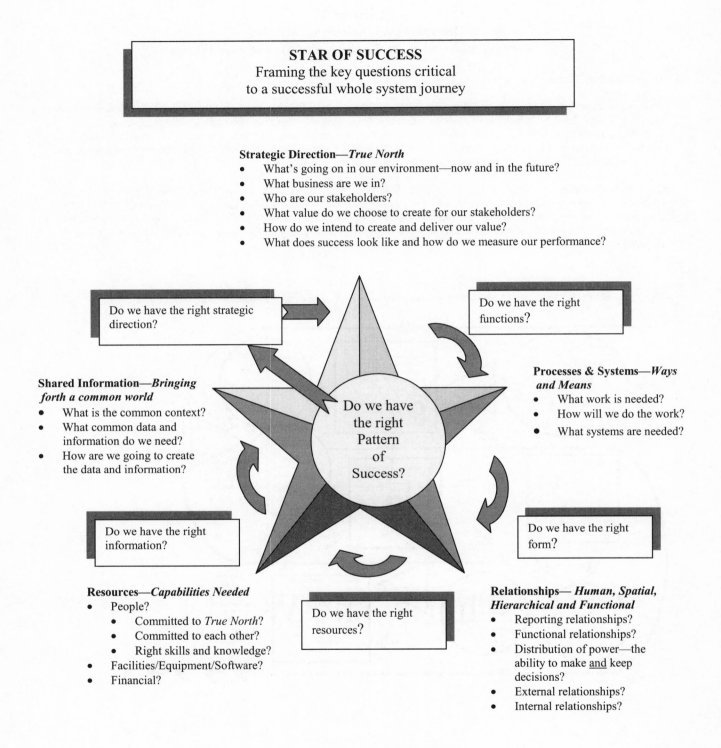

Do we have the right strategic direction?

Do we have the right functions?

Shared Information—*Bringing forth a common world*
- What is the common context?
- What common data and information do we need?
- How are we going to create the data and information?

Do we have the right Pattern of Success?

Processes & Systems—*Ways and Means*
- What work is needed?
- How will we do the work?
- What systems are needed?

Do we have the right information?

Do we have the right form?

Resources—*Capabilities Needed*
- People?
    - Committed to *True North*?
    - Committed to each other?
    - Right skills and knowledge?
- Facilities/Equipment/Software?
- Financial?

Do we have the right resources?

Relationships— *Human, Spatial, Hierarchical and Functional*
- Reporting relationships?
- Functional relationships?
- Distribution of power—the ability to make <u>and</u> keep decisions?
- External relationships?
- Internal relationships?

That's The Way!

WORK DESIGN IMPLEMENTATION ROADMAP (Whole-Scale™ Change applied to Work Design)

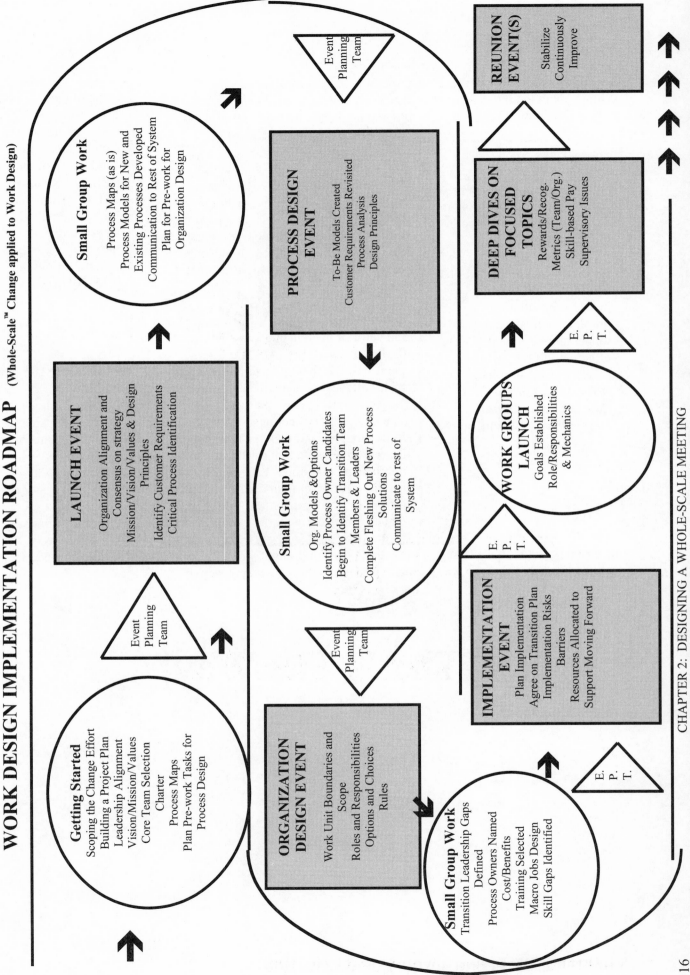

Getting Started
Scoping the Change Effort
Building a Project Plan
Leadership Alignment
Vision/Mission/Values
Core Team Selection
Charter
Process Maps
Plan Pre-work Tasks for
Process Design

Event Planning Team

LAUNCH EVENT
Organization Alignment and
Consensus on strategy
Mission/Vision/Values & Design
Principles
Identify Customer Requirements
Critical Process Identification

Small Group Work
Process Maps (as is)
Process Models for New and
Existing Processes Developed
Communication to Rest of System
Plan for Pre-work for
Organization Design

Event Planning Team

PROCESS DESIGN EVENT
To-Be Models Created
Customer Requirements Revisited
Process Analysis
Design Principles

Small Group Work
Org. Models &Options
Identify Process Owner Candidates
Begin to Identify Transition Team
Members & Leaders
Complete Fleshing Out New Process
Solutions
Communicate to rest of
System

Event Planning Team

ORGANIZATION DESIGN EVENT
Work Unit Boundaries and
Scope
Roles and Responsibilities
Options and Choices
Rules

Small Group Work
Transition Leadership Gaps
Defined
Process Owners Named
Cost/Benefits
Training Selected
Macro Jobs Design
Skill Gaps Identified

E. P. T.

IMPLEMENTATION EVENT
Plan Implementation
Agree on Transition Plan
Implementation Risks
Barriers
Resources Allocated to
Support Moving Forward

E. P. T.

WORK GROUPS LAUNCH
Goals Established
Role/Responsibilities
& Mechanics

E. P. T.

DEEP DIVES ON FOCUSED TOPICS
Rewards/Recog.
Metrics (Team/Org.)
Skill-based Pay
Supervisory Issues

REUNION EVENT(S)
Stabilize
Continuously
Improve

CHAPTER 2: DESIGNING A WHOLE-SCALE MEETING

16

In the EPT meeting, you take on the role of process consultants. The wisdom about the purpose and content of any organizational event lies in the participants. You will want to combine the microcosm's multiple realities to create an image of the organization's reality.

In your blending of the EPT's content wisdom and your process wisdom, you create a "joint diagnosis" that helps the team determine the purpose, outcomes and agenda for an event that will move the organization forward in significant and meaningful ways.

The dynamics in the EPT are a pretty good indicator of the dynamics that will occur during an event. If you have a true microcosm of the organization on the EPT, their collective voice will represent the voice of the whole organization. They will provide a window into the larger culture. The thoughts and feelings that arise during the EPT meeting are the same thoughts and feelings that will emerge in the larger event for the whole organization to address. Being connected in this microcosm, individual EPT members begin to see the world though perspectives other than their own, and thus they begin to see a larger picture of the organization. At the end of one EPT meeting a member, reflecting on the two days shared, said, "I came in thinking it should be a certain way because I'd seen it done a certain way. As the group began to make changes, I thought, 'They're doing it wrong"...As I listened to hear their views, I realized I was the one who was wrong by seeing only my own perspective."

Event Planning Teams: The Whole-Scale Approach

Typically it's best if two consultants work together as external consultants to an EPT. Working in pairs brings your own multiple realities to the intervention and thus models your beliefs for the client. You can then engage internal consultants because combining their realities with your own and building infrastructure reduces dependency on you.

> Edgar Schein in his book *Process Consultation: Its Role in Organization Development* defines process consultation as: "a set of activities on the part of the consultant which help the client to perceive, understand, and act upon process events which occur in the

The organization selects members of an Event Planning Team to foreshadow the group that will be at a Whole-Scale event. This microcosm needs to be a snip of the DNA of the larger group: they need to represent diversities, different cultures, different roles, different locations and organizational levels, different attitudes (including the cynics and skeptics), and different experiences. Clients typically seem to understand how to create this kind of group without much difficulty.

Sometimes internal consultants struggle with getting the authorization for, or time for, a good, representative Event Planning Team meeting. Because there can be so many significant people involved in the larger meeting – and that makes the stakes especially high – you do not want to miss the mark. Therefore, you will need to explain the vital importance of having the wisdom of a microcosm planning team. Real time in the EPT meeting, ask members whether the present group is a true microcosm. If not, ask, "What voices are missing and what can we do to get those voices into the conversation?" If you cannot get a true microcosm team, it is not the end of the world, but it means you will have to work especially hard to gather additional data and continuously check out your purpose and design with various other members of the client organization.

During the EPT meeting, work hard to engage all voices—especially the quiet voices and the voices of the fringe. Frequently they make the most valuable contributions because they espouse views that are controversial and help break paradigms. They help discuss the "undiscussable." When *they* believe the agenda for the event will really work, there's a high probability that it *will* work! The work the EPT does serves as a pilot for the Whole-Scale event, because the EPT will take the same journey that the larger group will take. Design and facilitate the EPT meeting using similar processes and the same underlying principles you use during any Whole-Scale event. The EPT's reactions help determine what will and will not work. Their experience will be an accurate foretelling of the larger group's learning and developing experiences.

The EPT's job is to figure out both what the organization needs to accomplish during the Whole-Scale event and how to develop it. Build an agreement with the EPT that the group will make all decisions in the two days of the planning session by true consensus. The team needs to understand that there can be no agreement on the "right" agenda until *everybody* agrees. The wisdom about what needs to happen next flows from these discussions, even though some members of the team grow impatient and are uncomfortable with the dissenters. Nevertheless, each person's voice needs to be heard and integrated, even when you find yourself wishing the dissenting person(s) would just agree with everyone else! Each person on the planning team will be a representative of a wider group in the organization, and therefore you want to consider his or her truth seriously, as it has more "visceral weight" than just "one-voice." Changes you reach through this kind of acceptance and discussion will be the right ones for the larger group.

> *Some organizations are so resource constrained that they will not give up people for two whole days. Keep to the concept of using the microcosm to plan, and take whatever time is available. Work with the system to find creative ways for the organization to uncover and own its own data and design ideas, while staying whole.*

It is particularly important to be clear about your role and the roles of the EPT members at the beginning of the work. It is important for you, as external consultants, to be the "process" experts, and it is important for the internal team members to be the "content" experts. If you can keep your roles clear, the EPT will produce an effective design, by linking and combining what the process experts know about how to do this kind of session with what the internal content experts know about where this company is right now and what it needs to deal with in order to move ahead. When agreement/consensus is reached in the EPT on the agenda of activities to be used, we (the external consultants) need to be part of that consensus…you do know more about adult learning than they probably do and you need to hold out for what you know.

Event Planning Teams: Why they play a critical role

EPTs play a critical role in accelerating whole system change because they do the following things:

- *Create Empowerment and Participation* - By using an EPT, you inform and empower a microcosm within the organization. This microcosm makes meaningful decisions about their future and the future of the organization. The EPT process builds ownership and commitment not only for the event but also for the actions that come out of the event.
- *Create Community* - When you foster an environment where employees can come together, they can create and believe in something larger than themselves. The use of an EPT brings voices from across the organization into conversation in a way that builds a sense of community.
- *Create a Shared Preferred Future* - When a group connects around creating a collective "image of potential" for the future, that image will form the basis for action today. People will truly support what they have been part of creating for the present and for the future. Combining and uniting around common yearnings is the basis for incredible power in any group. The EPT creates an image of how the world will be different as a result of a Whole-Scale event, and they translate that image into the event purpose. They begin to see how all their actions need to support the purpose in order to bring about meaningful change.

The EPT Meeting: Underlying process models

Three models work simultaneously to guide your work with the EPT. The first model is MCG (*Membership – Control – Goals)* because it helps you build a team. Second is D-P-P-E (*Data - Purpose - Plan - Evaluate)* because it evokes the data and provides the framework for designing the event. Third is D x V x F > R because it guides the flow and content of the conversations that need to take place.

MCG - Membership, Control and Goals

In your work with microcosms of all sizes, you need to focus continuously on helping the microcosm, in this case an EPT, become a real team. The MCG model for team development is an adaptation of Jack Gibb's Continuous Concerns Model (Gibb, Jack. *The Basic Reader: Reading in Laboratory Training.* Detroit, MI: Province V, The Episcopal Church, 1970.) The model depicts Membership issues, Control issues and Goal issues that you need to address continuously by getting appropriate data flowing in the kind of conversation that will enable good formation of a team. This model will guide you in creating an effective group of any kind or size. MCG will help you both to build an effective EPT and to guide the flow of the event agenda. See Figure 3 below.

FIGURE 3: WHOLE-SCALE MODEL FOR TEAM DEVELOPMENT
Entry/Initial Reason for Coming Together

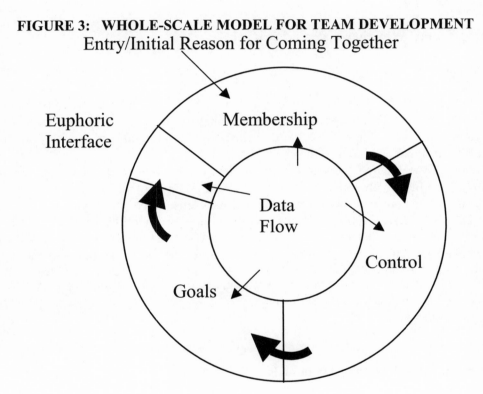

Some Questions That Team Members Ask In Each Phase

Data Flow
- What's new?
- What do we need to share to have a "level playing field"?
- Different data has to flow at each stage (membership, control, goals, and the Euphoria stage)

Membership
- Do I belong in this group?
- Do I want to belong in this group?
- Who else is here?

Control
- Who's in charge?
- What style of leadership are they using?
- How much control will I have/want?

Goal Formation
- What do we want to accomplish?
- What do I want to see happen?
- How will we know we've been successful?

Euphoric Interface
- Boy, aren't we a good team?
- Followed by a need to restart MCG again on a deeper level.

Adapted from Jack Gibb's "4 Continuing Concerns in a Group" in *The Basic Reader: Reading in Laboratory Training*. Detroit, MI: Province V, The Episcopal Church, 1970.

Membership

The concept of membership addresses questions such as: Do I belong in this group? Do I want to belong in this group? Who else is here?

In the EPT during the personal introductions and throughout the process of building a common database, team members have an opportunity to share why they are there, what they bring and their hopes for the future—as well as listen to thoughts from the other members around these same issues. In this process, people are checking out whether the other people in the EPT share their values. They may ask themselves, "Is this a group that I'd be proud to be part of? Will they be glad to have been connected with me?" When people feel comfortable about the answers to these questions, they are ready to move on to the next concern area: control.

Control

The concept of Control addresses such questions as: "Who's in charge? What style of leadership are they using? Do they care about other's opinions? Will I have too much control? Too little?"

The EPT has a significant say in the design of the Whole-Scale event. They tell you what you need to include and who needs to attend. They identify the key stakeholder voices that the organization needs to hear. During the actual event, the EPT continues to play a critical role in reviewing daily evaluations and making decisions regarding the design for the next day. If they do good work as a team, the impact they will have on the leadership team will surprise them. If the group gets a "livable" answer to the control concerns, they will then be ready to move to the final area of concern: goal agreement.

Goals

The concept of Goals addresses such questions as: "What do we want to accomplish? What do I want to see happen? How will we know we've been successful?"

The EPT develops the purpose statement for the event, which drives everything else, and identifies the outcomes to achieve during the event. At the event itself, max-mix tables and the room as a whole will have the opportunity to add their own yearnings to the community pot.

When you feel the EPT has addressed its goal concerns, help them move into a "holding area"—a "Euphoric Interface," a time when they are saying to each other, "We do good work. We're a good team." From this phase, a healthy group will move ahead to deepen the relationships and commonalties they have developed.

The organization *must* continue to focus on continuing concerns. One team-building event is never enough. Teams must nurture themselves. Ways to do this include on-going max-mix teamwork, reunions of a launch group or any work team, or continuous removal of old barriers to communication. The minute you have ceased building the team, people will begin to revert and go backwards: they will question common goals, the distribution of power and finally, whether they even want to be connected to this organization. This team process holds true with marriages, as well as teams and communities, and it speaks to the importance of keeping open communication toward a common data

D-P-P-E - Data-Purpose-Plan-Evaluate

We use D-P-P-E as a fail-safe way of planning a meeting, large or small. What we learned at the National Training Labs in Bethel, Maine, in the 1960s that caused many of us to change how we did process consulting was the absolutely powerful nature of consensus on "purpose"…"if you don't know where you're going, any road can take you there!" This D-P-P-E model helped many of us get there. "If you're having trouble agreeing on a Purpose, go back and get more data and you'll find it to be much easier." There is often a point in an EPT meeting when the consensus seems to be "stuck", when we will ask the question: "Do we have the right people in the room? Maybe we need more data from a different viewpoint." Probably the most important thing we learned in those early NTL days was that most of our energy and time was put into the Data-Purpose part of the model. It turned out to be astonishingly easy to come up with a Plan when we had done the first two steps well. Within the EPT meeting, the model provides a framework for actually designing the event. Within the event itself, you will use the model to facilitate the event. Like Plan-Do-Check-Act, D-P-P-E is an excellent process model for working any phase of a change effort.

Data
The first element, data, is about "getting your finger on the pulse" of the organization. The table below illustrates the various purposes for which you may use data with the EPT.

Consultants need data to plan the EPT Meeting	*The EPT needs data to* ▪ *Build itself as a team (MCG)* ▪ *Design the Event*	*During the Event everyone uses data to evaluate whether the organization is meeting its purpose & to tweak the design*
▪ What does the leadership yearn for? ▪ What outcomes do they desire? ▪ What's the scope of the change?	▪ What data needs to inform the event? ▪ Who does the organization need to hear it from? ▪ Who needs to attend?	▪ What's the energy level? ▪ Is it the appropriate kind of energy for the activity?
▪ What's in bounds? ▪ What's out of bounds ▪ What kind of microcosms is available to work with?	▪ What's our own data about how we see the organization now and in the future? ▪ What outcomes are our leaders looking for? ▪ What outcomes do we need to make the event worthwhile?	▪ Are people actively involved at their tables? ▪ What do written evaluations from all participants, customized to each day, reveal? ▪ Where would participants typically be in a successful change journey? ▪ Are people there? ▪ Are people coming back from the breaks? ▪ What is the EPT seeing and hearing at their tables, at breaks?

NOTE: If you cannot sit down with a true microcosm Event Planning Team and have them teach you (and each other) about the organization, you can simply pull together whomever you can get, and treat them as if they were a real Event Planning Team. This will work if you keep constantly aware, and keep the team constantly aware, that the team is not a true microcosm and might not have the right data. Keep asking the group questions like, "If the people from 'such & such' were here, what would they be saying?" The group usually does a pretty good job of role-playing in that fashion. Sometimes, though, you will become aware that you really have a lack of data, and it becomes necessary to send a "pick-up team" out to get more data from folks who can't be there...or in some cases to go out and get them to come to the EPT meeting, if needed. In any case, you as external consultants need to work very carefully to stay free of making your own judgments or interpretations. In other words, work hard to remember that "Each person's truth is truth" and to make sure the EPT remembers as well.

Purpose

Purpose drives everything in the event. Continually ask, "What has to be different in the world because this group met?" Keep asking that question as you are scoping a project to see it through the eyes of the leadership and the organization, when you are working with leadership teams, preparing for EPT meetings, and designing and facilitating events.

Always ground the purpose in data. Use data from the leadership to understand their overarching purpose for the change effort and to construct the purpose for the EPT meeting. The EPT, supported by you as consultant, uses data to construct the purpose for the event they are planning. Both the EPT purpose and the event purpose support the overarching purpose of the change effort.

In the planning meeting, once the EPT has a basic feel for the organization and has "their fingers on the pulse," help the team to define, in words, the underlying reason for convening a critical mass of the organization. Continue to ask the question, "What has to be different in the world because these people came together?" When you discern compelling results (rather than simply a list of activities), this will lead to a succinct purpose statement, which will serve as a beacon (or North Star) for the team to follow as it creates the event design. Without a clear, compelling purpose that the team has come to by true consensus, it isn't possible to make accurate decisions about what to pull all of us together for three days!" They will be excited by the proposed results, even if skeptical that they are possible.

Plan

There's a plan for the project (driven by the overarching purpose), a plan (agenda) for the meeting with the EPT (see generic agenda pp. 26-38), and a plan for the event itself. Purpose drives each plan—*What will be different because the organization does this?*

In the planning team meeting, with the event purpose clearly defined, the EPT will do the detailed planning. As you help them plan, constantly check the activities you design into the meeting against the purpose to see if you are still on track. Also, you can ask the EPT to put on a participant's "hat" to ask questions like, "Is this what I would want to be doing now? Am I interested in what is happening? Do I need a break?" The EPT will determine what is appropriate based on their knowledge of the organization, its history, its culture and what the participants will be thinking at that time in the event. Listen to see the world through their eyes, and you will hear the wisdom you need to hear, as an "outsider." Each design will follow the D x V x F > R model for change flow, but the activities in each event will be unique because, of course, the purpose is unique and driven by the realities of the client system.

Evaluate

Evaluation occurs throughout the event planning process, the event itself, and indeed, the entire change effort. You can evaluate at various times using a variety of techniques:

- Evaluate the event purpose by "road-testing" it outside the EPT, especially with the leadership group.
- Evaluate your design ideas by using the EPT to truly agree on that design to achieve that purpose, and sometimes by checking it out with other key stakeholders in the organization.
- Evaluate how the group is working together as an EPT after each day of meetings.
- Finally, gather written evaluations from participants after each day of a Whole-Scale event.

Members of the EPT, as well as members of the leadership group, play an important role in reviewing participant feedback at the end of each day during a larger event and help to formulate changes, if necessary, in the event design for the following day.

The Lippitt brothers (Ronald and Gordon Lippitt, The *Consulting Process in Action,* Second Edition, 1986, Jessey/Pfeiffer, pages 23 and 24) are very clear in their thoughts about evaluation and feedback: "Feedback is only helpful if it is utilized rapidly to re-examine goals, to revise action strategies, and, perhaps, to activate decisions concerning the mobilization of additional resources and changes of assignments and roles. Collecting evaluation data is really a waste of time unless some planning and energy are put into processing and using the findings, rewarding those who have made relevant efforts, and revising and improving plans for the next stages of action."

As the Lippitts suggest, it's effective to use evaluation in the intervening evening at each event, summarizing it and reporting it back to the whole group the next morning, along with any changes you've made overnight based on the feedback. Be committed to having the right people hear the feedback in order to get the right voices into the plan for any changes. The feedback belongs to the whole group, in order to help them build toward "one-brain and one-heart" as they go along.

The Meeting Planning Journey

$D \, x \, V \, x \, F > R$ – A Model for Change

This formula for change from Chapter One is also relevant for the EPT because it guides the design and flow of conversations and activities in the event.

The two days of an Event Planning Team are a journey of discovery. The discovery is around the elements of the change model: Dissatisfaction with the way things are right now (D) x Vision of what things could be that inspires and unites the group (V) x First steps that all can see as worth doing (F) > Resistance to change (R). The change formula suggests that when you can get the EPT to see themselves and their organization in terms of a common understanding of Dissatisfaction, Vision and First Steps, they will be able to design an event that will, by definition, overcome their organization's resistance to change. All people resist change when any one of the three elements is missing, or is not articulated.

The Event Planning Team Meeting

A Whole-Scale event is very important in the life of an organization. It is vital to ensure that the time people spend is valuable. What will be different in the world because these people came together? Your job is to help the EPT to make sure the results are worthwhile.

The EPT meeting—a journey of discovery as well as a planning process—has a movement similar to the movement of an accordion. The meeting opens to gather as much data as possible to allow the team to create a common database that reflects the richness of all their perspectives. Then the meeting narrows to a specific purpose, expands to identify all of the possible appropriate "chunks of the agenda", and then narrows again to specify next steps needed to pull off a successful event.

For most events, an EPT optimally needs to meet for two successive days. If this is possible, the results are almost always an event design that is appropriate to the larger organization's needs and culture. And, if it's not possible to get a microcosm for two consecutive days, one day is certainly better than no meeting at all. Having a generic EPT meeting agenda ensures that you take full advantage of the available time, energy and resources during the event.

A typical agenda for an EPT meeting agenda flow might be as follows: (Detailed step-by-step agenda below in
   Figure 4.)

Day	Agenda	D-P-P-E At Work
Day 1		
8:00 a.m.	Welcome & Purpose—Leadership Kickoff	
	Purpose—Agenda—Norms	*Data*
	View from EPT team members	
	Overview of the Whole-Scale approach	
	Desired Outcomes	*Purpose*
	Event Purpose	
5:00 p.m.	Evaluations and Close	
Day 2		
8:00 a.m.	Feedback on Evaluations & Review of Work from Day 1	
	Refining Participants List	
	Elements Brainstorm (Given the Purpose, what questions need to be answered?)	*Plan*
	Laying out a "Chunked" Agenda (flow of elements)	
	Developing a Detailed Design (content, process and logistics)	
	Leadership Team Review	
	Next Steps / Loose Ends	
5:00 p.m.	Evaluation / Debrief / Close	*Evaluate*

Developing a Detailed Design - An event design is a sequence of activities that lead the group to achieve their event purpose. Each activity ("chunk") must meet certain quality criteria that ensure the integrity of the whole design. Keep these criteria constantly in your thinking as you work with the EPT to develop the "chunked" agenda. Also keep them in your thinking as you facilitate an event. They are your way of staying client-focused. The quality criteria are:

- *Purpose* - Everything you do leads to this, the organization's "North Star." Purpose helps define the shift the organization is seeking. From the point where the EPT agrees upon the purpose statement, they make every decision—from deciding what customers the organization needs to hear from up to how long lunch will be—with the purpose in mind.

- *Theory* – The models such as DVF and D-P-P-E shape the design and the ways you will work with the EPT participants in the larger event.

- *Empowerment* - As one of DTA's colleagues, Barry Camson, put it, "The work is about a sincere, deep, abiding, unwavering, and non-faddish view of empowerment." Constantly look for ways to increase participation, to ensure that people feel listened to, to help them see that they have choices and feel wise enough to make those choices. All of these lead to an individual's increased capacity to act.

- *A Positive Atmosphere* – Additionally, you will want to create an environment where there are no negative learnings. As Lippitt and Lippitt (p. 49) put it: "One should not intervene to influence an individual member of the group unless the effect is at least neutral, if not positive, for the total group, and one should not intervene to influence the total group unless the impact will be at least neutral, if not positive, for each individual in the group." In your decision making, therefore, think about both the appropriate level of intervention and the potential side effects."

- *Shared Common Database* - Every activity should add to this database, build community and systems thinking, give the group a shared picture of the organization's business situation and therefore enable the whole to move forward.

- *Teambuilding* - Continually look for ways to make the team stronger in both their shared view of the organization and their ability to self-manage. Everything you do is an opportunity to build teams— both the functional and work teams as well as the cross-functional team. Staying in the same table configuration allows participants to go deeper with each other as they learn different perspectives from each other. Schein (p. 98) says, "Every act on the part of the process consultant constitutes an intervention."

- *Risk* – Keep risk to an acceptable level that builds as the event builds, as in the practice of yoga, where there is a difference between a healthy stretch and a painful stretch. At the beginning of an event, ask questions of one level of risk and build on these. At the end of an event, you'll be asking folks to commit to specific actions.

- *Learning* – Adhere to good adult learning process. Work hard to create an environment where folks feel—and are—smart. Rational people with good information make good decisions.

▪ CHOOSING INDIVIDUAL DESIGN ELEMENTS

In 1982 when we first invented the concepts of Whole-Scale, Bruce Gibb, Al Davenport, Chuck Tyson, and I were the external consultants who worked with internal Ford consultants, Nancy Badore and Cynthia Holm. We came together to design a seminar that could help Ford move to new way of working, connected around knowledge and passion for the future. We designed, with all six of us, and we agreed to design by real consensus; if anyone disagreed, the discussion would go back to its roots and start over again.

None of us remembers why we decided on that process, which certainly seemed cumbersome at the time. Consensus was usually reached after a fierce, confronting battle...and we always hung in and did it. After we began having startling success with these seminars, we began to wonder why. One of the answers, which emerged, was that it was the way we designed events built on a consensed purpose with modules, each representing a part of one of our own passions.

In order for a module to be included, each of us had to agree that it was the right thing to do at that moment and a good way to do it. What we created were design modules that included every principle and belief that any and all of us had...it was a struggle that fully paid off, and we even still cared about each other. I remember when Bruce would come up with an elegant theory that he thought would educate and develop people appropriately and I would say, "Boring! We want them to be empowered, not asleep." And all the color would fade from Bruce's face. And thus, the design struggle continued.

Here is our "umbrella" concept of design principles. It contains a checklist of characteristics to check against each proposed module in an event design. The importance of the umbrella is that everything is driven to accomplish the Purpose (the tip of the Umbrella in our model) and the various interactions are following the path of our Model For Change (the paradigm shift model) called DxVxF>R which is the handle of the umbrella. The third, and critical, concept is that every module of an event must respond to all the beliefs expressed in the points of the umbrella...

- Each module has to be focused and contributing to the purpose;
- Each module has to contribute to empowerment, meaning that people feel more powerful, more important, more knowledgeable than before;
- Each module has to have some risk embodied in it, enough risk to keep people alive but not so much risk that they'd hit the bushes to hide;
- Each module has to be designed around adult education principles: treating people like adults and getting them working on issues they knew so that they wouldn't feel "dumb";
- Each module has to be based upon good solid tested theory, not focused on today's "fad";
- Each module needs to add to the common database, so we end up with everyone knowing what each one of us knows;
- Each module needs to contribute in some way to building teamwork: either at a microcosm table, in a functional team, or at the very least, strengthening the team defined by the boundaries of the people in the room.

Working with an Event Planning Team, we can create an event that combines the right activities in the right order to create a genuine paradigm shift. Any one of us can design a module of an event that will work on one point or even two. It takes a team to combine all of their passions in the best learning experience possible.

Kathie Dannemiller

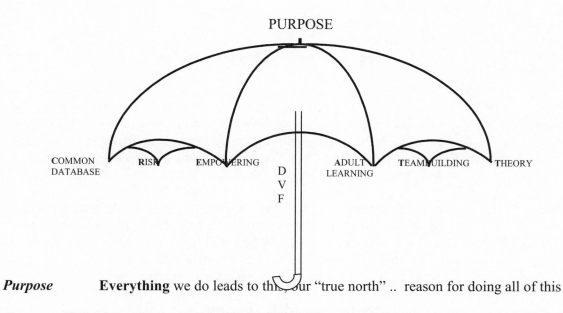

Purpose   **Everything** we do leads to this, our "true north" .. reason for doing all of this

Common Shared Database Builds community/builds systems thinking; is what enables the whole to move forward; gives us a shared picture of our business situation. There are no throwaway lines, everything must add to the common database.
Example: Telling our Stories

Risk   An expectable level that builds as the event builds, e.g. yoga and the difference between a healthy stretch and a painful stretch. Tie this to building the team and why we stay in max-mix: the longer we are together the more open we are, the more we speak up, and the more we are willing to confront.
Example: Telling our Stories is the foundation level of taking risk and throughout an event it builds to the point of being able/willing to commit to action plans.

Empowering	Increased participation Sense of wisdom Being listened to Having choice Increasing our capacity to act NO negative learnings **Example:** Open Forum gives them voice and control
Adult Learning	Good adult education, we work hard to create an environment where folks feel and are smart. Rational people with good information make good decisions. **Example:** Panels and Open Forums before we get down to doing work gives us different views so we begin to think as system not just individual.
Team Building	Continually making the team stronger and everything we do is an opportunity to build the team, both the work team and the table cross-functional team. This is way we stay in max-mix here and in a real event it allows us to go deeper with each other as we learn more about each other. **Example:** Rotating roles at table (facilitator, recorder, etc…)
Theory	Intellectual integrity, the models we believe in **Examples:** DVF, DPPE, and MCG

Event Planning Team Meeting: Getting Started

Purpose for the EPT meeting – To work together to ensure that the results the organization achieves at the Whole-Scale event are the ones it needs to achieve.

Logistics for the EPT meeting – The EPT meeting typically occurs at the client's facilities. A hotel meeting room is also an option to consider, as is your own office if its size is adequate. Depending upon the size of the group, you will sit around one table or create "max-mix" tables similar to the ones you will use in the Whole-Scale event itself. (Max-mix is simply a maximum mix of participants at each table so that each table is a microcosm of the whole room.) The only supplies the EPT team needs are a flipchart for each table, markers, and tape to hang flipchart sheets as team members fill them up (if you don't have the kind that stick to the wall). Post-it notes are handy for brainstorming and moving around ideas.

What follows is a generic design for an Event Planning Team meeting.

In spite of the detail, our generic EPT meeting design is simply a model – a starting place. The design is not an "off-the-shelf" training manual design. It will not work effectively if you try to run it exactly as it is written. You must tailor—or in some cases even radically change—it to make it relevant for your particular organization and circumstances.

GLOSSARY

Max-Mix –

Used to describe an actual microcosm of the real organization: all of the levels, experience, attitudes, locations that will be represented in the larger group meeting. We think of the max-mix group as having the same DNA as the total room will have.

Arthritic Theory –

Referring to a theory written by Kathleen Dannemiller years ago, which compares a hierarchical organization to the human body...as it ages, calcium tends to build up at the joints. It gets difficult to flow energy and blood around that build up. Kathie's theory suggests that the same happens in old-line organizations, where people have existed in "chimneys" or "silos" for a number of years. It gets difficult to see what's happening in other parts of the company because of the calcium blocks...just as it does in the physical body.

Valentines –

Describes a module we invented to get communication flowing past the arthritic blockages. It encourages people in one organization ("arthritic box") to ask for particular support from other boxes, and sets up a process to make commitments to change. The processes are based on Kathie's theory for dealing with conflict: Most conflict occurs because we are unable or unwilling to listen to (and honor) each other's needs. If we can get people to listen to see the world through the other group's eyes, a "win-win" solution is very possible.

Glad-Sad-Mad –

Describes a module we invented that allows the whole group (and individuals within that group) to get a system-wide picture of how each of us and all of us sees the organizational processes. It's the quickest way we know to get that kind of system view.

FIGURE 4 *Day 1—EPT Meeting*

7:30	**Continental Breakfast**	Post the EPT Meeting Purpose & Agenda Depending on the size of the group, provide: ■ One or more tables ■ Markers, tape, 3x5 post-it notes ■ Video player/monitor	If the group size is over 16, consider creating "max-mix" tables (a maximum mix of participants at each table so that each table is a microcosm of the whole room). Sit at a table with the group.
8:00 (30)	**Welcome/Purpose – Leadership Kickoff** Have organization leaders, both management and union, if appropriate, informally talk about: ■ What they think are the important outcomes (for them personally and the organization as a whole) of the larger event this group will be planning ■ Why they want it to happen ■ Who's here today and why they asked them to help plan ■ What they need to see accomplished by the event ■ What, if any, are the boundaries/conditions for the meeting This half-hour might also involve some question and answer, if it feels appropriate. Before they leave, leaders need to close their remarks by saying they are looking forward to returning and seeing what the group produces for the organization and to hear what the group needs from them. Then they need to introduce the consultants.	■ Decide who the EPT needs to hear from in order to legitimize the process ■ Coach the speaker(s) to talk about the outcomes they need from the larger event. (For instance, if union members are involved, union leadership will need to articulate their outcomes even if management is putting on the event.)	If not the organization's leaders, what key stakeholder(s) might convene the EPT meeting? Coach leaders on their role to set the tone for the EPT meeting: ■ Don't use viewgraphs ■ Keep it informal ■ Speak from the heart ■ Emphasize that the two days are about joining together to design a good meeting for everyone. The leadership's outcomes will not necessarily be the answer to the event's purpose—but it is important to include the leaders' yearnings in the purpose. If the leaders are able to be

| | members of the EPT, which is rare, have them share their role during the meeting.

Coach the leader regarding their role on the EPT:
■ They are a participants with a specific view of the organization
■ They should avoid as much as possible giving "the answer"
■ Rather, they should engage in the exploration to find an answer |
| Leaders can then leave until the next day. Occasionally they want to stay, and if they are willing to be there the whole time, it is very helpful. | |

| 8:30 (15) | **Agenda/Logistics/Norms**
Present a loose agenda for the two days and describe how the group will work together:

■ Be purposeful in describing agenda activities—bring the agenda to life!

■ Describe the role of the EPT before, during and after the event

● Design decisions by consensus (they have the content; you bring experience with the process)

● Explain that this is an informal meeting; break as needed, use restrooms when needed, etc.

● Emphasize that each person's truth is truth. The more open people can be with each other, while really listening to understand all the different perspectives, the better the Whole-Scale event will turn out to be…and the better this two days will be, as well. | Participants will have varying degrees of understanding and knowledge about an EPT. This is the opportunity to get all of them on the same sheet of music…a time to take the mystery out of these two days. Explain why you are here, how you were chosen, how the group needs to work together to plan a good event and what the outcomes from these two days will be. |

8:45 (until done)	**View from Event Planning Team Members (Telling Our Stories)**	The purpose is to build a composite picture of multiple realities from the diverse individual perspectives represented in the room.	**Purpose:** an opportunity for team members to connect, to begin to build themselves as a team, to hear perspectives other than their own and to begin to build a common database. (MCG)
	▪ Go around the table having each person speak about what is working and what is not working in the organization, and what needs to come out of the Whole-Scale event.		The questions that you ask individuals to use to introduce themselves are designed to uncover their yearnings for the organization and their participation in the organization and to get at their frustrations as well as what they are proud of. Craft these questions ahead of time.
	▪ Allow for questions of understanding from other team members, and feel free to ask them yourself, based on getting to the point where you can see the world through each person's eyes.	You know you are truly done with this process when you have your "finger on the pulse" of the organization: when discussions become somewhat predictable and there are no gaps in what you have heard you feel need to be filled.	
	▪ Once everyone is heard, end with a summary by listing "What We Think We Know" about the organization. "What did we hear as common themes? What were some significant differences? What are we saying we want to accomplish in a larger event?"		(See framing tips in Chapter 5, Day 1)
	▪ If you have more than one table, get them to report out to each other around common themes, differences and desired outcomes.		Each Person's Truth is Truth
	This activity can easily take two or three hours.		Be careful to ask questions that will tap each person's knowledge and yearnings (This makes the person feel "wise" instead of feeling "inadequate" —and helps people to feel wiser about each other and the organization instead of feeling "diagnosed")
	Sample questions could be:		Tip: If your event planning team is over 16 members, you might consider organizing it into tables of eight and following the process
	▪ Your name, how long you've been here, what roles you've held and what role you hold right now		
	▪ What you've been able to accomplish in the organization the past year that makes you proud		
	▪ What has happened in the past year that has frustrated you, kept you from being as effective as you wanted to be		
	▪ If you had a magic wand that gave you the power to make it happen, what you would change about the way things are going right now in the organization		
	▪ Based on all of that, what would you like to see as outcomes of the event you are planning, things that would make it worthwhile to pull that important group together?		

CHAPTER 2: DESIGNING A WHOLE-SCALE MEETING

	This is a time to listen, not debate, to see the world that the speaker sees. It's not that the speaker is right or wrong; rather it's his or her unique view and therefore important in creating the whole picture.	in Chapter 3, Day 1. Consultants might want to join a table -- you'll learn a lot!
10:35 (15)	Break	Depending on how long the "Telling our Stories," goes, build in a break.

Time	Activity		
11:35 (25)	**Overview of Whole-Scale** When the last person has told his or her story, ground the whole group in some basics of Whole-Scale. Showing a videotape of an event may help the group to visualize what they can design. Walk through some of the basic models over the two days together—when it's the "teachable moment." At this point, it's a good idea to walk through D x V x F > R to give them a flow of the change journey. Link the model to their story, which you've just unfolded together. You might also walk through any other models that are appropriate to this kind of change effort—the Whole-Scale Strategic Planning Model is sometimes helpful here…see it at Page 73.	Any handouts? (You might have handouts of models available for those who like to take notes – DPPE is a useful model to give the group because you can use it to help them understand the journey they will be taking in the meeting. Err on the side of giving handouts of various models, like DxVxF, or Strategic Planning. Those who like models will be grateful; those who don't need them won't read them until later.	What you say depends entirely upon the make-up of the Event Planning Team and what they know about the processes ahead of time. Use your judgment about what to present here without driving them into passivity…don't talk too long. You may want to send out some pre-reading to help them be ready.
	"Wild Card"		
12:00 (45)	**Lunch**		What other kind of grounding might the team need? E.g., ■ an update on what task teams have been doing

12:45 (60)	**Desired Outcomes for the Whole-Scale Event**	Help the Event Planning Team push their boundaries by looking at the opportunities created by the large group being together, by stating outcomes as results rather than activities, and by checking on whether the outcomes are realistic and achievable, yet still stretching.	After everyone has shared his or her story (the answers to the questions the consultants posed) and listened to see the world through each person's eyes, the EPT as a whole will be able to look at the yearnings and desired outcomes for a Whole-Scale event from a systems perspective.
	A room-wide brainstorm based upon the common database the group built before lunch works well here		
	You might ask participants: "What will be different at 5 p.m. on Day 3 of our larger event because we had the event?"		Tips: Remind them of the rules of brainstorming; both consultants record in order to write as fast as people talk. Feel free to try different techniques for this brainstorm, depending on group size and disposition and learning styles:
	This room-wide callout will need a couple of people to write on newsprint and will be a brainstormed one...each person's truth is truth. You will find that the outcomes feel different (though related) from the ones individuals have identified earlier, because they have listened to each other and have already expanded their database of expectations and needs for the event.		■ room-wide ■ introverted brainstorm using post-it notes ■ small group (table) brainstorm ■ affinity diagramming

1:45	**Event Purpose Statement** You might begin by having a brainstorm of phrases or words that need to be in the purpose, or having individuals or groups draft possibilities. The result needs to be true consensus on a statement of why the organization is having the Whole-Scale event…what has to be different in the world in order to make the event a true "accelerator of change." Have the whole group test the purpose by having someone read the purpose "with passion!" Ask, "Does this describe the meeting you really want to come to?"	Depending on the number of people on the team, do this activity as a whole group or in subgroups. Either way this activity can take a bit of time. It's time very well spent, as it is this purpose statement that will drive everything else that the EPT will do to plan and execute the event. Developing the purpose statement can take quite a while. Ideas may need to soak overnight and be revisited the next morning. It is worth taking enough time to get the "right answer" It is critical that the EPT reach true consensus on the statement of purpose for the event. Break as needed. A purpose will generally start with a "To…." And end with "in order to…" Some examples sometimes help, but it is important not to give them the answer. The struggle to agree on the purpose is vital to the success of the planning. Usually you will be able to get agreement…and even excitement…on a purpose statement by the end of the first day. Sometimes it helps to send the group home thinking about it, and revisit the purpose the next morning. Overnight insights are often wonderful.
4:45	**Evaluation/Close**	

CHAPTER 2: DESIGNING A WHOLE-SCALE MEETING

	Have each person say something.	
Do a Gestalt-type closure, going around the room to ask: "How is this going for you so far? What's one word that describes how you're feeling as we leave?" When you have heard from each person then ask for any advice for tomorrow…and go home.		

Day 2

Time			
8:00 (15)	**Revisiting the Agenda/Logistics/Purpose Statement for Whole-Scale Event** If the group did not complete the purpose on Day 1, you will need to finish it now – and it might take longer than 15 minutes!		Even if you have finished the purpose, it is worth reviewing and reaffirming it after a night's sleep.
8:15 (10)	**Refining Participants List** Now that the event purpose is clear, take another look at who will be attending the Whole-Scale event. Identify any additions, changes. Lippitt and Lippitt (p. 21) say it best: "One of the more critical and neglected phases of planning is an anticipatory rehearsal. It helps to answer the question of who (from inside or from outside the system) should be involved in order for a plan of action to have the best probability of success. Once you have identified these targets for involvement in planning, a second question becomes how to involve them. This sets up a new planning sequence and new goals that are concentrated on an involvement strategy."		
8:25 (30)	**Design Elements** Brainstorm activity ideas for the Whole-Scale event. What are all the ideas the EPT (consultants and representatives) might have for people the group needs to hear, conversations people need to have with each other in the room, things people need to learn from their leaders, their customers, etc., strategy the organization might need to unite around, system-wide action planning and back-home team activity plans it need to develop and share, etc., etc. You might ask:	Post-it notes can be handy here.	The purpose of this activity is to build a common database of possible options. You as process consultant usually take the lead based upon experience. This is not a time to worry about details such as sequencing of activities; here you want to encourage lots of creativity in thinking.

CHAPTER 2: DESIGNING A WHOLE-SCALE MEETING

	• What questions need to be answered during the event to help us reach our purpose? Who can answer them? • What work needs to happen? • What activities could lead us to our purpose? • What conversations need to take place?	
8:45 (105)	**Laying out a "Chunked" Agenda** Starting with the first day and the Welcome/Purpose/Agenda/Logistics, ask: "What would you want to do next?"	Do not worry about detail at this point. Break as needed. Remember: you need to help the organization build a common database during the first two days of the Whole-Scale event. Keep in mind key issues the EPT identifies, as well as key models you may have given to the team, such as the Arthritic Theory, the DVF change model, and the Strategic Planning Model. If you have a suggestion, frame it with "How about….?"

10:30	**Detailed Designing** Go back over "chunked agenda" and add detail. (Who, what, how) You can keep the group whole and work through the details. Planning Team members could self-select to work on specific chunks. Provide structure, guidelines to help them contribute where they feel wise and you need their specifics. Break out groups might work on: ■ Specific questions for Telling our Stories ■ Topics for "Organization Diagnosis" (Glads/Sads/Mads) assignment ■ Key messages to include in invitation letter – other communication ideas ■ Special considerations – e.g., how to accommodate language differences in the meeting ■ Prework assignment – if prework makes sense ■ Who should speak and what they need to speak about (list specific topics for each speaker) ■ Groupings for "Valentines" **Lunch**	Since you will often not have enough time to complete the detailed design during the two day EPT meeting, focus on the issues that only the internal members of the team can answer, such as pre-work assignment (if any) and questions that panelists and speakers would address. You can finish the detailed design and get it back to the Event Planning Team members in the days after the meeting, so the team doesn't need to sweat all the detailed logistics stuff. Talk in terms of possibilities!
12:00		

12:45	Detailed Designing (continued)		
3:15 (45)	**Reviewing the Design with Leadership** To ensure that leadership "owns" the design, the EPT walks them through the purpose and agenda, explaining rationales and making adjustments as necessary with leadership a part of the consensus. Give the planning team time to get ready. They could break into four teams: one team to walk through the process the EPT used and the outcomes & purpose they created; the other teams each walking through the flow of one day, explaining along the way the rationale behind the EPT's decisions and link to purpose. They include any coaching tips for the leadership as participants and presenters during the event.	Keep the setting informal and inclusive so leadership integrates with the planning teamg.	If leadership has problems with some of the team's work, do not take it personally. It is a signal that you and the group simply missed some important data. Usually the leader's response is, "Wow, that's great! Now, what do you want me/us to do?" To the extent possible, make adjustments by consensus right in that moment with leadership and the EPT. Otherwise, it will likely be your job to find win-win solutions later and get approval from the key stakeholders. Coach leadership ahead of time; coach EPT members on presentation purpose & process.
4:00 (45)	**Next Steps/Loose Ends** Review the role of the EPT and the consulting team before, during and after the event. This is the time to do whatever needs doing for the Whole-Scale meeting. Things to consider might include: 1. Do we need to meet again? When? Where? 2. What are the arrangements for staging day?...primarily for logistics folks and consultants 3. Who will get the logistics team leader? Workers? Should the external consulting group supply a logistics leader who has done it before?	Get agreement on who will accomplish the "to-do's" the EPT agrees on, as well as how and when.	

CHAPTER 2: DESIGNING A WHOLE-SCALE MEETING

	4. Who will create max-mix and other seating? 5. Who will invite and brief speakers? 6. What are the issues regarding the venue? 7. How will participants be invited? Who will write the letter? Etc.	
4:45 (15)	**Evaluation/Debrief/Close** Get each person to speak to a couple of questions: ■ How did we do? ■ How confident are you that the Whole-Scale event will be a success?" ■ How will you talk about these two days and the upcoming event? What will you say when you get back to work tomorrow? This last question gets folks thinking about how each individual can help generate excitement and enthusiasm for the event.	There should be a lot of warm feelings about how the team meeting went – and hope and confidence about the larger event. Expect to hear some frustration with the design process itself (it is not straightforward and easy) and some skepticism about whether the Whole-Scale event will really result in anything different. Most employees of organizations have a long history of disappointments, so their skepticism is understandable and appropriate.

Chapter 3
Facilitating: Whole-Scale Style

(Before, During, and After the Meeting)

Process consultants facilitate all the time. However, this chapter focuses specifically on facilitation you will do (before, during, and after the event) in direct support of a large-group meeting. We've realized over the years that there's no difference between large and small group in terms of how we facilitate. The principles we use in large groups are for the most part the same principles that we apply to small groups. Ron Lippitt, who taught many of us small group process, clearly articulated one of the disadvantages of being an outsider as lacking the context and history of the particular system and its operational problems. We learned how to utilize internal planning teams in order to counteract that dilemma. The wisdom about the purpose and content of any organizational event lies in the participants of the event. Edgar Schein in his book *Process Consultation: Its Role in Organization Development* (p.9, Addison-Wesley 1969) defines process consultation as: "a set of activities on the part of the consultant which help the client to perceive, understand, and act upon process events which occur in the client's environment." With these thoughts providing the context for the Whole-Scale consulting approach, let's now focus on large-group meeting facilitation.

The first and foremost rule of Whole-Scale consulting and facilitation is that you NEVER work alone. During a large-group meeting the consultant has many roles to balance: relationship building, designing ahead, gathering and interpretation of data, coordinating with logistics, teaming with other consultants, balancing stakeholder needs, facilitating small groups, coaching leaders and presenters and leading from in front of the room. It would be impossible for one individual to give each of these roles adequate attention to ensure the success of the meeting.

Coaching Is Important

Coaching is one of the most important roles of the consultant. You will coach event planning teams, leaders, presenters, the logistics team and each other or other consultants working with you. What follows are the important coaching considerations to think about as you approach an event. The coaching tips cover the times before, during and after the event itself. The lists are not intended to be complete. You will certainly think of others things you might do as well.

COACHING: BEFORE THE EVENT

- For Presenters/Leaders:
  - Contract for time keeping (cued or on his or her own, etc.)
  - Emphasize the importance of good time keeping (short presentations and lots of Q & A)
  - Contact ahead of time, at least by phone, to coach /understand the purpose and outcomes, roles, and content guidelines for any presentation suggested by the Event Planning Team (EPT).
  - Paint the picture of what to expect during the event
  - Describe the kind and style of presentation that works:
    - no slides
    - no overheads
    - from the heart – "Honesty is the best charisma"
    - open forum process
  - Help people who are presenting rehearse beforehand, if necessary, or if the group wants it (A staging day to get ready is very helpful)

- For the Event Planning Team:
  - Instruct them to come a few minutes early to help greet attendees
  - Paint the picture of what to expect during the meeting
  - Make sure they understand what their role in the larger meeting is
  -
- For the Logistics Team/Czar:
  - Paint the picture of what to expect during the meeting
  - Make sure they understand their role in the meeting
  - Walk through the meeting design with the czar/czarina and/or whole logistics team

COACHING: DURING THE EVENT

- In the morning, provide coaching for:
  - Czar/czarina of logistics
  - leader
  - EPT
  - other consultants on the team

- Be clear and precise in your communications—use direct language

- Coach everyone to be a good listener ("see the world others see")

- As panels of presenters show up, consultants meet them and do final preparation (*helpful tip: assign a specific consultant to be the liaison to each panel*)
  - Explain how the process will work when they begin
  - Arrange for time signals – contract or re-contract

- Discuss each of the presentations with the panels beforehand: Did they get at the points the Event Planning Team had hoped for?

- Coach people (presenters and the logistics team) on how to use microphones

- Coach the logistics team and the presenters on how to handle questions from an Open Forum

- Keep the panel together during first part of open forum (table discussion)
  - Say "The more questions you answer in open forum, the more satisfied participants will be"

- Throughout the day, provide coaching for:
  - Participants
  - Presenters

- Coach the participants in the meeting to make sure they get their questions answered (Always check back to the table to make sure the question has been adequately answered, before moving on)

- During table preparation for the Open Forum:
  - Roam the room to hear the questions participants are likely to ask (you can also coach presenters to do this)
  - Think about how the Q & A process will take shape

- Coach presenters on how to answer questions during the Open Forum:
  - Speak from the heart
  - Admit it if you do not know the answer
  - Give short and simple answers

COACHING: AFTER EACH DAY OF THE MEETING

- While reading evaluations:
  - Show people how to read for themes in the evaluations
  - Remind readers not to focus on the negative
  - Let them know that the purpose is to learn, not to critique

- Discuss next steps/continuation with leaders and event planning team
- Give tips on summarizing the last day evaluations and preparing to give everyone the feedback

- Discuss with Event Planning Teams and others what their post-session roles will be
- Offer suggestions on how to synthesize the data from the meeting and put it into some kind of usable fashion

Large Group Vs. Small Group Facilitation

Most consultants are well grounded in the skills for small group facilitation and training. When you go from a group of 16-24 to a group of 160-2600, however, important differences in methods and approach emerge.

Focus on People and Process
One thing that stands out about Whole-Scale facilitation is that you, the facilitator, are *not* the center of attention. The process and the people are the center – the action is not up-front with the facilitator. In small group facilitation it is possible to have direct contact and conversation with each person. In large group facilitation you just can't do this – you may be talking to 300-400 people in the room.

If you "grew up" in the world of small group facilitation you may feel lonely with this style—another good reason never to work alone. As a facilitator of large group events, the payoff and rewards come from watching real empowerment come to life in the room. People see and understand the issues, create the future possibilities, decide on the actions and commitments they need to take and experience ways to conduct effective meetings with their max-mix table group.

The facilitator of a large group event has to trust the design for the event—a relatively easy task in the Whole-Scale approach because you, the facilitator, didn't design the meeting alone. You designed it with an Event Planning Team (EPT) that knows best what needs to happen and what will work in their culture. Remember that anguish and chaos, when they appear, are not negative; they are part of the Whole-Scale process and indeed part of any large group meeting. Trust the process and rely on the daily evaluations, the work with your partner and the EPT to know if the design is working and what to change if it's not.

The rest of this chapter focuses on bringing to life the differences between the two. Some of those differences are listed below:

Small Group Facilitation

The consultant /facilitator can:

- Check with the group for understanding of instructions
- Make the working of assignments informal
- More easily use visual aides
  - Overheads
  - Computer modules
  - GroupWare brainstorms
- Adjust timing for small groups
- Give instructions orally or put them on flipcharts
- Control the logistics
- Get feedback from interaction with individual participants
- Handle the facilitation from the front of the room
- Work alone

Large Group Facilitation

The consultants /facilitators:
- Give instructions only one time
  - No throw-away lines are possible

- Use precise verbal framing and appropriate written language
  - ➢ The wording of instructions can make a huge difference
- Give assignment instructions in verbal **and** written form most of the time
- Use visuals only rarely
  - ➢ Overheads sap energy
  - ➢ A handout for each person of what would have been on the overhead is much more empowering…and the person can even take notes
- Never allow one table to hold up the entire room
  - ➢ Quick recovery is not possible
- Use a logistics plan and team
- Constantly get—and use—feedback from the Event Planning Team, the leaders, the participants, and the whole group energy
- Encourage facilitation to occur mostly within the table group
- Never work alone

Now let's walk through each of the bullets under large group facilitation above.

Give instructions only one time. In small group facilitation you are close enough to the participants that if something isn't clear you can take questions and probably not lose more than two to three minutes. It is easy to call a "Stop Action" in a room of 15-30 people. They can hear you and see you, and you can quickly get their attention. In a group of 300-400 people, however, calling a stop to their work is a little like trying to stop a herd of elephants. If your instructions are not clear, you might never know it in a room of 300-400 people. Or as a Dannemiller Tyson Associated consultant experienced – it is possible to give instructions, watch folks go to work assuming they are on track, only to walk around the room as flip charts begin to fill up and find that half the table groups are doing one thing while the other half are doing another. This is definitely an experience to learn from, not to repeat! Make sure that everything you say in front of the room has meaning and relevance to the assignment you are about to give, and spend significant time and energy getting it "just right" before you stand up to give the instructions. Everything you say counts: there can be no "throw-away lines."

Use precise verbal framing and appropriate written language. Providing good written instructions is closely tied to giving oral instructions, as assignments are both written and verbal. It is critical to frame the assignment appropriately. Framing means creating the context and the energy for people to do the work you are asking them to do. There are several components of framing and introducing the assignment:

- **Tie the assignment to the event purpose** – how does what the group is about to do move them closer to achieving the purpose of the meeting/event?
- **Tie the assignment to what has come before** – how does what the group is about to do support the work they have been doing to this point in this meeting/event?
- **Tie the assignment to what will be done later** – how will the group use the products of this activity as they moves forward?
- **Give specifics of how the activity will be done** – this includes giving directions, providing clear expectations for work output and establishing an environment for this activity.
- **Spell out the time frame, the location of the assignment and roles for the groups** – how long will participants have to complete this activity, where will they do their work and what process roles will be helpful to them as they work?

An example of good framing can be found in the Open Forum Model, depicted in Figure 2. Open Forum provides a good example because of its importance in almost every Whole-Scale meeting.

To frame, read aloud through the written assignment, which participants will find in their in-box, placed there by the logistics team "just in time" for the work to be done. If participants have the assignment in hand, you might ask, why read it from the front of the room? As you know, different learning styles take in information in different ways. The more senses that are involved in understanding the assignment, the better the chances are that people will understand it. Plus, depending on your environment you cannot count on everyone in the room being able to read.

The EPT has designed the assignments prior to the event to make sure the language is clear and fits with their culture. In contrast, you will need to develop framing during the event as it pulls from relevant information coming out of the event to that point. Meaningful framing and clearly worded assignments contribute significantly to the success of the event. Five minutes of talk may require as much as 60 minutes to write—to get it right.

Good framing is an "art." Some of the components of this art are:

- It's an invitation
- It enables the audience's diversity
- It opens rather than closes possibilities
- It offers flexibility and inclusiveness (critical)
- It's empowering
- It builds relationships

The consultant doing the framing needs to keep the following principles in mind:

- Be authentic
- Be very clear about what the Event Planning Team or Leadership Group needs to do up front – pre-work is key
- Know and understand your audience
- Know the emotional tone of the group
-

Finally, this is another point at which not working alone comes into play. Write out your framing and then bounce it off your co-consultant for refinements – take very seriously the phase "no throw-away lines."

Use Visuals Only Rarely. Be leery of using visual aide equipment in a large group event. From your own experience think about what happens to your energy when the lights go down in a meeting. Multiply that by 300-400 people, and you have a room full of low-energy folks. On very rare occasions it may be appropriate to use visuals. We once worked with a VP for Finance who was scheduled to present. Two days before the event, his mother died. He took the time to make a 10-minute video of his presentation. Given the circumstances, that video went a very long way to creating credibility.

Another reason for not using overheads is that rarely does the person speaking create his or her own slides. When you have the whole organization in the room, people need to see their leaders and perceive them as sincere and speaking from the heart. The leader's sincerity rarely shines through when he or she is speaking from overheads someone else has prepared. Participants see though this and say, "Same old, same old." In addition, presenters often buy into the myth that people will be able to see the slides from a large room. Handouts work much better.

Never allow one table to hold up the entire room. Never sacrifice the room for an individual or a small group…an axiom that applies in both large group and small group work. It is much easier in the small group setting to adjust time, stop for questions, even process an activity. In large group meetings, be concerned far more with the critical mass of participants. Where are they in the process? If 20 tables are working diligently to complete the assignment and two are struggling, trust that the 20 will come up with answers that the two will be able to live with. In a meeting of 300-400, one individual or table of eight *cannot* hold up the entire room.

Encourage facilitation to occur mostly within the table groups. Set up tables from the start of a large group meeting to be self-managing. Everything you are doing is based on the underlying purpose of building capacity in the client system to carry on when you are gone. Thus, do not have professional facilitators at the tables. Starting with the first activity, ask table groups to choose process roles such as facilitator, timekeeper, recorder and spokesperson. Rely on the table groups. Most participants will understand the assignment and work with those that don't to ensure clarity. In the rare instance where the table group remains unclear, people can seek out one of the consultants for clarification.

Give assignment instructions in verbal and written form most of the time. Using flip chart paper to give instructions works great for small groups where everyone can see the chart. In a room of even 100 participants the folks in the back or sides of the room can't read instructions on a chart in the front of the room. If participants have their own handout of the assignment they have a place for notes and can follow along with instructions from the front of the room. If they choose, they have the assignment to take back to work. Getting handouts to participants is the work of the logistics team. They do it on a "just in time" basis, so that when the work is to be done, the instructions are available. For copies of handouts for an event, encourage the client to use different colored paper for different assignments. The facilitator from the front of the room will then be able to say, "In your inbox you will find a blue handout – pull it out." Do everything possible to make it easy for participants to focus on the work and not the logistics.

Use a logistics plan and team. If you think back to the roles identified at the beginning of this chapter, you will realize that it would be impossible to also worry about the logistics in a room of 300-400 people. The logistics team (See Chapter Six for more detailed information about logistics teams) are like stage-hands in a play. They are there to ensure that participants have what they need when they need it. If the team has done its job, logistics people will be inconspicuous during the event except for a "thank you" at the end. The structure of the consultant team and the logistics team is hierarchical in that the consultants get information to the team through the Logistics Team Czar/Czarina. It is then the czar/czarina's responsibility to delegate the work to the logistics team. Consider making the logistics czar/czarina part of the consulting team during the Event Planning Team meeting. As the design of the meeting unfolds, he or she will have good ideas on the logistics of how to do the work. It is critical that the consulting team and the logistics czar/czarina constantly share the same image of the process, activities and timing for the meeting.

Constantly get—and use—feedback from the Event Planning Team, the leaders, the participants, and the whole group energy. Remember that as an external consultant, if you are, causes you to be "lacking the context and history of the particular system and its operational problems," as Ron Lippitt would remind us. Base your event designing and even redesigning on this principle. Do not make decisions about the event design, or make changes during an event, on your own. Our DTA way of making sure that we are keeping the voice of the organization paramount in our decisions is through the following method: At the end of each day of an event, we will hand out a one-page, three-question (generally) evaluation that we ask each individual to complete anonymously. The logistics team collects these evaluations as folks leave the room. The EPT, consultants (internal and external) and logistics czar then sit in a circle and pass the sheets around the circle, read all the evaluations – all of them. After you've read them, ask yourselves two questions: "What are they saying about today?" And "What if anything do we need to change for tomorrow to allow us to achieve our purpose?" Facilitate that group, of course, and you will get the answers to anything that needs to change for the next day. Consensus will be required, as usual, and it can take an hour or so to get there. It's worth it. Sometimes when the group has made a decision, the consultants may have to stay around longer to create new handouts and new design flow.

The other type of changes that you will face during an event are changes to the environment: i.e., "It's too hot /cold in here." You will hear these complaints either directly or through the logistics team. Do not act on one lone comment. Follow a rule that says "Don't do anything for an individual that takes away from the learning of the whole, and don't do anything for the whole that takes away from the learning of an individual." As you might guess, following this guideline is at times not easy. An isolated comment may be just that – one person's experience. Hold off until you hear the same comments from other locations in the room and then act. Your job is to make the meeting work and be meaningful for everyone—and genuine physical discomfort can be very distracting.

In summary, all the partners at Dannemiller Tyson Associates came out of small group facilitation and all would now say that large group facilitation is much more rewarding. The principles outlined in this chapter work – for small groups and large! They honor the individuals and the organization by building their strength to carry on without outside help. DTA hopes you find the same fulfillment in using them as it has.

Figure I. The Roles Consultants Balance

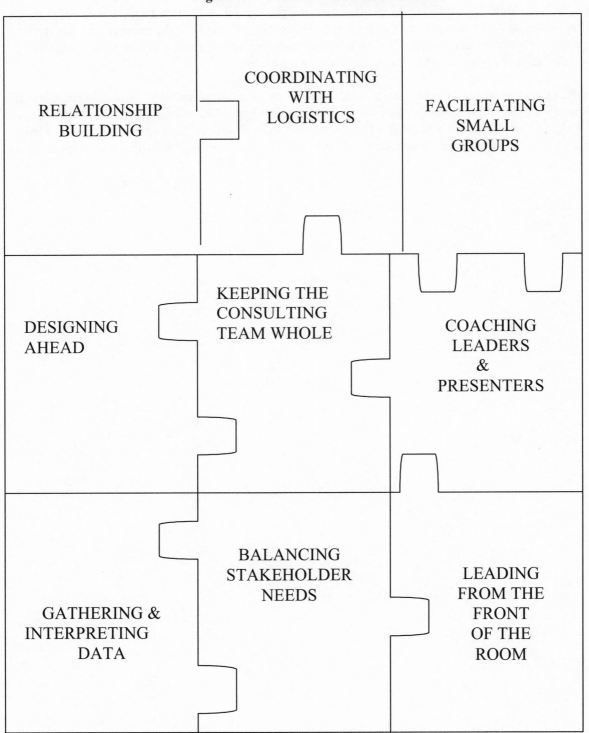

CHAPTER 3: FACILITATING: WHOLE-SCALE STYLE

Figure II Open Forum: Tips and Advice

The Open Forum is an adaptable method for having participants integrate information. It is especially effective when a speaker or a panel makes a presentation. Its basic format is as follows:

CONTENT/ACTIVITY	NOTES	WHO
Introduction of Speaker	Let participants know that they will have an opportunity to discuss and question what they hear. This interactive process is part of building shared understanding. Also ask them to listen for understanding.	Facilitator
Talk by leader / stakeholder	Encourage speakers to keep remarks to about 20 minutes or less. It's best if there are *no* slides, viewgraphs, etc. Encourage the presenter to speak "from the heart" in order to ensure that it will carry impact. Participants can always tell the difference. .	Leader / Stakeholder
Table discussions	Table discussions work best if each table appoints a facilitator, recorder, and question asker. Give them about 15 minutes to discuss: ▪ What did we hear? ▪ What are our reactions? ▪ What questions of understanding do we want to ask? Of whom?	Participants
Question /Answer Session	Each table's "Question Asker" poses the table's questions to the speaker. This process works best if the facilitator moderates, by identifying tables that have questions, being sure that the questions are for understanding - not debate or speechmaking by the question asker, keeping time, etc. Check back with the question asker to see if the answer actually got to their question. (Note: This does not necessarily mean that the response pleased the questioner.)	All

ADDITIONAL TIPS AND NOTES ABOUT OPEN FORUM

Some of the advantages of Open Forum are:

- It promotes a "message" being sent and received.
- It inhibits interruption during a talk.
- It ensures that the speaker will get well thought out questions.
- It encourages participants to process what they hear. Different people will hear and key in on different things, have different "hot buttons", etc. The table discussion acts as a leveling tool and enables participants to help each other with things they may have missed or misconstrued.
- It reduces the likelihood of disruption by "difficult" participants. Most questions that people at the various tables ask or the comments they make become those of greatest importance to the most people.
- It helps build community. In addition to listening for understanding, participants get to hear the questions and concerns of others and can gauge how similar those are to their own.
- It enables the speaker and other participants to assess how clearly participants received the intended message, or where misunderstandings occurred.

Other Tips:

- The Open Forum format is an excellent way of having people integrate complex information.
- Participants can rearrange themselves to allow for cross-discussion, e.g., discussion with people who have different points of view within a "community"
- The consultant can redirect the Open Forum process by asking different questions, e.g.: "What common themes did you hear?" "What new insights/understandings did you get?" "Which issues stand out as most important your group now?"

Three important things happen in the communication process of an open forum:

- Everyone hears the same brief presentation
- 15 minutes of discussion help people synthesize the data they have heard
- Everyone in the room hears and understands the answers to the questions people ask

Chapter 4
Logistics: Freeing Participants to be Creative

Logistics that work are critical to the success of any Whole-Scale event—large or small. In successful "Whole-Scale change" meetings, activities *must* flow like clockwork. All the meeting components—participants, speakers, consultants, and materials—*must be* <u>where</u> people need them *when* people need them. Participants will experience anything less as chaos. They will either feel "herded around," or they will feel that no one is in charge and thus infer that the meeting is not important. You need to have a well-organized, well-briefed logistics team to carry out the behind-the-scenes activities that ensure a "seamless" event for the participants. (The work of the logistics team includes administrative matters before the session as well.)

The number of people you will need on your logistics team depends upon the complexity of your meeting design, and a rule-of-thumb to use is one logistics person for about every 40 participants. Additionally, it is important to have a designated logistics czar/czarina to manage the logistics team, serve as liaison to the consulting team and coordinate arrangements with the meeting facility.

This chapter includes generic checklists of logistics issues you will typically need to address prior to the session, immediately before the session, and during the session. . Also in this chapter you will find samples of handouts to use in registration packets and for the more complex assignments. *Note: As this is generic information, the actual logistics and handouts you develop for the event you are leading must respond to your specific agenda design.*

Some of the things suggested here will not make sense unless you have an overall feel for the flow of the meeting. We recommend that you peruse the other parts of the field book if you have not already done so before you read any further.

ADMINISTRATION BEFORE THE SESSION

The bold-faced numbers following some of the items below refer to the more detailed notes following the checklists.

Logistics Personnel
__ Have you identified a logistics "czar/czarina"? **1**
__ If you have a czar/czarina who is external to the organization, have you identified an
internal counterpart to coordinate arrangements? **2**
__ Have you identified and briefed a logistics team? **3**

Facility Arrangements
__ Have you booked a facility?

Space Requirements
__ Is your main room big enough? **4**
__ Do you have enough breakout space? **5**
__ Is there enough space for meals? Refreshments? **10**
__ Will you be able to keep the meeting room overnight (or will you need to store materials?)
__ Do you have space for a "logistics headquarters"?
__ Have you arranged for a meeting room for the Event Planning Team on the staging day?
__ Have you arranged for workspace for the leadership team for the evening of Day 2?
__ Does the facility management know you will be taping flipchart sheets to their walls? **6**
__ Are there adequate phone and bathroom facilities?

Equipment Requirements
__ Will the lighting be bright enough to help keep up the participants' energy level?
__ Will the sound system be adequate? **7**
__ Have you arranged for other equipment as needed? **8**
   __ Audio/Visual (main room and breakouts)
   __ Computer/Printer
   __ Copier
__ Will there be adequate coat racks for all participants?
__ Will you need risers or platforms? If so, how many?

Set-Up Requirements
__ Have you arranged the room set-up? **9**
   __ The right number of round tables for eight, with numbers on table stands
   __ Podium/panel table for front of room on the long wall
   __ The right number of registration tables outside the room
__ Have you arranged for tables to be set and refreshed as needed?
   __ Numbers on stands
   __ Water
   __ Pads and felt-tip pens
   __ In-boxes
__ Have you arranged a mechanism to get messages to participants?
__ Can you get into your space with enough time to set up?

Food Requirements
__ Have you arranged for meals and refreshments? **10 and 11**

Participant Needs
__ Has the organization identified the participants?

Information
__ Have invitations gone out to participants far enough in advance (including start and end times, dress code)?
__ Has pre-work (if any) gone out to participants at the appropriate time?
__ Do participants have all the pre-meeting information they might need?
    __ Travel information, map to facility
    __ Parking information

Seating Assignments for the Meeting
__ Are your seating assignment lists prepared for all configurations? **12**
    __ Are *all* the participants included?
    __ Are the lists up-to-date, given substitutions or late additions?

Materials 13
__ Have you ordered all the materials you will need to support your design, or do you have a plan to get them?

___ In-Boxes:	One for each table in the room and breakouts
___ Flipcharts and easels:	One for each table in the room and breakouts; two in front of the main room
___ Extra flipchart pads	
___ Markers (Mr. Sketch) Watercolor, not permanent☺	2-3 for each table, + extras
___ Masking tape:	1 roll for each logistics member + extras
___ Myers-Briggs books:	One for each participant + extras
___ ¼ inch red dots and gold stars:	For voting as needed
___ Crayons:	One dark color for each participant for voting
___ 3 X 5 inch "Post-It" notes:	½ pad for each participant
___ "Flair" type felt-tip pens:	One for each participant + extras
___ Scratch pads:	One for each participant + extras
___ Name tags:	One for each participant + extras
___ Banners for posting results:	As needed depending on design

Presenter Needs
__ Do you know what speakers will want for their presentations?
   __ Podium
   __ Style of microphone: lavaliere, cordless, etc.
   __ A/V equipment
   __ Handouts/materials they will want to distribute

STAGING DAY (OR BEFORE)

__ Are you working from the final (or most recent) version of the design?

Facility Arrangements and Room Set-Up
__ Have you finalized your plans with the facility?
   __ Audio/Visual (main room and breakouts)
   __ Meals and refreshments
   __ Room set-up (main and breakouts)
   __ Table set-up and refreshments
__ Have you checked the lights and sound system (and other equipment as needed)?
__ Have you posted the purpose, agenda, and planning model up front if they are not on a handout?
__ Do you know where the breakout rooms are?
__ Do you have a plan for extra people?

Meeting Plans
__ Do you have a plan for participant registration? **14**
__ Do you have a plan for how people get to their first assigned seat?
__ Do you have a floor plan that shows how the tables are set up?
__ Have you divided it into sections for open forums? **15**
__ Do you have a plan for how people find their breakout rooms?

Materials and Equipment
__ Are nametags ready at the registration table? Do you have extras?
__ Do you have all your registration packets stuffed?
__ Do you have all the assignments that need to be there either on handouts or on flipcharts?
   __ Telling Our Stories
   __ Valentine packets
   __ Nightly evaluations
   __ Others
__ Do you have all the materials and equipment you will need?
   __ From list above
   __ Computer/printer/extra disk   __ Trash cans
   __ Extra copies of design   __ Copier paper
   __ Extra copies of breakout room maps   __ Staplers and staples
   __ Extra copies of handouts   __ Pen knife
   __ Scissors   __ Rubber bands

STAGING DAY – DATE – LOCATION

The purpose of Staging Day is to get everything set up and ready to go. On this day, the logistics team will become absolutely clear on its roles and goals and the agenda flow for the upcoming days of the event. The Planning Team, the Leadership Team, the presenters and the consultants will connect with each other and make sure everyone has a common understanding of what will happen and has done everything he or she is supposed to do to ensure that the event will go smoothly and will achieve its purpose.

It may be a good idea to develop a pre-reading package for the members of the logistics team to help orient them to the facility. This is also the time to move supplies and materials to the facility.

The generic schedule below describes the typical things that happen on Staging Day

. Time	Content/Process	Logistics
9:00 a.m.	**General Meeting of Logistics Team, Leadership Team, presenters and consultants**	▪ Make general announcements ▪ Make sure everyone understands the purpose of the day and what his or her role is ▪ Give pre-reading packets to logistics team members

	Logistics Team Meets with Consulting Team and Logistics Czar/Czarina
	▪ Build yourselves as a team:
	  ➢ Introduce everyone
	  ➢ Get clear on Logistics Role and expectations of each other
	  ➢ Describe how you expect to communicate as a consulting team and a logistics team—e.g., the Logistics Czar/Czarina is the key link to the consulting team
	▪ Walk through the meeting agenda design so logistics team members will understand the flow and identify key logistics actions. (It's the Czar/Czarina's option to ask consultants to stay for the walk-through.)
		▪ Plan continental breakfast, breaks and lunch (Note: It's easier to order food brought in.)
		▪ Provide a copy of the agenda design for each logistics team member
		▪ Have a list of Logistics Team members for all on the team

	Then Czar/Czarina & Logistics Team begin to work to: ▪ Identify specific roles ▪ Inventory supplies and handouts ▪ Sort and label handouts for each day	▪ Logistics Roles could be: ➢ Audio ➢ Handouts ➢ Microphone People (three to four) ➢ Recorders (three to four) ➢ Laptops ➢ Climate ➢ Food ➢ Documentation
	While the facility sets up the room, ▪ Check the room layout and tweak as necessary ▪ Set up a logistics "command center" ▪ Do anything else you can think of to get a head start	▪ Set up the Logistics "command center" ▪ Provide laptops, printer, copier and other supplies: ➢ Two to three rolls of 1" masking tape ➢ 3 x 5 post-it notes—1/2 pad per person ➢ Crayons for voting ➢ Dots for voting (15 red & 15 green per person) ➢ Flair-type pen for each person to write on post-it notes ➢ 10 pair of scissors for turnaround ➢ Scotch tape ▪ A Logistics supply kit is handy, with things like: ➢ Stapler and staples ➢ Paper clips ➢ Rubber bands ➢ Business-size envelopes, if called for in the design ▪ Two step ladders make hanging headers easier

	After the facility sets up the table and chairs, logistics team members can do the following things: ▪ Put handouts on tables ▪ Place an In-Basket at each table ▪ Station flipchart easels around the periphery of the room	*Check Table Seating:* ▪ Number of participants divided by 8 equals the number of participant tables you will need ▪ Provide an extra table for last-minute shows ▪ Also provide a table for the consultants and observers, if there are any,. and provide a table for the logistics team

	Logistics team continues to work to: ▪ Set up and test microphones ▪ Train microphone people on the Open Forum process and make sure they know how to operate cordless, handheld microphones ▪ Train one person overall to work the audio/visual system with an a/v technician ▪ Make a drawing of the room layout ▪ Make copies to refer to for planning breakouts, quadrants for Open Forum, etc. ▪ Make the Open Forum grid. Post the grid on the podium ▪ Set up the registration table outside the room. Lay name tags out in alphabetic order ▪ Make headers ("banners") for the stations to post when needed. ▪ Make headers for Glads/Sads/Mads (G/S/M) ▪ Have a game plan to quickly take down the headers from External View 1 and put up the G/S/M headers if the design calls for speed. **Meanwhile, you as the Consultant may do the following:** ▪ Check in with the Logistics Czar/Czarina to hear what's happening in the organization (members of the Event Planning Team? The Leadership Team?) ▪ Tweak anything you need to ▪ Review everything and be ready ▪ Touch base with anybody you need to (presenters, leaders, etc.)	*Provide Participant Lists for Czar/Czarina:* ▪ Alphabetical list of participants ▪ Table list of participants ▪ List of participants by Dept/Division *Make Nametags:* ▪ Place on registration tables ▪ Put the appropriate table number on each name tag *Get microphones ready:* ▪ Set up cordless, hand-held microphones ▪ Put a mike at the podium ▪ Provide two to three mikes for the panel table *Have a full-time AV technician* *Set up VCR and Monitors, if needed* *Prepare the front of the room:* ▪ Provide a riser with the podium ▪ Place Open Forum Grid on the podium *Set up Easels:* ▪ Have one available for each table ▪ Set charts up around the periphery of the room to start the day ▪ Provide three additional t easels up front *Prepare the tables:* ▪ Put an in-basket, table number and marker pens at each ▪ At each place setting, place a folder with handouts: 1. List of Event Planning Team members; list of Operating Committee & Staff Group on reverse 2. One-page handout of Purpose/Agenda for the days of the event with Roles of table facilitator, recorder, spokesperson on the back, along with Rules for Brainstorming. 3. "Case for Change" if created 4. D x V x F > R model 5. Strategic Planning Model 6. Map of the facility
5:00 p.m. or when finished	**Adjourn and get a good night's sleep!**	

IMMEDIATELY BEFORE AND DURING THE SESSION

Final Check: Set-Up
__ Are the tables spaced adequately in the main room? In breakouts?
__ Are the tables set as desired in the main room? In breakouts?
__ Is the chart paper in position in main room? In breakouts?
__ Is the front of the room set up as desired?
__ Do participants have access to the perimeter of the room to hang flipchart sheets?
__ Are all the mikes working? Do you have extra batteries?

Ongoing Needs 16 and 17
__ Do you have a plan for moving easels in and out of the table area?
__ Have you identified team members to hand out/reveal assignments?
__ Do you have an adequate number of copies of all handouts?
__ Are your handouts and materials counted out into table-size sets for fast distribution?
__ Have you identified team members to carry microphones?
__ Do you have a plan for collecting, labeling, saving, typing & distributing work participants do during session? **18**
__ Are you keeping the easels clear of "old" work?
__ Are you minimizing your movement and noise so you do not distract the participants?
__ Are you freshly supplying all materials both in the main room and breakout areas as they are used up or lost?
    __ Chart paper
    __ Markers
    __ Tape
__ Are you keeping aisle ways and perimeter of room clear so participants can move around easily?
__ Do you have a plan for spreading out voting assignments as much as possible?
__ Are you giving breakout groups time warnings & getting them back to main room as needed?

NOTES

1. Logistics Leadership
To streamline communication and minimize conflicting instructions between the logistics team and the consultants, designate one person as logistics team "czar/czarina" to coordinate all communication, work, and assignments and serve as liaison to the consulting team and facility staff. The logistics czar/czarina is like a stage manager in the theater. Professional trainers or meeting planners need to be particularly open to new ideas if one of them happens to be the czar/czarina because they usually have a different paradigm about how to run a meeting. *You will get regular feedback about how unusual the kind of meeting described here really is.*

2. Internal Logistics Resource

The client may handle many of the logistics arrangements directly. These include such items as contracting for the facility and food, sending invitations and arranging for presenters. It is essential, therefore, to establish a single internal point of contact for coordinating logistics with the logistics czar/czarina. It is important to be in frequent contact with the internal contact between the event planning team meeting and the event.

There are two major benefits from having an internal logistics coordinator:
- The internal coordinator is familiar with the system and can get things done easily and quickly.
- Working with an internal coordinator makes it possible to begin transferring skills to the client system as they do the practical leg work needed to prepare for an event.

Make sure that the internal logistics coordinator has enough help. There is nothing worse than getting to the day of an event and finding out that a task has not been done because the internal coordinator, overwhelmed by other organizational demands, did not see it as important. Examples are arranging for max-mix seating, preparing nametags and making sure that meals can be served very quickly.

3. Logistics Team Members and Responsibilities

It is helpful to a company-wide change effort to select as logistics team members people who will not be participants but who will benefit from being part of the session. Team members should understand that logistics work is demanding and fast-paced!

As soon as possible after the organization has identified the logistics team, brief them on the nature of a Whole-Scale session (what you are trying to accomplish, what kind of environment you are trying to create, what you believe are some of the critical success factors as related to logistics activities) and the logistics team's role in the process.

In general, the logistics team is responsible for:

- Providing all materials and handouts
- Preparing and posting assignments on chart paper as required
- Preparing and distributing assignments on handouts as required
- Helping to direct participants during lunch and breaks
- Relaying phone messages for participants and consultants
- Responding to minor catastrophes as they arise (e.g., room arrangement)
- Handling registration
- Distributing name tags
- Leading groups to breakout rooms
- Moving easels to and away from the participant tables
- Organizing the feedback on the draft strategy at the end of Day 2 for the leadership
- Typing, copying, and distributing the final goals and objectives before the session resumes on Day 3. (It is important to contract with some team members in advance to cover the "evening" shift.)
- Making copies of the Action Plans on Day 3 to distribute to the participants
- Walking cordless microphones to participant speakers during open forums and report outs
- Periodically checking flip charts for paper supply and replenishing as needed
- Collecting, labeling, and storing participants' output
- Giving breakout groups time warnings and shepherding them back to the main room
- Performing other tasks as they arise (flexibility is important!).

4. Main Meeting Room Size

The room must be large enough to accommodate the number of participants seated at round tables of eight. Furthermore, there must be sufficient aisle and perimeter space to allow people to easily move around and to accommodate flipcharts. This usually means that you need more space than the hotel thinks you do because they only give enough space for waiters and waitresses to get through, which can lead to fairly tight quarters. Multiplying the number of participants by 25 square feet per person will give you the approximate capacity for your purposes. You will need extra space if you plan to use video screens, cameras, etc. Be careful that the facility doesn't switch meeting rooms on you without your knowledge! Try to avoid rooms that are too long and narrow (the "bowling alley" effect). The "front" of the room should be on the longest wall.

5. Size, Number, and Location of Breakout Rooms

In the main room, given enough "elbow room" between tables, groups will be able to stand the noise level for short assignments, but for many activities, relatively private meeting space works better (for groups of various sizes) so participants can hear each other well enough to accomplish complex or delicate assignments.

Make sure that "breakout rooms" are adjacent to the main room so that traveling between them is quick and easy. If they are not close by, they may not get used much because the agenda design cannot accommodate the additional travel time required.

Although the number of breakout rooms you will need is driven by the actual agenda design, the number of participants, and the availability of facilities, these rules-of-thumb will help you maintain flexibility in the face of uncertainty:

A. Try to have space available to send about two-thirds of the largest subgroups to breakouts where they will have plenty of elbow room. (Some groups can stay in the main room.) Groups larger than eight people have a particularly hard time hearing each other if they are in a loud environment.
B. If your meeting is not planned before you need to book a facility, maximize your design flexibility by holding two to four big, open spaces that will each comfortably hold one-third to one-half of the participants at round tables. This is *in addition* to the main room and lunch room.
C. Avoid trying to give breakout groups privacy by dividing open spaces with curtains or screens: they make the noise issue worse because groups do not get the visual reminder of their impact on each other.

At the meeting itself, it is important to help participants find their breakout rooms quickly and easily. Include a map of the facility in their registration packet and hand out lists of breakout assignments, as they are needed. Also, members of the logistics team often act as guides.

6. Taping to Walls

Many facilities have rules about taping to their walls. You can usually get permission from the facility to tape things up since they want your business. For the most difficult situations, 3M makes some special tapes guaranteed not to take off paint or leave residue. (One option is Scotch Brand drafting or painters tape which is pretty easy to find.)

7. Sound System

Use hard-wired mikes for the front of the room and cordless mikes for the audience. You will need one mike for the podium, one for every two people who will be sitting at a panel table, and three to five cordless mikes depending on the size of your meeting. Be sure to check the requirements for mikes in breakout rooms also.

Since the meeting depends upon people being able to hear each other, it is critical to have a full-time audio technician to run the sound system. Many in-house systems are inadequate for one reason or another. You may want to use an independent system with dedicated technicians. Be sure to train one member of your logistics team to understand the system so he or she can function as a back up to the technician.

8. Equipment

You may need some audio/visual equipment at the last minute. Usually a facility can handle this. Also, you may change a design in mid-stream if it is not working. A redesign may call for new or altered instructions on handouts for each participant. To be prepared for changes and to turn around the new strategy before Day 3, have a computer, printer, and copier at the disposal of the logistics team.

Video taping the event is often useful for sharing the work of the day with others and for orienting new employees later on. If you do decide to create a video, make the camera work as unobtrusive as possible. Be sure to tell your camera operator to cover more than just what happens up front. Close-ups of table conversations, brainstorming sessions, report outs and voting will help bring the event to life for those who did not experience it. On the day of the event, mention that a video record is being made and why.

9. Meeting Room Set-Up

Participant Tables
To promote easier discussions and work, use round tables, each seating eight people. Number the tables and ask the facility to display the numbers on table stands so that you can see them easily from a distance.

Arrangement
To enable the largest number of participants to easily see the speakers and the speakers to make eye contact with the largest number of participants (which keeps everyone more involved), place the "front" of the room on the long wall in a rectangular room

(Note: Facilities often have trouble comprehending this type of arrangement – their tendency is to place the front on the short wall (classroom style) or at the end opposite the entry doors no matter where they are.)

Have the facility fax a drawing of the room to you. Using that map, draw how you want the facility to arrange the stage, refreshments and tables. Provide the facility staff with the drawing of the room arrangement you desire, but also be prepared to rearrange the room when you arrive the night before or early the day of the session. The most frequent problems you will encounter are tables too close together and tables too close to the wall.

> ---- Leave space for
> movement around
> room perimeter

10. Meals

Have meals served in a room other than the meeting room (but still close by - see "Breakout Rooms") to avoid delays caused by meal set-up and clean-up. The goal is to serve people as quickly as possible (in fewer than 10 minutes, preferably in 5 or 6!) regardless of the group size. Meals served buffet style are the quickest, but only if there is a sufficient number of lines and a sufficient amount of room. (At a Ford session, 350 people were all eating within 10 minutes. They had eight buffet lines.) If you decide to have meals served, have as much as possible of the food preset (e.g.: salads, desserts, and rolls). If it is impossible to serve meals in a separate room, use box lunches—clearly labeled and easily accessible. These lunches greatly simplify the process of serving and cleaning up. Make sure lots of trashcans are available!

Find out if the leadership and others will want meals on the evening of Day 2 during their work that night.

Remember to include vegetarian and other special diet requirements in your planning.

11. Refreshments

If there is enough space, place the refreshment table right in the main room. During the session, encourage people to do whatever they need to do to stay alert, so it helps if they can get some refreshments quickly and easily. At the very least, have coffee be available throughout the day and make sure that pitchers of water are regularly replenished at each participant table and at the speakers' (panel) table. If you decide to provide snacks, participants really appreciate some low-fat options.

12. Seating Configuration

Some combination of the following five types of seating configurations work well during Whole-Scale sessions:

"Functional"
Individuals who perform the same or a similar function across divisions such as industrial relations, finance, engineering, and manufacturing.

"Max-Mix"'
A maximum mix of participants, at each table, creating a microcosm of the whole organization at each participant table. Make up tables of eight individuals who are as representative as possible of functions, organizations, and levels. In order to encourage free-flowing discussion and exchange of ideas, do not put anyone at a table with their immediate boss. Be sure to assign the top leader to a table, hopefully with none of his/her direct reports seated at the same table.

"Organizational"
Intact work teams with a boss and subordinates. When it is not possible to bring together such a group, the key criterion for forming a work team is its members' interdependence. (Sometimes this is the same as functional.)

"Program" or "Project"
Usually a cross-functional team responsible for accomplishing or carrying out a specific project or program.

"Self-Select"
Groups formed by participants at the session based on each choosing a particular topic on which to work.

13. Materials May Include:

Markers
People cannot read flipcharts written with red or green markers from a distance. Use dark colored markers (Mr. Sketch water color markers, not permanent!), especially when making signs.

In-Boxes
An "in-box" on each table provides a consistent place for groups to find handouts and supplies. Use plastic trays, or box tops.

Keirsey-Bates
Two booklets, **The Sixteen Types** and **Temperament in Leading**, allow you to do Myers-Briggs work simply. Order them from:　　Prometheus Nemesis Book Company
Post Office Box 2748
Del Mar, California 92014
760-632-1575

Post-It Notes
There are a number of uses for sticky notes. 3M Post-It Notes are the most popular brand. The 3x5 size works best. In most cases one-half pad per participant for each activity requiring Post-Its is a good rule of thumb. Remember that in high humidity these notes may not stick well.

Dots and Stars
You will typically use about 20 stars and 10 dots per person. The quality of commercially available stars and dots vary. Some do not peel off easily and others do not stick well. Pre-test your supplies before the day of the event.

Name Tags
There are two tasks connected to name tags: making the seating assignments and actually creating the tags. Creating max-mix table assignments requires familiarity with the participants so they can be grouped to maximize diversity of function, length of service, level, race, gender, etc. No one should be seated with his or her direct supervisor. The Event Planning Team or someone else internal to the organization may do the seating assignments.

When participants arrive at the event, they should find a pre-printed nametag showing their name and their table number. In some cases there will be two table numbers for different seating at different points in the event. Be sure to assign these two tasks well in advance. *Don't ever wait until staging day to start doing this for a 500-person event!* Also, have extra nametags and be ready to print them out for unexpected participants. An alternative is to have nametags on the tables and have the participants fill them out.

14. Registration Packet

You will want to give the participants any information they might need in a folder they receive at registration or at their tables when they first sit down. In addition to company-specific information such as strategy statements, consider including:

- The meeting purpose and agenda
- The role of facilitator, recorder, spokesperson and rules of brainstorming
- The strategic planning model

15. Open Forum Process

A process that works well to get questions from the floor in a structured way when you are working with a very large group is the "grid" method:

On the floor plan of your room, divide the tables into four or five relatively equal, contiguous sections:

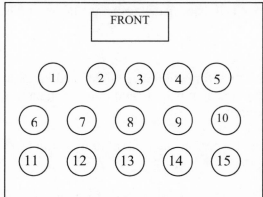

Next, list each section's table numbers in columns in a random order:

3	8	14	11
1	5	10	15
4	6	9	12
2	7		13

Give a copy of this "grid" to each mike handler and tape one to the podium. (Try to keep extra copies around, too.)

Then, during a question and answer session, call on tables from each section of the room – two at a time: call the first table number and alert the next table number to be "on deck." In the example the facilitator would say: "Table 3 is first, with table 8 on deck." Then, "Table 8, with table 14 on deck," and so on. As a table asks a question, check it off the grid so you can keep track of who has not had a chance to ask a question. This process enables you to give all the tables a chance to ask a question sometime during the three days and enables the logistics people to be ready at the next table with a microphone so you can keep moving quickly.

You will find it particularly important when you use this approach to leave ten minutes or so for "burning" questions when you open up the process to *any* table. Logistics should have a clear contract with the consultant at the podium about how this will work. By increasing the "hype" as each question gets asked ("You will not be able to go on if you do not ask this?") you still make room for participants to ask the important questions and end up with a feeling of closure. Abrupt endings ("OK, that is all the time we have.") seem to leave people feeling cheated.

Whenever you have more than one question and answer session, you can pick up where you left off on the grid, and you can start again from the top of the grid after you have made it all the way through.

16. Participant Materials During the Meeting

Work hard to make sure participants have what they need exactly when they need it for two reasons: you want them to be able to concentrate on the task at hand (content) rather than on how to do that task (process), and you want the logistics to facilitate their success rather than get in their way.

Specifically:
Easels
Although each table of participants will get an easel for themselves, easels tend to end up in odd concentrations around the room. The logistics team needs to provide assistance to get the easels to tables quickly – and out of the way when people are not using them.

Another task involving the easels is to keep the aisles, perimeter of the room, and any voting areas clear as possible during "post and read" and voting activities. The easels tend to be in the way, so a quick sweep of the room can make a real difference in participants' ability to move around…especially during voting.

Handouts
The logistics team and the consultant giving an assignment need to have an agreement about when to hand out written instructions or new seating lists. The issues that come into play when deciding when to hand things out include making sure participants will not misplace things if they are handed out too soon, making sure that participants are not reading when they should be listening to a speaker, and having a system to distribute the materials as quickly as possible.

(Note to Logistics Team: It is often helpful if the handouts are copied in different colors for easy reference, but check with the consulting team first.)

17. Pacing
Lags in the proceedings of a large meeting are amplified by the size of the room: picture 600 people all waiting for something to happen. Therefore, you will want to work hard to keep your pacing crisp and quick. You can do this a number of ways:

Handouts
Before you need them, count out the appropriate number of handouts for each table and crosshatch these "packets." Assign specific logistics team members to distribute packets to specific tables and shoot them out when agreed—either on cue or during an appropriate break in the action.

Microphones
Make sure the next table to ask a question or the next group to report out already has a mike in the spokesperson's hand, ready to go.

Speakers
Make sure whoever is speaking next is right up by the podium. Avoid the long walks up from the back of the room.

18. Preserving the Work and Documenting the Meeting

You will want to save and publish some of the work participants do. Usually this includes the Glads, Mads and Sads, the Valentine Responses, the System-Wide Action Plans, and the Back-Home Plans. Find out from the Event Planning Team what they want to keep . (If you cannot get an answer, *save everything*! You can always throw things away later.)

Although you will ask the participants to label their work, it will be enormously helpful to devise a labeling scheme of your own so that you are sure of where things came from (activity, page, group) after the meeting. When you have collected all the work that needs to be saved from a given activity, roll it up, rubber band it (tape makes a mess when you unroll it), and label the outside of the roll with the activity name.

The sooner someone types this material and distributes it back to the event participants, the better. If it is back soon enough, they will use it to explain what happened at the event to people in the organization who were not able to attend the meeting, thereby adding "leverage" to the changes the participants are trying to bring about.

Important! Before leaving the event, contract with someone inside the client organization to take custody of all the work products (charts, post-its, etc.). Have a very clear understanding of who will be responsible for typing up the content and by when. People are both exhausted and euphoric after many of these events, and there is a high risk that this material will be gathering dust in someone's office two months later if you don't ensure that it won't. Part of the responsibility of the leaders to the participants is to make sure that they do something with their feedback.

Note: You and the client should consider arranging for documentation of the event in real time. Having computer "scribes" in the room makes it possible to have results compiled at the end of each day. Participants see a new model of communication feedback when they are able to have data from one day typed and ready for them at the beginning of the next day. It also jump starts the follow-up process.

SAMPLE REGISTRATION PACKET:

Example of Participants' Agenda

Purpose

To work together as leaders of this organization to:
- Build a picture of where the organization is right now,
- Explore and agree on where it must be in the future if it is to be successful, and
- Make commitments to each other on what people in the organization need to do differently, individually and collectively, to get there.

	Day 1
7:30 am	Continental Breakfast
8:00 am	Welcome/Purpose
	Agenda/Logistics
	Telling our Stories
	Environmental View
	View from our Customers
	Organization Diagnosis
	Celebrating Diversity
5:00 pm	Evaluation – Day 1

	Day 2
7:30 am	Continental Breakfast
8:00 am	Feedback of Evaluations/Agenda for the Day
	Stakeholder "Wild Card" Module
	Strategic Planning Model
	View from the Leadership
	Organization Strategy: Revisit
	Feedback on Strategy by Participants
5:00 pm	Evaluation – Day 2

	Day 3
7:30 am	Continental Breakfast
8:00 am	Feedback of Evaluations/Agenda – Day 3
	Response from Leadership Group: "Finalized" Strategy
	Panel of Possibilities
	Preferred Futuring
	System-Wide Action Planning
	Valentines: Inter-Group Requests
	Back-Home Planning
5:00 pm	Wrap-Up/Evaluation/Close

Example of Roles of Facilitator, Recorder and Spokesperson

Rules of Brainstorming

Facilitator
- Help keep the group on task
- Watch the time to assure that the group completes its task
- Assure that everyone is able to participate-no one dominating, no one excluded
- Remind people to listen as others are talking
- Encourage people to respect and use their different perspectives and views

Recorder
- Listen for key words; do not edit-use exact words
- Capture the basic ideas, essence
- Write rapidly
- Write legibly, 1 to 1-1/2 inches high
- Number each sheet; reference topic, group
- Do not worry about spelling

Spokesperson
- Be sure you understand what you are expected to report
- Listen carefully to the discussion
- Report out key points as requested at the end of the session

Rules of Brainstorming
- Do not discuss ideas
- Do not judge ideas (good or bad)
- Repeat ideas are fine
- "Piggybacking" off someone else's idea is fine
- Wait for the silences to end: the greatest creativity follows
- The more ideas, the better

Example of Strategic Planning Model

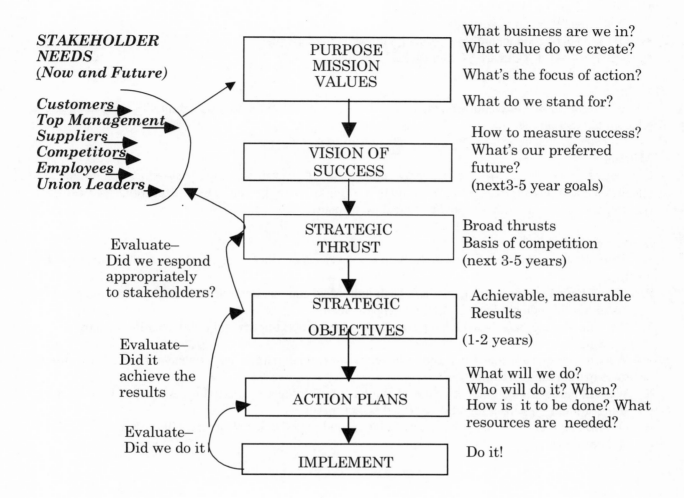

STAKEHOLDER NEEDS
(Now and Future)

Customers
Top Management
Suppliers
Competitors
Employees
Union Leaders

PURPOSE
MISSION
VALUES

What business are we in?
What value do we create?

What's the focus of action?

What do we stand for?

VISION OF
SUCCESS

How to measure success?
What's our preferred
future?
(next 3-5 year goals)

STRATEGIC
THRUST

Broad thrusts
Basis of competition
(next 3-5 years)

Evaluate–
Did we respond
appropriately
to stakeholders?

STRATEGIC
OBJECTIVES

Achievable, measurable
Results

(1-2 years)

Evaluate–
Did it
achieve the
results

ACTION PLANS

What will we do?
Who will do it? When?
How is it to be done? What
resources are needed?

Evaluate–
Did we do it

IMPLEMENT

Do it!

Example of a 'Strawdog' Strategy

Principles
- PEOPLE are our key resource
- INTEGRITY is our way of life
- QUALITY of product and of customer support is fundamental
- TECHNICAL EXCELLENCE must guide design

Vision
To be recognized by our customers and competitors as a world-class provider of quality computing and telecommunications services.

Mission
Company's mission is to satisfy our customers' requirements by providing computing and telecommunications services of superior quality. Quality includes meeting or exceeding the customers' requirements for cost, schedule, and technical performance.

Strategic Goals
1. Continuous improvement in the quality of our services, products, and processes will be our way of life.
2. We will create an environment where each individual can make important contributions and achieve his or her full potential as part of the Company team.
3. We will take a proactive leadership role in developing and implementing information system strategies.
4. We will achieve a leadership position in selected external markets with financial returns and growth rates better than our competitors.
5. We will make timely, innovative use of available technology, emphasizing responsive, user-friendly solutions and systems integration of off-the-shelf products.
6. Our management systems, policies, procedures, and organization structure will be simple, effective, and consistent.

SAMPLE ASSIGNMENT: Valentines

To:_____

(Specific Group Name)

These are the things we need you to do differently in the future in order to help all of us achieve our goals...."

From:_____

(Specific Group Name)

SAMPLE ASSIGNMENT: Preferred Futuring

It is _____ – _____ years from now. We are pleased and proud of how effectively we have achieved this objective. What do we see happening? What are people doing that lets us know we've reached our objective?

- Use one "Post-it" note for each idea – but write as many ideas for each objective as you can think of. There are more "Post-its" if you run out. Write the objective numbers at the top of the "Post-its". Logistics team members will be coming around to pick up your ideas. Keep creating ideas until you have "emptied" your brain -- all the ideas you have carried in your mind that no one seemed to care about before. Get them all on Post-It sheets.

- As you write your ideas on the "Post-its", be as clear and specific as you can.

SAMPLE ASSIGNMENT: System-Wide Action Planning

Assignment: As you will see around thee room's walls, there is a chart sheet with e table's number on the bottom. The Post-It sheets have been distributed equally across the tables. Each table has been assigned to one of the organizational goals and the Post-It sheets have been sorted accordingly.

Now, at your table, choose a facilitator – the best one you've had in the past few days – and a recorder. The recorder will go to the sheet with your table's number on it and bring it back.

1.. Sort your "Post-its" into themes.

2. Based on those themes, develop a preferred future statement representing your own beliefs and the input you have received on the "Post-its".

3.. Focusing on the preferred future you just developed:
   A. Brainstorm all of the things happening right now in the organization as a whole that will help you move toward your preferred future.
   B. Brainstorm all of the things happening right now that are going to make it more difficult to achieve your preferred future.

4. Now: Brainstorm all of the ideas you have about what we could do differently as an organization in the next six months in order to really "move the needle" on this goal.

5. Using your last brainstorm of ideas, agree on a specific, detailed plan for this goal (including what actions, who is responsible, by when) that you recommend for the whole group's consideration.

6. Create a self-explanatory flipchart report of your preferred future statement (step 2) and your action recommendations (step 5). Leave a four-inch margin on the left side of your sheets for voting. Hang your sheet under the goal header for the goal you've been exploring.

SAMPLE EVALUATION: Day 1

How did today go for you:

What were the Highs?

What were the Lows?

What advice do you have for us for tomorrow?

SAMPLE EVALUATION: Day 2

What were your most important learnings today?

What still feels unfinished for you?

What advice do you have for us for tomorrow?

What were the most significant outcomes of these three days for you?

On a scale of 1 to 10, how confident are you that we will carry out our commitments to each other?

Not a   Watch
snowball's   1-------2-------3-------4-------5-------6-------7-------8-------9-------10   our
chance...   dust!

Why did you mark it where you did?

What do we need to do from here to sustain our momentum?

Chapter 5

Design Possibility: A Generic Three-Day Event Plan

In order to create an agenda you will need to describe a purpose and flow of work (which the EPT has created). This example provides ideas about how activities might flow. You will always, of course, design based on your particular purpose. Notice that each module has a purpose and an underlying philosophy. Each module is described in four columns: Time, Content, Process, and Tips.

GENERIC DESIGN: DAY 1

Purpose

To work together as leaders of this organization to:

- Build a picture of where the organization is right now
- Explore and agree on where it must be in the future if it is to be successful
- Make commitments as to what people in the organization need to do differently, individually and collectively, to get there

Day 1   Expanding the organization's world view – building a common data base about each other, the organization, its stakeholders and its environment

- Welcome Purpose
- Agenda/Logistics
- Telling Our Stories
- Industry Trends
- View From Our Customers
- Organization Diagnosis
- Celebrating Diversity
- Evaluation – Day 1
- Read/Act on Evaluations – Day 1

Day 2   Ensure the organization is connected as "one brain and one heart" and able to develop a new direction together built on that connection and expanded worldview.

- Feedback of Evaluations/Agenda for the Day

- Stakeholder "Wild Card" Module (suppliers, union, program managers, et al)
  View from . . . . .
- Strategic Planning Model
- View from the Leadership
- "I Have a Dream" speech from the leader
- Organization Strategy: Revisit
- Feedback on Strategy by Participants
- Evaluation – Day 2
- Read/Act on Evaluations – Day 2
- Leadership Work on Response to Input

Day 3   Become whole about the strategic direction of the organization, shift its paradigm and create a full system commitment to change.
- Feedback of Evaluations/Agenda – Day 3
- Response from Leadership Group: "Finalized" Strategy
- Panel of Possibilities
- Preferred Futuring
- System-Wide Action Planning
- Valentines: Inter-Group Requests
- Back-Home Planning
- Wrap-Up/Evaluation/Close

WELCOME/PURPOSE OF THIS MEETING
(total time = 10 minutes)

Purpose
To signal the importance of this meeting and why the group is together. The change champion will have an opportunity to communicate his/her commitment and need for support from everyone in the change process.

Underlying Philosophy
This module sets the tone for the remainder of the event. Because you will often work with hierarchical organizations, the group almost expects the leader to welcome participants and legitimize what they are going to do. You can, however, use this module as an opportunity to signal that things will be different by changing who presents and/or adjusting the tone, style, and content from whatever is typical for that organization. In addition, participants will usually be at max-mix tables, which also sets a different tone.

Time	Content	Materials/Logistics	Tips
7:30	**Registration/Coffee, etc.**	Registration table with name tags	
	Participants receive their "max-mix" seating assignments.	Have a sign at doors with "max-mix" seating assignments by name or include assigned table numbers on individual name tags	If participants will switch tables at any time during the event, you may want to include the other table number (e.g., back home group) on the back of the nametag.
	The EPT will have identified the packet contents ahead of time. Packets might include: ■ Purpose and Multi-day agenda (headlines) ■ Telling Our Stories assignment ■ Table Roles (facilitator, recorder, spokesperson) ■ Rules of Brainstorming ■ Relevant models, e.g. DVF, Strategic Planning, etc. ■ Any other data needed for the kick-off	Put a packet at each person's place Place table numbers, in-boxes, and open forum questions on tables along with individual packets. Put pens, pads, markers, and masking tape on tables. Set up the podium with microphone and a table grid. Also, set up the panel table with mikes if needed.	Talk to A/V technicians and ask that they remain at least through the first activity that requires mikes to ensure that the equipment is working properly.

CHAPTER 5: DESIGN POSSIBILITY: A GENERIC THREE-DAY EVENT PLAN

Time	Content/Process	Logistics	

8:00 (15)	**Welcome/Purpose**	The speaker is a sponsor of the three-day session, a real or a virtual leader of the change process. He or she could be:	• It's helpful if the speaker uses "I" messages and speaks to the purpose as if it were his or her own.
	The speaker does the following things:		• Prior to the welcome, make an agreement with the speaker about timing and a process to indicate when time is up. You cannot stop people while they're talking if you haven't contracted with them in advance.
	• Explains why the organization is having this launch meeting and what everyone has done to get ready. He or she describes how the organization chose the EPT, and the purpose the team developed for these three days.	▪ A hierarchical leader ▪ A union leader ▪ An EPT member ▪ A program director ▪ Etc.	
	• Describes what the purpose means to him or her, and why it's important.		• Stand near the front of the room because trying to signal from the back of the room is fraught with danger!
	• Describes how he or she hopes the group will work together during these three days.		• Make sure that participants understand that the event has been planned by members of their own group.
	• Tells what he or she personally hopes to walk away with at the end of the third day.		• It is important that leadership stay throughout the whole meeting, assigned to a max-mix table.
	• Introduces the members of the EPT by name and function and have them stand up one at a time.		
	• Describes his or her participation. For example, he or she might say, "I will be at a max-mix table myself, and I will be here for the whole session. Let's make this session a great one!"		
	• Introduces the lead consultant.		
	.		

AGENDA/LOGISTICS
(total time = 35 minutes)

Purpose
To provide participants with an overview of the meeting so that:
- You reduce the mystery about what will happen in terms of process and content
- You identify what they will be doing during this meeting that will be different from the passive role they may have played in other meetings

Underlying Philosophy
To identify norms that describe how the group is going to be working together. These norms include the awareness that participants will be able to be responsible for their own learning. Participants will hopefully begin to understand that they can shape and influence the outcomes of the meeting.

8:15 (15)	**Agenda** Introduce yourself and other consultants.	Lead consultant walks through the three-day agenda, guiding participants through a map of the journey that the whole group will be taking together during the next three days.	- Give enough information about yourself to reduce the mystery of who you are before you walk through the agenda. - Include beginning and ending times for each day. You need flexibility during the actual meeting so do not include times for the activities including breaks and lunches as you may not always be precisely on schedule and that would disturb some people. - Reassure participants there will be breaks and lunch so they don't panic.
8:30 (10)	**How the Group Is Going to Work Together:** You might say, "Let me tell you why you're seated the way you are: You are in a max-mix seating arrangement,		You want to explain to participants why they have assigned seats and what the

Time	Content/Process	Logistics
	which means your table represents the maximum mix –a microcosm– of the whole organization. With any luck at all, you are seated with people you normally do not see very often and you are not seated with your direct boss/employee. The purpose for sitting this way is to enable each of you to get a broader database by seeing the world through the window presented by other people from different parts of the organization. We want you to be able to begin to see the organization as a whole system rather than merely from your own perspective. At various points during the three days, you may change the table where you sit to enable you to have different perspectives as needed. Certainly at some point in the session you will return to your 'back home' groups. Let's take a five-minute break now and give people an opportunity to move to their assigned tables if they're not already there. You will be far more successful if there is a microcosm at each table."	benefit is to them. When you explain why this is important, people are inclined to go along with it. You want to help the participants understand how important it is to share information across functional lines in order to plan more effectively for the future. If your internal resources tell you that everyone is seated where they supposed to be, consider skipping this part.
(10)	Logistical Tips: Be sure you give the participants the following messages: • "Here is how you can check for messages… ■ If you have to smoke (assuming it's permitted), take three puffs and come back quickly because your table group needs your point of view. ■ If you need to make a phone call, likewise, come back quickly or your table will not have a full perspective. ■ The restrooms are…."	

Then you can continue: "The most important thing we will be doing together is building a common database by *'listening to each other in a way that will enable you to see the world through each other's eyes.'* " "Do whatever you need to do to stay focused. If you need to use the restroom, get up and go. Don't wait for a break. If you are falling asleep, stand up and stretch, go to the back of the room so you can still listen. Come immediately back; your table mates need your input."	

Time	Content/Process	Logistics
	TELLING OUR STORIES *(total time = 70 minutes)* **Purpose** To begin to build a real learning community as a team at each table and in the whole room by: • Beginning to build a common database • Connecting at each table across organizational lines • Enabling participants to think whole system by giving them a broader base of understanding • Ensuring each person has the opportunity to clarify and express his or her own views and needs **Underlying Philosophy** This module addresses several key points: • Building the cross-functional table groups into a team that functions well and is increasingly open with each other over the three days: a safe place to try out ideas and reactions with people from diverse parts of the organization. • Broadening the picture that each person sees of the whole, so that, as the module unfolds, everyone sees a bigger picture of the whole. • Signaling to the participants that this is their meeting. The message is: "If it is to be, it is up to me."	
8:40 (30)	**Assignment & Table Work** The lead consultant then introduces the first assignment. He or she might say: "Take two minutes to prepare to introduce yourself to the rest of your table group: • Give your name, job, and background • Tell how long you have worked at the organization • Look back over the past year, and tell what you have accomplished that makes you proud • Likewise, tell what has been frustrating for you this past year • Imagine you have a magic wand, and tell what you would change to help this organization be more successful in the future • Given all that, tell what you need to see accomplished during the next three days to make this meeting	Use max-mix seating. Put handouts of assignment in each packet. You may want to change the questions based on what the EPT is yearning to know about people in the organization. The questions can be a little risky but with enough room to choose how much you want to reveal. Try for questions that will speak to what each participant knows so that they will feel smart when they answer. Think about questions that add to the common database of the organization as a whole. Ask people to listen carefully to see the world through the eyes of the

CHAPTER 5: DESIGN POSSIBILITY: A GENERIC THREE-DAY EVENT PLAN

		warning.	
	worthwhile Now, each person takes three minutes to share your answers with your table group. Choose a facilitator to keep time and ensure that everyone has three minutes."	other people as they talk. It is important that they empower a facilitator to keep people on time so that each person has a full three minutes. Note: If there are ten people at a table, each person will have only two minutes to present.	
9:10 **(10)**	**Summary Process** "Now take 10 minutes as a group to record common themes, significant differences you heard from each other and what your table needs to make this meeting worthwhile. Choose a recorder and a spokesperson. The recorder gets a flipchart to write on and sets it up at the table. Choose a spokesperson to shout out the table's answers to the three questions."	Ask participants to remove the handout from their packet that describes the roles of table facilitator, recorder, and spokesperson and the process of brainstorming.	
9:20 **(20)**	**Room-wide Database Building** Work the crowd to get the answers to each of the three questions. Call on people who have raised their hands until people have articulated the whole story. Then you can pose the following questions: ■ "What did you hear in common?" ■ What did you hear differently?" ■ "What does your table need to get out of this session?" At the end of the callouts, thank the writers and tell the group they'll be getting copies of the data captured on the sheets later in the day.	■ Move flipcharts to perimeter of room. ■ Have three flipcharts/markers and writers (from the logistics team) up front on the risers ready to go. ■ That trio will need to orchestrate their writing so that they're taking turns and moving as fast as possible. ■ As the consultant doing the callout, keep an eye on the writers to make sure they're keeping up and speak into the microphone every time you get an input so the writers can hear it clearly.	A large group may need mikes, but it works better not to use them in order to discourage people from giving long speeches. In any event, you will need to repeat callouts into the microphone and make sure the writers are getting everything down. If they miss one, repeat it. Your goal here is to have everyone feel heard and affirmed by everyone else in the room. At the end of the callouts, you can expect to feel an energy shift in the room—people are more alive, they feel supported, and they are

Time	Content/Process	Logistics
		beginning to understand that this meeting is different from the passive ones they've attended in the past.
		■ You will end up with data that can be typed and handed out later.
9:40 (05)	**Change Model** Finish up the expectations with: "I'd like to share a formula for change that the Event Planning Team used to plan this session. It is an adaptation of work from Dick Beckhard at MIT. If you want to bring about change, you must have **'D'**, a multi-faceted picture of dissatisfaction with the way things are right now; multiplied by **'V'**, a combined vision of the way we yearn to be in the future; multiplied by **'F'**, which stands for first steps that we all believe we can take in order to get to that combined vision. The product of those three elements has to be greater that **'R'** which stands for resistance to change. The key to the formula is that if any of the three elements, D, V, or F, is zero, the product will also be zero and will not be greater than 'R', because we all resist change. This is an individual change model as well as an organizational one. In order for me to change, I need to be dissatisfied with what I'm doing right now, have a vision of what I could be doing that would be rewarding for me, and know some first steps that I believe will get me moving in that direction. If all of these things are in place, I will change. If any of them is missing, no change will take place. [Note: Helpful to give a personal example.] ■ If you have D but no V or F, people will be angry and frustrated, but will not act	Have formula on a handout for each person or write it clearly and large up front as you talk: **D x V x F > R**

	<ul><li>If you have D and F but no V, then you'll get busy going nowhere!</li><li>If you have V and F but no D, people will just sit around talking philosophy.</li></ul>
	If the change needed is organizational, a critical mass of the organization needs to agree on the dissatisfaction with things as they are now; see a common vision of their preferred future; and agree on some first steps that will begin to move the organization in the right direction. When these three needs are met, change will take place. That is the purpose of your journey together. Let's see if we can help you build that critical mass together in these three days."
9:50 **(10)**	**Break**

Time	Content/Process	Logistics

INDUSTRY TRENDS

(total time: Option I = 65 minutes, Option II = 90 minutes)

Purpose

To build a common database of what's happening in the environment now and in the future that will allow the group to make more informed choices regarding strategy

Underlying Philosophy

This module defines trends in the organization's industry as part of the environmental scan in its strategic plan so that the organization can see further into the industry and the future. If the Whole-Scale event is taking place in a subsidiary, it is critical that this module focus on the subsidiary's industry, not the parent companies. What participants need to hear in order to open up their thinking that would not be sufficiently covered elsewhere has determined the content of this module (e.g., in the view from the leader's bridge, view from the customer's bridge, etc.). Appropriate topics could include global, economic, or political issues; technological trends specific to the industry; competitors' data; etc.

Design Choice Points

The who: You need to decide who is the best source for this information. Note: "Best" is defined by credibility, knowledge, and breadth of "view."

- Do the participants themselves possess the necessary data and does the data need to be made explicit?
- Would an "industry expert" be a most appropriate choice? If so, should this person be from outside the company, or from corporate; from the marketing department, or another internal source?

The how: You need to decide what is the best method to facilitate sharing the information. Note: "Best" is defined by the ease and depth with which participants understand the material and the extent to which everybody sees the "big picture."

- Would a pre-reading get the participants' "juices flowing" on the topic?
- Would handouts make the presentation easier to follow?

Time	Content/Process	Logistics
10:00 **(5)**	**Option 1: Speaker(s) as Expert** **Introduction** "As you hear from an industry expert(s), please begin practicing a different kind of listening. We are all trained to evaluate what people are saying as they talk: to decide whether we agree or disagree, whether they are right or wrong. Throughout our session we will ask you to listen instead for understanding – not to judge but to try to see the world through the eyes of the speaker. We will give you plenty of time later to add your own opinions as well.	Use max-mix seating Make sure speakers have what they need, e.g. podium, mike, etc. Logistics should coordinate distribution of handouts with speakers. Don't forget to make a deal with the speaker to give him/her a warning	Brief speakers ahead of time regarding the content and process for their presentation and their part in the overall three-day design. Coordinate timing and content if there is more than one speaker. Tailor topics to the specific situation and client: what do

	(e.g. five minutes, then one minute), and then let them know when time has expired.	people really want to hear? Coach speakers to keep presentations brief. This will help participants stay tuned in, integrate the data into their own thinking, reenergize themselves, and ask only what they need to know more about during the Q&A.
		Advise speakers that handouts are far more effective than slides or overheads–turning down the lights on a big group is a guarantee for passivity!
	Distribute handouts if the speaker has provided them.	Make sure speakers understand the open forum process and how the Q & A session will work. Since this is the first time the participants will be listening to a presentation and doing an open forum, it is helpful to really hype listening for understanding: to see the world through the speaker's eyes.
But first, listen to see if you can let other perspectives in – not to sway your thinking, but simply to understand how others see the world. We will help you listen by using an 'open forum' process throughout the meeting. For each open forum, you will have fifteen minutes to talk about what you have heard, your reactions, and to prepare questions of understanding for the speaker. Then we will put the speaker back up front and you will get a chance to ask those questions and push for clarification of the things you do not understand. OK, with that, let me introduce our speaker. Remember to see the world through his/her eyes…"		

Time	Content/Process	Logistics
(15)	**Presentation** "These are trends that I see in the industry…" (Examples): ■ Demographic shifts ■ Competition ■ Government/regulatory ■ Labor ■ Technology ■ Any other meaningful areas	
(15)	**Open Forum** Table Discussion: "Now take 15 minutes to talk about: ■ What did we hear? ■ What are our reactions? ■ What are our questions of understanding? And for whom? Select a new facilitator, recorder, and spokesperson. The facilitator's role this time is to move the group through the three questions and to make sure one outspoken person does not dominate the discussion and take up the entire 15 minutes. The recorder's role is to capture the table's questions and the spokesperson's role is to ask the tough questions, given the anonymity of representing a whole table group."	Place open forum questions on table tent cards. Move easels to tables.	Since everyone picks up slightly different information from a speaker, this activity gives participants a chance to integrate what they've heard and to prepare to ask better questions. It also energizes the group. Participants need to know that roles will rotate with each new activity and therefore they will not be "stuck" in these roles for the entire event. Knowing this will encourage greater participation at the table. Asking questions posed by a table group creates a safe environment for participants to ask tough questions.
(30)	Q & A with Speaker(s)	Provide table and chairs for speakers.	Give as many tables as possible a chance to ask one question. It

		is important to help every table feel that they are involved. Spreading questions around will lead to most tables getting all their questions asked.
		Check with the table that has the floor to ensure the question was satisfactorily answered before moving on.
		Announcing that time is running out and opening up the process for burning questions leads to a feeling of closure better than an abrupt announcement. Emphasize that "burning question" means just that. It's not a time for just any question. Try to end on time but use your judgment about slipping a little. It is better to be late and have a common database than to be on time and miss something.
		The open forum process helps create a sense of closure and of being heard for the participants.
"What questions of understanding do you have? This is not a time to slip in an editorial!"	Provide wireless microphones for logistics. It helps the pace to create a "grid" which divides the room into quadrants and lists table numbers within each quadrant. Moderate the Q/A process by calling on a table within the first quadrant and then moving to another table in the next quadrant, etc. following the grid. The grid stays on the podium throughout the three days. Check off tables as they ask questions. Don't call on a table again until all others have had a chance. This gives all tables an opportunity by the end of the session. Logistics team delivers wireless microphones to tables in the sequence they will be called on using the grid. When only about 10 minutes are left, open the rotation for "burning questions," i.e., allow any table to ask a question that must be answered now or they won't be able to go on. (See "Open Forum Process" in logistics notes.)	
10:00	**Option II: Participation**	Post list of topics on flipcharts up	Instead of speakers, this module

Time	Content/Process	Logistics
(5)	**Instructions** "It's time to consider other things that are going on in your environment, i.e. organizations and situations that affect our industry. We call these 'other things' events, trends, and developments –(ETDs.). To get as broad a perspective as possible of the various ETDs that affect your organization, we would like each table to pick a different topic from this list and identify its impact on you and the issues surrounding it that you must consider as you develop your strategy. We would like each table to do the following: ■ Brainstorm the events, trends, or developments that are happening in the topic area or are resulting from actions being taken within the topic area. Record these. ■ Once you have your list, pick the most important ones to discuss (without recording) what you know about these items. ■ After the discussion, identify and record implications of these events, trends, or developments for this organization. What do you think this will mean for your business or organization? ■ Prepare a three–minute report of your ETDs and implications. ■ Select a new facilitator and recorder." "Now take a minute at your tables to decide what topic you'd like to work on. Keep a second choice in mind in case you don't get your first choice."	front. (Use handouts if participants cannot easily read the list up front.) Sample: ■ Demographics ■ Competition ■ Government/Regulatory topics ■ Labor ■ Technology ■ Etc. (including subdivisions of the above) taps the wisdom of the participants to address events, trends, and developments (ETDs) that are, or have potential for, affecting their organization. It is not crucial that the participants distinguish accurately or agree whether a specific topic is an event, trend, or development. For example, a merger among competitors might be an "internal" event; a change in U.S. defense policy is a development; an expanding market segment is an example of a trend. Create a brief table-group assignment, which will allow participants to share and pool their collective wisdom. It is critical that it fit for the organization culturally and that it stimulate the people to unleash their brains. For example, what are all the leading-edge trends in our industry? What's new and exciting? The Event Planning Team may compile the initial list of topics with review by the sponsor(s).

(10)	**Groups Select Topics** Call out topics and ask for tables that want to work on them – or have them send someone up to put their table number on the list as soon as they have made a decision.	Move easels to tables. Tables choose a new facilitator, recorder, and spokesperson.	With a very large group, there may be more than one table per topic. Letting tables choose, even if you have to force the distribution by limiting the number who may sign up for each topic, gives the participants a greater sense of ownership then if you randomly assign the topics.
(40)	**Groups Work**		
(35)	**Table Presentations** Call on one table from the first topic.	After each topic report, ask for significant differences from other tables that worked on the same topic (only value-added additions).	Alternatives to reports would be a post and read process or a post/read/vote process.
11:30	LUNCH		

Time	Content/Process	Logistics

VIEW FROM OUR CUSTOMERS
(total time = 110 minutes)

Purpose
To hear from a key stakeholder – customers – about what is happening in their environment and what they will need from the organization in order to help them face their challenges in the future.

Underlying Philosophy
To do good strategic planning, the participants need to hear directly from their customers and engage in a dialogue of understanding. In order to be more effective in supporting the customer, the participants need to see the customers' world and the challenges they face. Ordinarily, dialogue with customers is problem-focused. In this session the key is in having "live" customers so that the participants get a visceral connection with these key stakeholders.

Design Choice Points
Decide on which and how many customers you need, who should invite them, and what to include in their invitation letter. Be clear that they know what to expect and what you expect from them: a large group, a short presentation and a long Q&A session. Make a decision as to who is the right person in the organization to introduce the customer, who will clearly signal that they are valued customers.
Three customers is a good number. If you decide you need four, limit their presentations to 10 minutes each. You will need to get a cross-section to connect with the diversity of the audience (products, geography, etc.). You want customers who will offer new and/or important data. The EPT members should ask themselves, "What do the participants need to hear? Should there be internal and/or external customers? Which businesses have the most urgent need for data?" What you want to do is give them three different voices for the broadest customer picture possible.

Time	Content/Process	Logistics
12:00 **(5)**	**Introduction** "These are key stakeholders. Please listen carefully to see the world through their eyes. You will have an opportunity to discuss what you hear, share reactions at your table, and generate questions of understanding at the end of the panel presentation."	Seat customers at panel table with mikes. Customers should receive the specific questions you want them to address and be advised of how much time they'll have well in advance of the session.
(45)	**Introduction of Customer Panel:** Plan on three or four presentations in response to the following questions: ▪ What are the challenges and opportunities your organization is facing in the next few years? ▪ What will you need to be doing as a result of these	The leader or a member of the leadership team introduces the customer panel. Make sure someone from the organization is prepared to greet the customers upon their arrival, show them to their seats, etc. Each of the customers has 15 minutes to present (or 10 minutes Coach the customers on the importance of telling their own

	challenges and opportunities? ■ What will we, as suppliers, need to do differently to be more helpful to you?	each if you have four customers). Contract with them in advance regarding timing and warnings.	stories. Participants need to understand what their customers are facing. The main focus is "What can we, the suppliers, do differently in the future?" rather than "What have we done poorly in the past?" Describe the open forum process so speakers will know what to expect from the Q & A session. Repeat the name of each customer just before he or she begins to speak so participants are certain of whom they're listening to. Name placards on the panel table are generally too small to see.
12:50 **(15)**	**Open Forum** Table Discussion: "Now take 15 minutes at your tables to talk about: ■ What did we hear? ■ What are our reactions? ■ What are our questions of understanding? And for whom? Select a new facilitator, recorder, and spokesperson."	Put open forum questions on table tent cards. Bring easels to tables.	

(30)	Q & A with Speaker(s)	Logistics team is ready with wireless mikes. Begin the open forum with the next table according to the grid. Save the last ten minutes for burning questions.	

CHAPTER 5: DESIGN POSSIBILITY: A GENERIC THREE-DAY EVENT PLAN

Time	Content/Process	Logistics

| 1:35 | **Break** | |

ORGANIZATION DIAGNOSIS (*total time =70 minutes*)

Purpose
To begin building a common database around management processes that link the participants across the organization. To allow participants to identify what they see the same and what they see differently about these processes. To open discussion around management issues that participants normally don't talk about and to begin building a critical mass of participants who agree on changes that the organization needs to make to help them become more successful.

Underlying Philosophy
Participants begin to feel "I am not alone–others agree with me on these issues." Specifying this common dissatisfaction early in the session can focus the motivation for change (DVF model.) Using "glads, sads and mads" language is helpful in the venting process because it targets participants' child ego state. In some organizations using "prouds and sorrys" or "successes and frustrations" might be a better fit culturally. This module also validates the wisdom of the participants by permitting them to act as their own experts. They are diagnosing themselves rather than having an outsider tell them what is right and wrong in their organization. This process generally leads to less resistance from participants in owning the assessment.

Design Choice Points
Topics assigned to the tables for this activity need to be ongoing processes that link all parts of the organization and impact all participants. If you do not choose processes, participants will have trouble brainstorming because their answers will tend to be single judgments: "Pay is too low," or "Didn't hear anything back from the employee survey." Your interviews and input from the Event Planning Team will give you the hot topics, although don't work the list to death. Overlapping processes are fine, and participants will find a way to say what they want to say no matter which topic you have assigned to them!

1:45 (5)			
	Instructions "This activity will greatly add to your common database about the current state of this organization. Each max-mix table represents a microcosm of the organization and the perceptions and experiences represented are quite diverse. This will give you a more complete picture of how things really are system-wide. You are going to tap into your collective experience by analyzing some of the basic management processes that each of you encounters every day as you go about doing your work. We are going to ask you to agree on a working definition of your topic in order to ensure everyone at your table is talking about the same thing. Then we will ask you to brainstorm all the things you are glad about, sad about, and downright mad about as you think about your topic over the last year. And don't hold anything back! If you want to be better, you have to make an honest and complete assessment of yourselves.	Arrange max-mix seating. Post headers for topics. Possible topics: ■ Communication ■ Planning ■ Problem solving ■ Quality ■ Decision making ■ Training ■ Resource allocation ■ Leadership ■ Performance management ■ Participative management ■ Rewards/recognition ■ Career development ■ Rewards/Recognition ■ Teamwork	In very large meetings, many tables will work the same topic. When this is the case, randomly assign the topics evenly across the tables, and within each topic designate one table to summarize all the voting. If the number of tables is close to the number of topics, you may let them choose a topic based on interest: put the topics on a flipchart sheet with sign up slots, and ask each table to send up a
	"In your in-boxes you will find an assignment sheet with the list of processes you will be analyzing and a card assigning one of them to your table. Please pass them around and make sure everyone knows which topic your table has been assigned. (If your card has an 'R' on it, your table will need to select two spokespersons to "report" the results of this activity. I'll say more about their assignment later.) "Everyone find your topic? Good. Let's quickly review the rules for brainstorming: ■ Piggybacking is OK ■ Add to the list whatever anyone says, no evaluating ■ It's OK to repeat	Place handouts in in-boxes with topic list and assignment for each person. Put Card in in-box with topic for table to work. (Put an "R" on the back of the card assigning a reporting table if the total group is so large that you need to limit the number of reporters.)	

CHAPTER 5: DESIGN POSSIBILITY: A GENERIC THREE-DAY EVENT PLAN

Time	Content/Process	Logistics
	• No discussion • Silence is OK	runner to put their table number by their choice.
	"So part of good brainstorming means that if one of you is glad about something and someone else is mad about the same thing, it gets recorded in both places.	
	"Here's the assignment: 1. Select a facilitator, recorder, & spokesperson. **Facilitator:** your job is to ensure you are brainstorming – be tough about it, encourage your table to simply call out everything they can think of and fill up a bunch of pages. **Recorder:** your job is to write your topic and working definition on the top of your flipchart sheet and then quickly record what you and your tablemates brainstorm using the three column format on your assignment sheet. After each item, make sure you leave three to four inches of blank space for voting and then draw a line so that it will be clear on which item you are voting.	Show the following format, and make it OK that items might appear in more than one column. Remind recorders to label every flipchart sheet with the topic on which they are working
		Ask recorders to put each item they write into a box since everyone will be voting on these sheets. Leave about three inches of white space in each box so that there is room for people to put their votes.

<table>
<tr><td colspan="3" align="center">TOPIC and DEFINITION</td></tr>
<tr><td>GLAD</td><td>SAD</td><td>MAD</td></tr>
<tr><td></td><td></td><td></td></tr>
</table>

Spokespersons: I'll talk about your job after you complete your brainstorms.

CHAPTER 5: DESIGN POSSIBILITY: A GENERIC THREE-DAY EVENT PLAN

		It's helpful to hype the mads a little so participants don't hold back: this is a time you really want participants to vent and put everything on the table.
	2. Agree on a quick working definition of your topic to ensure you are all talking about the same thing. (Don't get hung up and spend a long time on this!) 3. Brainstorm: As you think about your topic over the last year: 　■ What are you glad about? 　■ What are you sad about? 　■ What are you downright mad about?"	This need not be a textbook definition, just a working definition for the table group.
1:50 (30)	**Groups Work** "OK. You have 30 minutes to work: Agree on a working definition and then brainstorm glads, sads, and mads as you think about your topic over the last year. Grab a flipchart and go for it! As you fill up sheets, a member of the logistics team will come around to place them under the appropriate header on the wall."	Move flipcharts to tables. Logistics team spreads out to take sheets as they are filled up and post under the appropriate process header. Using the logistics team in this way helps the process move more quickly than having the tables responsible for hanging their own sheets. Also, you can ensure you are maximizing the spread of the sheets by using all the wall space while not hanging sheets on more than one level. This greatly facilitates the voting process.

Time	Content/Process	Logistics
2:20 **(20)**	**Post/Read/Vote** "Make sure all of your sheets are up on the wall. Now, each person take an 'IVI' – individual voting implement – and, for each topic in which you have an interest, vote on your two 'gladdest glads,' 'saddest sads,' and 'maddest mads.' In other words, as an individual, you have six votes total for each topic. Look over all of the flipchart sheets under 'communication,' for example, and then vote for your two 'gladdest glads,' 'saddest sads,' and 'maddest mads,' – six votes total – and then move on to the next topic.	Provide a dark crayon (IVI) for each person.
	Spokespersons: before you begin voting, please meet me here at the podium for the next few minutes so I can give you your assignment."	One table from each group that got the same topic assignment should have been designated as a reporter table. Each reporter table sends up two people, who will work together to circle the top two-to-three vote-getting glads, sads, and mads across all the flipchart sheets for their topic and prepare to report them out. Spokespersons need not count votes. Simply look for clusters, remembering that the same item may have gotten votes on more than one sheet
2:40 **(10)**	**Report Outs**	Have spokespersons stay under their header and report from where they're standing. Logistics will bring them mikes.
2:50 **(5)**	**Wrap Up** "We are purposely not going to let you solve the sads and mads. After all of the stakeholder analyses, you will work together on ways to do things differently. What you have just done will be used as data as you continue to work through the strategic planning process. We will collect these sheets and incorporate them into	Many participants will feel unfinished after this activity because, once they have identified so many problems, they want to go to work on solving them. It is helpful to remind them that this information is an important part

112

the permanent documentation of this session.	of the common database they are in the process of building – but it is only a part. Like putting together a jigsaw puzzle, the group needs to add a few more pieces before they start solving problems.

Time	Content/Process	Logistics

CELEBRATING DIVERSITY
(total time = 105 minutes)

Purpose
To better understand different ways of looking at the world and to learn to celebrate those differences for the positive things they bring to the organization.

Underlying Philosophy
Participants will get insights about themselves and an appreciation of the value of different approaches applied to the same problem/situation. This is a fun, fairly light activity which participants enjoy. It's a major paradigm shift for most of them: beginning to see that diversity among people is actually a strength. Because it is fun, this learning "sneaks up on them." This module also provides a consistent message regarding the stakeholder concept: people must listen to each other – see the world through the eyes of each other – to make the best decisions and set the best strategy.

Time	Content/Process	Logistics
2:55 **(5)**	**Introduction** "We are going to use a personality questionnaire that will help you start to see yourselves and each other in a different light. MBTI teaches you about different personality styles, e.g. how different people interact differently with other people, process information differently, respond differently to their environment, make decisions differently, etc. By gaining a better understanding of differences, you can learn to use them in ways that will help you work with others more productively. You will score the questionnaire yourself and keep the score. After you have done the scoring, we will explain the letters.	Use max-mix seating Place an easel and markers up front. Provide handout booklets for each participant. Refer to two booklets: *Temperament in Leading*, and *The Sixteen Types*. The questionnaire is in the back of each booklet. (Ordering information for these books is in Chapter 4, Page 67). Participants may be a little uneasy about taking a "personality questionnaire." Keep the introduction light and upbeat. Katherine Briggs developed this questionnaire back in the 1920s. She based it on the work of Carl Jung. Participants should answer, "as they really are" at work – not as they wish to be or as others wish them to be.

Time	Content	Facilitator	Notes
	Here are the instructions: ▪ Answer as frankly as possible. ▪ Answer as you see yourself in your work environment – not how you think you should be, but how you think you really are. ▪ When you have finished, score the questionnaire according to the directions in the book. ▪ Read the four-letter description in the book. If the description doesn't fit for you, don't worry about it.	Ask participants to tear out the answer page and record their answers directly onto it as they go. Ask them to be sure to record answers across the page, not up and down.	
3:00 (30)	**Participants Work** ▪ Answer questionnaire ▪ Score questionnaire ▪ Read about your four-letter type	Circulate among tables, helping with scoring as necessary	If any participants don't "recognize" themselves, it may be because they are very close on one or more of the scales. In that situation, you can recommend reading about the types the close letters suggest to see if the person likes better what those alternatives describe.
3:30 (20)	**Explain the Dimensions:** "Each dimension is a scale – you will have some of both, but favor or prefer or side on which you scored highest. Like right or left-handedness – you prefer or favor one hand, but you can still use the other.	Describe each dimension drawing on flipchart paper, and give examples. You can explain each dimension, but it is often better to do a little "skit" type presentation with two people, each with opposite letters, explaining themselves and having interaction with each other about the dimension. For each dimension, put emphasis on "why we need each other" as you explain the differences.	You are giving participants a framework for understanding the types. You are adding to what they have already read and are giving them new data about the opposite letter. The purpose is to help them see the interdependence people have on each other, how groups are stronger because they have the view and perspective of both types. That's why the "why we need each other" discussion for each dimension is so important.
	E ——————————— I Extravert Introvert	For each dimension ask for a show of hands about how many	Keep presentation light and upbeat. This is about celebrating differences,

Time	Content/Process	Logistics
	"Measures where you get energy: ■ Extravert: from outside world/through interaction with others ■ Introvert: by going inside/by thinking/by introspection Examples: ■ Going to parties. ■ Speaking up in meetings. ■ Dealing with conflict. In general population: ■ 75% are extrovert ■ 25% are introvert S ------------ N **Sensing Intuitive**	not judging each other. People will often laugh and nod in agreement as they recognize themselves or others in the descriptions. It's best not to invite participant questions and/ or input at this point. It's better to cover the basic data quickly. Interruptions could delay this part much too long. have each letter and how many "x" or even scores. Describe why different types are so important to each other. Ask for show of hands for each dimension.
	Measures how you gather data: ■ Sensing: like a camera, taking a series of pictures of the horizon and examining each carefully. ■ Intuitive: like a radar screen, scanning the horizon and looking closely only at an occasional blip. Examples: ■ Like seeing trees or forest. ■ Reading a book or long report. In general population: ■ 75% are sensing ■ 25% are intuitive F ------------ T **Feeling Thinking**	Describe why different types are so important to each other. Ask for show of hands.

Measures which kind of data is going to influence your decision the most. ■ Feeling: "fairness," what's right, ruled by the heart. ■ Thinking: "logical," pragmatic, ruled by the head. Examples: ■ Coaching a sports team. ■ Giving feedback on a presentation. ■ Buying a new home. In general population ■ 50% are feeling ■ 50% are thinking	Describe why different types are so important to each other. Ask for show of hands.	
P ———————— J Perceiving Judging Measures how you decide and your need for closure. ■ Perceiving: open, always looking for new input, low need for closure. ■ Judging: wants things wrapped up, finished, wants to move on, high need for closure. Examples: ■ Planning a vacation. ■ Being on time for an airplane. ■ Following a meeting agenda. ■ Reopening an already decided point. In general population: ■ 50% are perceiving ■ 50% are judging "Now please write your four-letter type on your name tag as a reminder to practice listening for understanding: if someone at your table is not making sense to you it may be that they simply have a different perspective to which you might need to pay more attention.	Describe why different types are so important to each other. Ask for show of hands.	Emphasize again that the letters (types) represent simply a preference. This will allow participants who fear being stereotyped to let go of their nervousness a bit. The goal is to see the value of all the different types so that participants can gain deeper appreciation of their differences and learn to build on them. Working with the four types in front of the group for the remainder of the event will help them all practice.

Time	Content/Process	Logistics	
3:50 **(5)**	**Leadership Styles** "In addition to the 16 types, there are four subgroups that describe leadership styles: "NF, NT, SJ, and SP." Assign each type to a breakout room "Here is your assignment: "Read your two-letter type description in the *Temperament in Leading* booklet and prepare a group report answering these questions: ■ What are your strengths? ■ What are your weaknesses (things to watch out for)? ■ Why does this organization need your type? ■ "Don't forget to select a facilitator, recorder, and spokesperson, and, although we want to hear about your strengths and weaknesses, choose a spokesperson who can come back and really sell the rest of us on why this organization needs your type."	Post breakout room assignments up front. Write assignment on a flipchart in main room and in each breakout room. Provide an easel and markers for each table. These are arrived at by linking N to F or T and S to J or P. Have participants show hands for which of the four types they are. It is helpful to further segment the SJs into SFJ and STJ. The SFJs should read the ISFJ or ESFJ description in the Sixteen Types booklet because the SJ description in Temperament in Leading mostly describes STJs. You may also want to split the STJs into ISTJ and ESTJ to keep groups down to a more manageable size. Even with those subdivisions, you may have multiple tables of ESTJs and ISTJs. See below for the methodology to use to keep the report-outs down to a reasonable number.	This activity deepens the participants' understanding of themselves and, during the report-outs, of others. Hype the "sales pitch" approach. This makes the report outs lots of fun.

3:55 (25)	**Groups Work**	Groups move to breakout rooms. While groups are working, select one table from those working on same types (e.g., ESTJ, ISTJ) that appears to be working especially well. Ask this table to be the reporter for their type. Tell the other tables of that type that another table will be reporting out and they are welcome to make additions if there is something significant missing, but they need not prepare a full report.

Time	Content/Process	Logistics	
4:20 **(25)**	**Groups Report Out**	Encourage applause after each report. Encourage groups to really hear and understand what the others say. You have asked them to present competitively but they must listen non-competitively. Each report takes about four minutes. When there are multiple groups for the same type, ask for additions if there are any.	When groups fail to list weaknesses, you may need to give some examples.
4:45 **(5)**	**Summary** "I hope this helps you see the positive power of your differences – that you need each other – that you are stronger because of your diversity. It would be a very strong team indeed that represented and really listened to all of the different types."	Caution participants to offer this activity to spouses, subordinates, and/or colleagues in a caring way – not a "Here! Take this!" approach. Better to let a spouse, for example, read the participant's four-letter description first. Then they likely will be interested in finding out their own type.	Urge participants to celebrate and appreciate their diversity. Encourage them to use their learnings about preferences and conflict as they proceed through the next two days. Expect a high-energy, positive group atmosphere after this activity.

EVALUATION–DAY 1
(total time = 10 minutes)

Purpose

To get 'a finger on the pulse' of the participants as they are leaving and to use the information as a common database shared by you and the Event Planning Team as you plan for tomorrow and shared by the participants when they hear the data tomorrow.

Underlying Philosophy

To get a reading on where the participants are. The purpose of the evaluation is not to critique the design. Instead, use the participants' data to plan for tomorrow. Use the information to adjust tomorrow's agendas to help the group achieve the purpose of the event. The evaluation also provides an opportunity for participants to vent if they need to do so. The use of written evaluations further empowers the group since their feedback serves to guide changes to the next two days' agendas.

| 4:50 (10) | "One more thing before we break for the day
■ The logistics team is coming around with a form for you to use to tell us how today went for you.
■ The leadership and Event Planning Teams will read your answers tonight and use the data to agree on any changes needed for tomorrow's design
■ We will also summarize the themes we hear and tell you first thing tomorrow what you said. In that way, each of us will have a better 'fix' on how you are reacting. Your reactions become another important part of the common database. So, be sure to "tell your truth."
■ Thanks. See you at breakfast at 7:30. Tomorrow's session will start promptly at 8:00.
■ Leadership and Event Planning Teams: please join us at a table to read the evaluations." | Logistics team hands out evaluation forms to each table. Before handing out, count out the appropriate number of forms per table and crosshatch the stack for easy distribution.

Logistics team puts boxes or stands at doors to collect evaluation forms. Team should also check tables in case some participants have left evaluations there and take evaluations to the EPT and leadership teams as quickly as possible wherever they're sitting. | Recommended questions:
How did today go for you:
■ Highs?
■ Lows?

What advice do you have for us for tomorrow?

If you change these questions, it's important that you use open-ended questions so that you can get your "finger on the pulse" of the group.

Inform the leaders and Event Planning Team beforehand that you would like them to stay to read the evaluations with you. |

Time	Content/Process	Logistics

READ/ACT ON EVALUATION
(total time depends upon how the session is going)

Purpose
To enable the EPT and leaders to understand where participants are as they leave today and to be sure all are on track for tomorrow.

Underlying Philosophy
By getting the leaders to read with you, you involve and engage them in the heart of the process. This helps them own the process and heightens their awareness of their role on Day 2 and how important that role is.

Design Choice Points
The design the EPT originally developed may not be "perfect" to achieve the session purpose. The data from participants enables the EPT to determine whether the purpose is being met and to revise the agenda if necessary. The leaders may ask you how long they need to stay. A response is, "As long as you can. It shouldn't take more than an hour. Will you just sit down and read the evaluations for about 15 minutes?" Say whatever you think you need to say to keep them there to read the evaluations. Tell them that tomorrow night they will need to be here all evening. "Give us what you can," is the message to communicate.

| 5:00 | **Read Evaluations and Vent** | Logistics team clears off a table and makes room for about 20 people. EPT and leadership team members sit in a large circle to read the evaluations and pass them around. Encourage everyone to vent about evaluations they don't like.

Consultants: look for implications for the designs on Day 2 and Day 3. Keep control by only raising issues that concern you. Don't ask "are there any changes for tomorrow?" | What you are looking for in the evaluations to show that you are on track:
Highs:
■ Opportunity to hear and ask questions of the leader
■ Celebrating diversity.
■ Being part of a team.
Lows:
■ These are usually varied (unless there was a particularly bad presentation by a leader or about industry trends).
■ May tend to have negative comments about not being able to solve problems identified in "mads & |

	Walk Through Chunked Agendas for Next Two Days Emphasize "revisit strategy" module on Day 2.	sads." Emphasize to leadership the importance of bringing the strategy to life for the participants tomorrow. Answer questions honestly and concisely.
	Summarize evaluations Consultant who will feed back evaluations the next morning should prepare the evaluation summary.	Summarize the main themes for each question and give a few examples of answers using the authors' exact words. When you report back the evaluations, do not explicitly or implicitly make judgments: give only the facts. Give a colorful commentary that is not judgmental. There are always three or four miscellaneous comments that the group needs to hear, in particular, negative comments. Give quotes, even if there is not a theme, to signal that you are listening to the negative comments too.

Time	Content/Process	Logistics

GENERIC DESIGN: DAY 2

Purpose (generic)
To work together as leaders of this organization to:

- Build a picture of where the organization is right now,
- Explore and agree on where it must be in the future if it is to be successful
- Make commitments on what people in the organization need to do differently, individually and collectively, to get there

Day 1   Expanding the organization's world view – building a common data base about each other, the organization, its stakeholders and its environment.

- Welcome Purpose
- Agenda/Logistics
- Telling our Stories
- Industry Trends
- View From Our Customers
- Organization Diagnosis
- Celebrating Diversity
- Evaluation – Day 1
- Read/Act on Evaluations – Day 1

Day 2   Ensure that people are connected around one brain and one heart and able to develop a new direction together built on that connection and expanded worldview.

- Feedback of Evaluations/Agenda for the Day
- Stakeholder "Wild Card" Module (suppliers, union, program managers, et al) View from .....
- Strategic Planning Model
- View from the Leadership
- "I Have a Dream" speech from the leader
- Organization Strategy: Revisit
- Feedback on Strategy by Participants
- Evaluation – Day 2
- Read/Act on Evaluations – Day 2
- Leadership Work on Response to Input

Day 3   Become whole about the strategic direction of the organization, shift its paradigm and create a full system commitment to change.

CHAPTER 5: DESIGN POSSIBILITY: A GENERIC THREE-DAY EVENT PLAN

- Feedback of Evaluations/Agenda – Day 3
- Response from Leadership Group: "Finalized" Strategy
- Panel of Possibilities
- Preferred Futuring
- System-Wide Action Planning
- Valentines: Inter-Group Requests
- Back-Home Planning
- Wrap-Up/Evaluation/Close

CHAPTER 5: DESIGN POSSIBILITY: A GENERIC THREE-DAY EVENT PLAN

Time	Content/Process	Logistics

FEEDBACK OF EVALUATIONS/AGENDA—DAY 2
(Total time = 10 minutes)

Purpose
To expand from an individual view of yesterday to a whole system view of where the organization is and be able to move to the next stage of change based on that wider picture.

Underlying Philosophy
Building to one brain and one heart requires moving constantly from the individual view to a whole system view and back again. In that process, people need to stay connected as they move ahead if the organization expects everyone to support the change. Participants need to understand that action research is not academic exercise. Individuals will be able to build on the whole group's feedback as they interact with each other. That's the principle of action research – the organization moves forward, it moves deeper, it stays whole. This process is the first stage of unleashing participants' desires to be empowered. Participants see that their input is valued and used. Such a participant might say, "I can influence as far as I can see."

Time	Content	Process/Materials/Logistics	Tips
8:00 **(08)**	Feedback of Evaluations Describe summary of feedback and give specific quotes from representative responses The purposes of this activity are: 1. To let participants know they have been heard 2. To add to the common data base 3. To model making feedback public - whether positive or negative 4. To show their feedback is being acted on - showing what changes are being made in today's agenda for instance.	Use the same max-mix seating as the day before.	Make it clear as you describe the summary what proportion referred to each theme. ("About a third of you thought the day went fast.") Do not make implicit or explicit judgments. Just the facts. (e.g. "Here were the most frequent responses"- not: "Here were the big winners.") The consultant who actually read and compiled the feedback should deliver this information. Be energetic and use an element of humor, if appropriate. Delivery matters.
.8:08 **(02)**	**Agenda**	Review the agenda "chunks" noting any changes in the design based on	You are taking them on a preview of a journey. Make it an

CHAPTER 5: DESIGN POSSIBILITY: A GENERIC THREE-DAY EVENT PLAN

	participant feedback.	interesting one. Be purposeful yet brief.

KEY STAKEHOLDER "WILD CARD" MODULE (SUPPLIERS, UNIONS, PROGRAM MANAGERS)
(Total time = 90 minutes)

Purpose
To broaden the participants' world, individually and as a group, to include the views through their remaining key stakeholders' eyes.

Underlying Philosophy
Before participants hear feedback on strategy, they need to have a full picture of what their stakeholders are experiencing and what they are expecting from the organization now and in the future.

Time	Content	Process/Materials/Logistics	Tips
8:10 (05)	Introduce the module and the panel. Describe the organizations the panelists represent. Suggested framing: "These are key stakeholders. Prepare yourself to listen to see the world through their eyes. You will have an opportunity to discuss what you have heard, share reactions at your table and generate questions of understanding." "Listen to see the world through their eyes," should be the last thing they hear from you.	Logistics should provide: ■ Chairs for presenters 　Table for presenters (optional) ■ Mikes for presenters ■ Name placards for presenters ■ Open forum tent cards at tables ■ Handouts on cue It is helpful, if possible, to have an A/V person there at all times (mikes usually crackle at these moments when you need them) Contract with presenters to agree that they will use handouts rather than overheads (which are deadly on energy in the room)	The EPT will have decided who the key stakeholders are and will have invited a panel from those groups. Identify panelists as they come in and make sure you confirm that they understand what the expectations are. Presentations are to "tee up" the questions. Have the presenters stand and speak from the podium.
8:15	**Panel Presentations**	Seat stakeholders at panel table	Contract with the stakeholders to

CHAPTER 5: DESIGN POSSIBILITY: A GENERIC THREE-DAY EVENT PLAN

Time	Content/Process	Logistics
(30)	Three or four presenters (total presenting time of 20, no more than 30 minutes); no overheads Ask them (ahead of time) to address the following questions: ■ What are the challenges and opportunities your organization is facing in the next few years? ■ What does your organization need to do differently as a result of these challenges and opportunities? ■ What will we, as a stakeholder, need to do differently to be more helpful to you?	tell them when their time is up (include some signal for a two-minute warning) with mikes. Well in advance of the session, give stakeholders the specific questions the Event Planning Team wants them to address. Coach the stakeholders to tell their own stories. Participants need to hear and see the world the stakeholder is facing. The main focus needs to be "What can the organization in the room do differently in the future if it is to most effectively meet its stakeholders' needs? Shaping the future is more important than punishing the past, though the past will provide good action research wisdom.
8:45 (15)	**Open Forum: Table Discussion** Choose a new Facilitator, Reporter and Recorder. Now take 15 minutes at your table to discuss: ■ What did we hear? ■ What are our reactions? ■ What questions of understanding do we need to ask? of whom?	Place assignment on table stands. Tell the recorder to get the flip charts. Give a two-minute warning to tear off the question sheets and move the easels back to the sides of the room. Remind participants of the importance of the three questions to be sure that everyone's views get articulated. You might say: "What did you hear?—you each will hear it differently—celebrate that and listen to each other! What were your reactions?—you each will have reacted differently depending on your position in the organization—celebrate that!

CHAPTER 5: DESIGN POSSIBILITY: A GENERIC THREE-DAY EVENT PLAN

			Now, based on all of that, what questions of understanding does your table have, that will allow you to see the world through the speaker's eyes?"
			Make sure you and logistics mike teams are in synch about which tables you are going to identify this round.
9:00 (30)	**Open Forum: Table Questions and Stakeholder Answers** "The purpose of this activity is for you to see the world that your stakeholder sees. If I call on your table, you will get a chance to ask questions of understanding." "Please have the reporter identify who the question is for."	Attempt to get at most of the tables, but you do not necessarily need to get to them all. Since participants are in max-mix seating arrangement, you should get to most of the questions. Save the last five minutes to address burning, unanswered table questions to ensure that you have covered everything you need to." After the panelist answers, ask, for example, "Table 15, did that answer your question?"	
9:30 (15)	**Break**	Logistics: Make sure the coffee is refilled before the break	
9:45 (90)	**Learning More About Our Organization** Purpose: To build a common understanding of what the organization has been up to, how it's been working, what other departments/functions really do, etc., to ensure that the organization is truly "one-brain, one-heart" Design Issue: During the planning the EPT has identified areas where people in the organization do not know everything about		

Time	Content/Process	Logistics
	what is going on, across functions, within certain function areas, etc. The question was: " What do people need to know to ensure a consistent and common data base that will help all participants have a system-wide picture of the whole organization?" Based on the answers to these questions, you have the 90 minutes here to address those questions. Possibilities could include, but not be limited to:	
	■ Arrange a competitive role-play. If you have decided that knowledge of the competition is the missing piece of the common database, one of the ways to fill this gap is with short role-plays of key competitors.	Get someone from marketing to put together information on the key competitors and then get someone on the EPT, or someone else in the organization, to "be" that competitor for five minutes, addressing: ■ What we see as changing customer needs or base. ■ What we see as our strengths ■ What we see as your weaknesses or vulnerabilities ■ How we are going to sink you/eat your lunch as a result.
	Functional teams meet for one-half hour to identify all of the things that the teams are doing that they want the organization to know about followed by report outs.	Assign each function a work area, e.g., a table or a breakout room to become one brain about what they want others to know. Each functional group chooses a reporter to educate the whole group. Each function gives a three-minute *passionate* report out to the whole room.

CHAPTER 5: DESIGN POSSIBILITY: A GENERIC THREE-DAY EVENT PLAN

	Functional groups prepare presentations ahead of time covering areas such as: ■ Our major responsibilities ■ Our challenges over the next six months ■ What help we think we will need to meet our challenges Use your creativity to figure out what needs to happen here.	Each function gets a "station" to make their presentation. At each station is a representative of that function to be the expert on the function. The presentation could be written, verbal or both and may have additional visuals, such as posters, samples of products, etc. Each max-mix table sends an "envoy" to each function station to learn about that function and to return to the max-mix table to teach everyone at the table about the function. The representative of a given function becomes the envoy to that function for his or her table.
11:15 (65)	**Wild Card Stakeholder Module** The EPT has decided who else needs to be heard from before the organization hears from the leadership. You can do this with a 20-minute panel followed by 15 minutes of table discussion (What did we hear, etc.) and 30 minutes of question and answer	
12:20 (30)	LUNCH	

Time	Content/Process	Logistics
12:50 (15)	**Strategic Planning Model** Purpose of this activity: To create a common language about purpose, process and the importance of strategic thinking, the purpose of organizational strategy is to get all members of the organization pointing in the same direction; in order to be effective competitors in the future. Ask participants to get the Star of Success and Strategic Planning Models out of their packets and begin a walk through to make sense out of the model. Suggested words: *Step one:* Sound strategy is based on whole system understanding. The questions the Star of Success raises provide a strong underpinning for sound strategy. Good strategic planning begins with an accurate picture of what the organization's stakeholders need from it right now and what they will need from it in the future. You will be hearing from one more key stakeholder shortly—the view from the executive leadership of the organization. ***Step Two:*** Based on stakeholder needs, the organization identifies and agrees on a description of: ■ Purpose-The organization's Fundamental	Put a strategic planning model and a Star of Success in each participant's folder. Have extra copies available so that logistics can replace them if necessary. Ground the Strategic Planning Model on the Star of Success. The Star is a graphic of whole system framing questions that underpin strategy. Walk them through a very basic, common sense roadmap of strategic planning which we learned from Peter Drucker back in the 70's. It doesn't matter what you call these various strategic elements—it only matters that you think strategically at each step on the roadmap. It's helpful for participants to use/understand the same language. Change the language as needed to fit the words the leaders use in their draft strategy. Purpose answers the question, "Why does this organization exist? Who's needs to do we care about and serve?"

[Strategic Planning Model diagram]

ENVIRONMENTAL TRENDS, STAKEHOLDER NEEDS (Now and Future)
- Customers
- Top Management
- Suppliers
- Competitors
- Employees
- Union Leaders

PURPOSE MISSION GUIDING PRINCIPLES
- What business are we in?
- What value do we create?
- What's our focus of action?
- What do we stand for?

STRATEGIC GOALS
- How to measure long term success?
- What's our preferred future? (next 3-5 year goals)

STRATEGIC THRUST
- Broad thrusts
- Basis of competition (next 3-5 years)

STRATEGIC OBJECTIVES
- Achievable, measurable, time-phased results (yearly results)

ACTION PLANS
- What will we do?
- Who will do it? When?
- How is it to be done?
- What resources are needed?

IMPLEMENT
- Do it!

Evaluate – Did we respond appropriately to stakeholders?
Evaluate – Did it achieve the results?
Evaluate – Did we do it?

[Star of Success diagram]

STAR OF SUCCESS
Framing the key questions critical to a successful whole system journey

Strategic Direction—*True North*
- What's going on in our environment—now and in the future?
- What business are we in?
- Who are our stakeholders?
- What value do we choose to create for our stakeholders?
- How do we intend to create and deliver our value?
- What does success look like and how do we measure our performance?

Do we have the right strategic direction?

Shared Information—*Bringing forth a common world*
- What is the common context?
- What common data and information do we need?
- How are we going to create the data and information?

Do we have the right information?

Resources—*Capabilities Needed*
- People?
- Committed to *True North?*
- Right skills and knowledge?
- Facilities/Equipment/Software?

Do we have the right resources?

Do we have the right Pattern of Success?

Do we have the right functions?

Processes & Systems—*Ways and Means*
- What work is needed?
- How will we do the work?

Do we have the right form?

Resource Relationships—*Human, Spatial, Hierarchical and Functional*
- Reporting relationships?
- Functional relationships?
- Distribution of power—the ability to make and keep decisions?
- External relationships?
- Internal relationships?

Reason For Being. This is a statement of key stakeholders' hopes, aspirations, yearnings, and longings that describe the organization's fundamental purpose and states what business it needs to be in order to serve its stakeholders' wants and desires. ■ Mission—Using Purpose as context, the mission will describe the focus of all actions the organization needs to take in order to create extraordinary value for all its stakeholders.	The handout in the folder will have a list of the key stakeholders of this organization at this time and participants will have heard these voices in the meeting itself. Include this same model in the folder people get when they arrive.	Mission answers the question, "What business are we in?" It defines the scope of the organization's activities - what we do and what we don't do. The story of the railroads in America in the 1960s and the 1970s clearly shows the importance of mission. What a difference it would have made if the leaders of the railroads had decided during their environmental crisis that the mission of railroads for the future was "transportation." They could have gotten into airplanes as that industry began to take over in the transportation industry. The railroad leaders apparently still thought of themselves as being in the "train track" industry…and that industry was shrinking.
■ Guiding Principles/Values — What are the principles and beliefs that the organization wants to stand for? The principles that will guide every member of the organization on its journey into the future.…		Values are the " How we want to work"" foundation upon which the organization's vision and mission rest. For an organization's values to have maximum impact, they need to represent the heart of the organization. Success depends on consistently living these values as a whole organization.

Time	Content/Process	Logistics
		If values have become a true statement of how people in the organization live, then everyone can take pride in how the organization makes decisions.
		Consider giving an example of a compelling vision from one of your own clients.
		Vision is the higher purpose towards which people work that provides meaning and inspiration for their collaborative work. The critical importance is to build a common vision of the future that will inspire and motivate everyone in the organization. "Yes! I would be proud to be part of this envisioned organization in the future!"
	Step Three— Vision of Success: If the organization is living out its purpose, mission, and values effectively, how do its members define success? What is the future they prefer for the organization in the next three to five years? What do they yearn to become three to five years from now based on their stakeholders needs and their competitors' challenges?	Many clients refer to these strategic thrusts as **strategic goals.** Whatever they are called, they answer the question, "What does the organization need to focus on improving in order to move toward the future its members want to create?"
	Step Four: Now that you are grounded in the **Mission, Vision, and Values,** the next step is to identify and agree upon strategic thrusts. The broad thrusts—products/services, relationships, processes/systems, the organization needs as its broad focus for the next three to five years. What does the organization need to change/improve?	You can also view these thrusts as "points on the compass" of

CHAPTER 5: DESIGN POSSIBILITY: A GENERIC THREE-DAY EVENT PLAN

system-wide wholeness, unified around its purpose and needed to help the organization realize its vision.

The language used in these strategic thrusts must allow each person to see how they can contribute towards success, no matter where they are in the organization.

Strategic Objectives are the deliverables the organization can achieve that show it is moving toward the future state. They are milestones on the journey. Without measurable objectives the change effort will lose direction and energy.

Action plans can be in functional areas or involve cross-functional activities. System-wide action planning is usually what is missing in the organization because everyone has been living in a departmental chimney. That is why you need to emphasize system-wide action planning in Whole-Scale events. Ad hoc teams or task forces can accomplish action plans through new kinds of cross-functional communication and cooperation. It is very important that leaders publicly support the

Step Five: Strategic Objectives--Describes achievable, measurable results in a one- to two-year time frame.

Step Six: Action Plans--With all of the above steps in mind, identify, agree, and commit to action plans:

- What will the organization do?
- Who will do it?
- When?
- How will they do it?
- What resources do they need to do it?
- When must it be finished?

Time	Content/Process	Logistics
	Step Seven: Implementation—Do it! Do what the organization committed to do!	implementation of the plans the organization makes in this process. That means sending clear messages, especially to middle managers, that the activities related to implementation are not a distraction from work, they are the work.
	Step Eight: A multifaceted Evaluation Process— ■ Did we actually do what we said we would do? ■ If we did what we said we'd do, were the results the ones we wanted to achieve? ■ If not, it's possible we had the wrong activities—Let's rethink it! ■ What progress have we made in meeting our stakeholders needs? Have we responded appropriately to each of the stakeholders? How do we know? How do we get appropriate feedback? Step Nine: Based on that feedback, you will be able to start another round of strategic planning, building on new needs you will have identified from the stakeholders."	What gets measured gets done. Unless there is a consistent effort to document effort and results, momentum will decline. It is unrealistic to expect everything to go as planned. Unexpected results are not failure, but a learning opportunity. Implementation of the plan follows the action learning model of Plan --Do--Check--Act. Leaders and others in the organization should think of themselves as being in a continuous improvement mode, learning and changing as they go.

VIEW FROM THE LEADERSHIP

Purpose
To ensure that each participant sees and is able to hear about the world that the hierarchical leader or leadership team sees…not because it's the right answer, but because the leader(s) will see things from their positions that others may not see. The idea is to continue working to build "one-brain" with each person knowing what all people know.

Underlying Philosophy
It is important to have worked with the leader(s) in advance, to ensure that they have a well-thought out sense of strategic direction for the organization. People in organizations nowadays are yearning for leaders they can believe in; leaders with vision, credibility and integrity; leaders with a demonstrated commitment to transform the organization to allow its people to achieve success. Traditional "Command and control," the old style of leading, is no longer "socially acceptable." People yearn for authentic, wise and competent leaders, not old-time dictators.

1:05 (30)	**View from the Leadership** Leader or leaders speak for a maximum of 30 minutes, about: ■ Challenges and opportunities facing the organization in the next few years ■ Challenges that the organization must address in order to be successful in the future. ■ The organization's strengths…areas where it definitely need to improve/change ■ The help the leader needs from the members of the organization	Logistics: Have table and chairs, one for each speaker, with several mikes…and a traditional podium with mike. If leaders have handouts to distribute, have copies put in in-boxes before they speak. Also provide copies of a draft strategic plan, if they're going to enrich it overnight.	Urge leaders to speak honestly, from their own heart, telling the truth, as they know it. A leader who speaks like that is compelling and will be truly respected and followed…and confronted appropriately if they are open to being confronted. Ask the leader(s) to speak without slides or overheads, using handouts for each person if they have data they want to share. Coach the leader, as needed, to ensure a heartfelt, honest "dream" speech. At the end of the speech, he or she describes the strategy document and asks for help in enriching it.
1:35 (60)	**Open Forum** 15 min. table discussion around the three questions: ■ What did we hear? ■ What are our reactions? ■ What are our questions of	Remind participants that this Q&A is not about argu the leaders, but to understand what they see and what they believe. What you are trying to do is have a complete picture of the organization's world so that people can be well-informed when they give their leaders	As in previous Open Forums, it is important to make sure participants are asking questions of understanding, not making a speech. You may need to ask, "What is your question?"

Time	Content/Process	Logistics
	understanding? Q & A 45 minutes with last five minutes for burning questions	feedback on the strategy in a few minutes. And, it is just as important to make sure the leaders are being responsive. "Table 4, does that answer your question or do you need to hear more?"
2:35 (15)	**Break**	
2:50 (15)	**"I Have a Dream" speech from the leader and Organizational Strategy Revisit** The leader speaks from the heart in describing what the organization would look like two to three years from now – "If we are really successful, I will see ……" the leader ends with a walk through of the actual draft strategy and a request for help to enrich the strategy.	Often the leader and his or her direct reports present the strategy. When union leadership is willing to participate, they can be a powerful advocate for the importance of the strategy on the future of employees. Leaders will have decided which parts of their draft strategy are open to input. If they believe the purpose is fine the way it is, just tell people…they'll all be fine with it. Most leaders are open to change on all parts of the draft strategy, but make sure they are truly open before you get the feedback. Do not raise people's expectations when there is nothing to expect.
3:05 (75) (10)	**Feedback on Strategy by Participants** Strategy Enrichment: Feedback from Participants *Introduction*: "You are embarking on a process James McGregor Burns of Harvard calls "transformational leadership". Under the traditional "command and	This is the moment where the participants can add their own insights and wisdom to the strategy. As a microcosm, they will see things that the leaders cannot see. In the process they will also struggle with the issues the leaders have been struggling with. The result will be a better strategy and participants who understand and can support it.

(20)

control" style of leaders, the leader gives direction for actions required and the follower asks for what they need to do the work. The leader agrees and the "transaction" has been closed.

Burns felt, in his writings in the 1970s, that the turbulence facing organizations in these times would require a new form of leadership, which he called "transformational." The leader studies the environmental trends, stakeholder needs (internal and external), and the competitive challenges, and decides on the strategic direction that will lead to success in the future. The leader then gives members of the organization that data, including the first view of what the strategy needs to be for the future to be successful. Then having ensured that everyone sees what the leaders see, he or she asks the people to respond. The leaders listen to the response and integrate the new data into their beliefs. At that point, the organization has identified a whole system strategy and built commitment. The organization will respond appropriately.

The leaders need your ideas and recommendations to create that whole system strategic plan."

Assignment:
At your table, brainstorm everything you believe should be changed, stay the same, or be added for each category.

Time	Content/Process	Logistics
	Choose a new facilitator to make sure you truly brainstorm and choose a recorder who will get an easel and document every idea as it's called out…leaving a 3" margin on the left hand side for room –wide voting	
	Voting Assignment: Walk around the room and read the input on the different portions of the strategy. Put a check mark by everything that you agree with. Your votes will tell the leaders which of these suggestions is most strongly supported so it will be clear what the people's priorities are.	Post feedback, under headers like "Purpose" "Mission" "Values" " Vision of Success" and "Strategic Thrusts" Logistics helps hang input under appropriate headers as the tables complete their work. Participants are saying "Yes!" to the suggestions that speak most strongly to them.
4:20 pm	**Evaluation – Day 2** Evaluation ▪ What were your most important learnings today? ▪ What still feels unfinished for you as you leave? ▪ What advice do you have for us for tomorrow?	After 15 minutes of voting time, logistics has placed the Day 2 evaluation forms in the in-boxes. Invite people to go back to their table when they're done voting and fill out the evaluations.
4:30	**Read/Act on Evaluations – Day 2** Get the EPT and the Leadership team to read the evaluations around a couple of	Logistics team arranges for dinner for the Leadership Team.

Time   Content/Process   Logistics

tables. Pass the evaluations around until everyone is comfortable that they know where people are. Walk through the design for the next day to make sure that it is okay or change it as needed.

Leadership Work on Response to Input

Discuss how the leadership team wants to do the strategy rework that night. Suggest that after dinner the Leadership Team divide into subgroups according to the strategic categories, i.e., purpose, mission, etc. to do the initial analysis. Each subgroup works for an hour to be sure that they hear everything that people are saying in the feedback. Each subgroup then prepares a presentation for the whole group to include:

- Here is what they said
- Here is what we recommend ought to be changed.
- Here is what we heard but did not change because......
- Here is what the rewrite could look like.

Each subgroup presents to the whole leadership team and helps work the team through to consensus – true consensus. The logistics team takes the version everyone agrees to and gets it typed.

The logistics team leaves someone behind to get the final version (arrived at by consensus) typed and copied so that each participant has a copy at their place when they return in the morning.

Time	Content/Process	Logistics

GENERIC DESIGN: DAY 3

Purpose (generic)

To work together as leaders of this organization to:

- Build a picture of where the organization is right now,
- Explore and agree on where it must be in the future if it is to be successful, and
- Make commitments as to what people in the organization need to do differently, individually and collectively, to get there.

Day 1 Expanding our world view – building a common data base about each other, the organization, its stakeholders and its environment.

- Welcome Purpose
- Agenda/Logistics
- Telling our Stories
- Industry Trends
- View From Our Customers
- Organization Diagnosis
- Celebrating Diversity
- Evaluation – Day 1
- Read/Act on Evaluations – Day 1

Day 2 Ensure the organization is connected around one brain and one heart and able to develop its future direction built on that connection and expanded worldview.

- Feedback of Evaluations/Agenda for the Day
- Stakeholder "Wild Card" Module (suppliers, union, program managers, et al)
- View from ....
- Strategic Planning Model
- View from the Leadership
- "I have a dream" speech from the leader
- Organization Strategy: Revisit
- Feedback on Strategy by Participants
- Evaluation – Day 2
- Read/Act on Evaluations – Day 2
- Leadership Work on Response to Input

Day 3 Become whole about the strategic direction of the organization, shift its paradigm and create a full system commitment to change.

- Feedback of Evaluations/Agenda – Day 3

CHAPTER 5: DESIGN POSSIBILITY: A GENERIC THREE-DAY EVENT PLAN

- Response from Leadership Group: "Finalized" Strategy
- Panel of Possibilities
- Preferred Futuring
- System-Wide Action Planning
- Valentines: Inter-Group Requests
- Back-Home Planning
- Wrap-Up/Evaluation/Close

CHAPTER 5: DESIGN POSSIBILITY: A GENERIC THREE-DAY EVENT PLAN

Time	Content/Process	Logistics

FEEDBACK OF EVALUATIONS/AGENDA—DAY 3
(Total time = 10 minutes)

Purpose
To continue building our common database.

Underlying Philosophy
Participants need to hear total group feedback on Day 2 in their own words (summary of Day 2 evaluations with direct quotes). "If I hear my own words, I trust the feedback more," a listener might say. Also, reviewing the agenda takes the mystery out of what the group will accomplish today and how the consultants will bring about appropriate group closure.

Time	Content	Materials/Logistics	Tips
8:00 **(5)**	Feedback on Evaluations	Logistics has a lot of work to do to prepare for this day: ■ Place a copy of the revised strategy at each place. ■ Post big headers around the room, one for each strategic thrust.	Make it clear as you describe the summary what proportion referred to each theme. ("About a third of you thought the day went fast.")
8:05 **(5)**	Day 3 Agenda	■ Around the room hang a flip chart sheet for each max-mix table in the room. The sheet is blank except for the number of the table in the lower right-hand corner. (Divide the number of tables by the number of strategic thrusts to know how many sheets to put under each strategic thrust header.) ■ Place a typed numbered list of the strategic thrusts at each place. ■ Place post-it notes and black Flair brand felt tip markers for each person in the in-box. Use 3"x5" post-it notes. About one-third of a pack per person usually works.	Do not make implicit or explicit judgments. Just the facts. (e.g. "Here were the most frequent responses" - not: "Here were the big winners.") This information could be delivered by the consultant or by a member of the EPT. Whoever delivers the feedback would actually have read and compiled it. Be energetic and use an element of humor, if appropriate. Delivery matters.

CHAPTER 5: DESIGN POSSIBILITY: A GENERIC THREE-DAY EVENT PLAN

	■ Seat participants at max-mix tables.
	■ Describe the journey the group is going to take today and the work products that it will develop.

CHAPTER 5: DESIGN POSSIBILITY: A GENERIC THREE-DAY EVENT PLAN

RESPONSE FROM LEADERSHIP: FINALIZED STRATEGY

(Total time=50 minutes)

Purpose
- For the leadership to demonstrate how effectively they have listened and to show how they have honored what they have heard
- For the entire organization to become aligned around the strategy.

Underlying Philosophy

This is the opportunity to create "one brain, one heart" around the strategy. Participants are willing and generally happy to let leadership "lead" provided they can see themselves in the strategy and understand the rationale for what leadership did and did not change in response to their input.

Time	Content	Materials/Logistics	Tips
8:10 **(5)**	Introduction	Explain the process that the Leadership Team used last night to incorporate participant input and feedback from Day 2.	Contract with leaders about timing for this presentation, but use your own judgment if they run over and you believe it is in the best interest of the participants to hear what they are saying. You and leadership must also agree on how to handle feedback during this piece, e.g. "Did we get it?"
8:15 **(30)**	Leaders Present Strategy	Member(s) of leadership team present finalized strategy and their rationale.	
		At the end of the presentation, a leader asks the participants, "Did we get it?" Stand by the leaders and join the leaders in deciding if they did "get it." If the eyes of the participants tell you that the Leadership Team did not get it, take over and work with the whole group to find out what they need. Usually discussions in	Don't let the leaders have to respond to the group if it appears that the Leadership did not hear the feedback. The leaders will most likely get defensive, which serves neither them nor the group.

the max-mix tables will produce the necessary data. Report outs from tables will inform the changes needed and move you ahead. Use your judgment to know when to move ahead.

Time	Content/Process	Logistics

PANEL OF POSSIBILITIES
(Total time=80 minutes)

Purpose
To open up new ways of thinking about change: anything is possible for this organization. ("I can influence as far as I can see and I need new ideas to release that creative energy from my brain," a participant might say.)

Design Issues
With the EPT, identify organizations that are doing innovative things that will speak to this organization. They do not have to be exactly the same kind of organization or function to release new ideas in this organization. The EPT generally knows who the innovators are and whom to invite.

Time	Content/Process	Logistics
8:45 (80)	**Panel of Possibilities** (05)Introduce the panel. Each speaks from his or her own change experiences, as follows: <ul><li>What was going on in the organization that caused you to contemplate change?</li><li>How did people respond to the idea of this change? What did you do to help people bring about the changes?</li><li>What did you learn from the experience? What would you do differently?</li><li>What advice would you give this organization as they face their change?</li></ul>(30) Panel Presentations (15) Open Forum Table Work (30) Q&A with last 5 minutes for burning unasked questions.	Get someone who knows the members of the panel to introduce them. The entire panel presentation needs to be no more than 30 minutes, so divide the time equally among the speakers and carefully control their time. See Day 1 Tips: <ul><li>Invite speakers to bring handouts and you can make copies for everyone.</li><li>Don't let the speakers use slides or overheads.</li><li>Brief the speakers before the session on the Open Forum process so that they know what to expect.</li><li>Remind speakers as they go up on the podium about timing and table questions.</li></ul>It will be important for an organization that has both management and labor to include both in the panel of possibilities.
10:05 (15)	**Break**	Be sure refreshments are in place before the break

CHAPTER 5: DESIGN POSSIBILITY: A GENERIC THREE-DAY EVENT PLAN

Time	Content/Process	Logistics
	PREFERRED FUTURING *(Total time=80 minutes)* **Purpose** To combine the yearnings of the participants to build a common database around a vision for the future – one that will motivate each individual and the entire organization. **Underlying Philosophy** Preferred futuring enables a paradigm shift when it comes at the right moment in time—after the participants have built a common database and are able to combine their yearnings to create an inspiring future. At this point they are working together to create the organization of their own choosing.	
10:20 (30)	**Preferred Futuring** Ron Lippitt, a behavioral scientist who was one of the founders of the National Training Laboratoriees in the 1950s, helped found the Institute for Social Research at the University of Michigan, did research on group dynamics. He recruited two different sets of leadership groups to test his theories on what it would take to sustain change. He gave the first set the assignment to identify all of the things that hindered them from being what they wanted to be and felt they should be. Then he asked them to identify the key hindrances and come up with solutions to those problems. The results in these groups were: ■ The longer these groups worked, the less energy they had to continue their work. (Their energy drained out their feet.) ■ The longer they worked, the more they blamed others for the problems (not my fault). ■ The results these groups tended to come up with were pain reduction solutions (stop the bleeding). ■ Over time it turned out that the groups did not feel personal ownership for the solutions and therefore	See: Lippitt, Lawrence L. (1998). ***Preferred Futuring: Envision the Future You Want, Unleash the Energy to Get There.*** Berrett-Koehler: San Francisco.

did not lead the charge for change.

Lippitt gave the second set of leadership teams the assignment to identify and agree on an image of what they wanted to become in the future. Then he asked them to agree on what they needed to start doing right now in order to help the organization move to that future.

The results in these groups were:

- The longer they worked together on this project, the more energy they had as a group.
- The longer they worked together on the project, the more responsibility and ownership they felt for the outcomes. (I know what I can do differently.)
- Their solutions tended to be innovative, ideas they had not had before.
- Over time, these groups led the changes needed to realize the future they had chosen. They no longer waited for "somebody else."

Time	Content/Process	Logistics
	Assignment: "Now, it's time for all of you to join together in creating the image of the future you prefer. Get your sheet of the numbered strategic thrusts, your package of post-it notes and your felt tip pens. Open up your brain and let all of your ideas out. It is _____, two years from today. This group is back together again. You are pleased and proud about how effective you have been in achieving each of the strategic thrusts. What do you see happening, what do you hear people saying that tells you the world is better? (30) Post-It note writing and collecting at the tables	You can make a handout for this assignment or you can give it verbally. It's your choice. Above all else deliver the assignment passionately in the moment of the future. "You are there. What do you see?" If you do that successfully, the answers will be innovation instead of problem solving. "Put one idea on each post-it. Be sure to include the number of the strategic thrust for your idea in the upper left-hand corner of the post-it so that logistics will know how to sort them. As you write your post-its, place them in front of you so that logistics can collect them." Logistics will circulate and collect all of the post-its, sort them into the appropriate strategic thrusts and then spread them evenly across the tables assigned to that thrust. Tip: When people have finished writing, if logistics is having trouble finishing the sorting, it sometimes helps to ask for volunteers to help get the post-its up on the sheets.

SYSTEM-WIDE ACTION PLANNING
(Total time=90 minutes)

Purpose
To unleash and combine the creativity and ideas of everyone in the room in a way that will enable participants to develop action plans for the organization as a whole.

Underlying Philosophy
The microcosm max-mix tables are now being asked to engage in transformational thinking in much the same way the leaders did last night. Their job is to take the ideas of everyone in the room that focus on a particular strategic thrust, develop a combined preferred future for that thrust based upon everyone's input. They will then be able to uncover and prioritize key system actions that will begin to move the organization toward that future. The key here is that they are listening to everyone as the whole organization speaking out of their own beliefs as they are shaped by everyone's input.

| 10:50 (90) | **System-Wide Action Planning** Instruct tables to go and get the sheet of post-its with their table number on it.

Assignment:
"Choose a facilitator and a recorder
1. Work together to sort the post-its into themes
2. Using those themes as well as your own beliefs, develop a preferred future statement for your thrust – What would success look like if the organization achieved it?
3. Focusing on that preferred future, brainstorm all the things you see happening right now anywhere in the organization that will help you move toward that preferred future?
4. Focusing on that preferred future, now also brainstorm all the things you see happening anywhere in the organization that could make it more difficult to achieve that future.
5. Now, brainstorm all of the ideas any of you have in your own mind or on your post-it notes about what | Remind participants of the rules of brainstorming. | |

CHAPTER 5: DESIGN POSSIBILITY: A GENERIC THREE-DAY EVENT PLAN

Time	Content/Process	Logistics	
	the organization needs to do to really move the needle on this strategic thrust. 6. Finally, using your brainstorm of ideas, discuss and agree on specific realistic actions that you recommend to the whole group. For each action, identify who needs to be primarily responsible and by when the action needs to be achieved. 7. Create a self-explanatory flip chart report of your future statement and your action recommendations. Leave a six-inch margin on the left side for voting by the whole group." Ask tables to post their report under the appropriate headers for the various thrusts.	Logistics can assist in posting the reports. As the groups are completing their final report, ask the tables to roll up the sheet containing the post-it notes, label it with the number of the strategic thrust and give it to a member of the logistics team. As the groups are completing their report, logistics distributes envelopes containing stars and dots for voting. Each person gets two to five gold stars (depending on the number of tables) per thrust meaning "These are the actions I believe will move the organization forward most effectively on this thrust in the next six months." Each person also gets two to five red dots to indicate, "You are not listening;	

CHAPTER 5: DESIGN POSSIBILITY: A GENERIC THREE-DAY EVENT PLAN

		this is not the way to go."	Someone always asks "Can we put all our stars or dots on one item?" Suggest that they probably wouldn't want others doing it, so it's probably not a good idea.
12:20 (60)	**LUNCH**, Post, Read & Vote Assignment: "Either go get your food first and then vote or vote and then get your food. Either way, you have an hour to eat and let your voice be heard on these proposed actions."	Explain the voting procedure (what the stars and dots mean). Tell the group that the leadership team will compile the results and report out the results after lunch. Get leadership team members prepared to report on the voting after lunch.	
1:20 (20)	**Leaders Report** Leaders form into teams to report on voting for each thrust. Leaders report out from headers on their favorite preferred future statement and the biggest hitters, positive, negative and mixed.		

CHAPTER 5: DESIGN POSSIBILITY: A GENERIC THREE-DAY EVENT PLAN

Time	Content/Process	Logistics

VALENTINES: INTER-GROUP REQUESTS

Purpose

For actual work teams to receive feedback on their actions from the organization as a whole and for the work teams to be able to use that information in preparing action plans that will help the whole organization be successful.

Underlying Philosophy

Conflict is best described as when people don't live up to each other's expectations. Generally the breakthrough into collaboration can occur if people can open up lines of feedback to each other. Often people are not living up to someone's expectations because that person has not clearly articulated the expectations and the reasons why they matter. Feedback is most effective when people give it in terms of behavior: "We need you to do more of ......, less of....." is a good format for giving feedback. Developing the feedback messages in the microcosm max-mix groups allows the messages of feedback to be multi-faceted, system-wide, and therefore more powerful to the recipients. Recipients need to truly listen to the requests, allow what people are saying to "get in", not because it's necessarily true, but because it is indeed the senders' truth. When people can listen in that way, they are able to see ways that they can respond in a "win-win" fashion...defensiveness grows out of not being able to see the statement as that person's truth.

It is a rare and wonderful opportunity a group to hear from all parts of the organization at the same moment in time. You will help groups use this data to make their departmental/office/program commitments for "next steps" toward the future they all yearn to create.

Design Choice Points

The EPT will need to identify, ahead of time, the specific groups who will receive the feedback. Look at the invitee list and choose groups according to the following organizing principles:

- They have an identity recognizable by others in the organization (e. g., Human Resources, Leadership Team, et al.)
- They have at least two and perhaps no more than 100 in the group who will be in the event together
- The event typically works best when a total of 10-15 groups are going to report out

Get consensus from the EPT about who needs to get feedback. This is never feedback for one person. It is for one function, one key part of the organization, one key part that can contribute to the organization's preferred future.

CHAPTER 5: DESIGN POSSIBILITY: A GENERIC THREE-DAY EVENT PLAN

| 1:40 (45) | Assignment to tables:
- "Look in your in-box. you will find a handout for each person at the table listing each of the groups that will open to feedback from your table. Hand those around.
- In the Inbox you will also find one valentine sheet for each function to which you will be writing. Do not hand these around. Give the entire batch to someone who is willing to be the recorder for this experience.
- Choose a facilitator who will make sure that everyone's voice will be heard and that you will really brainstorm instead of discussing with each other.

8 x 11 sheet
VALENTINE
To: (function)
From: Table number…

These are the things we need….

Brainstorm every idea any one at your table wants to give to this function. List them all on a sheet as fast as you can. You have forty-five minutes to write them. When the table is done, post valentines under the appropriate header using the tape provided

Participants circulate and read the ones that interest them. This gives them an idea of what people are saying to each other.

Back at their tables, participants get the back home table assignments out of the inbox. It's time for them to say goodbye to their max-mix table for now, take a break and | In the in-boxes place one valentine for each function, and one list of valentine groups for each person at the table.

Around the room logistics will place headers for each recipient group, with flipchart sheets and tape under each header.

While participants are working, | During the course of the EPT work, you will have decided on the message that needs to be part of the valentine form. For instance, one possibility could be:
- These are the things we need to see you do differently in the future in order to ensure that all of us are able to succeed…. or
- These are the things we need you to start doing that would help us be more successful…or
- Any other version that comes to their minds. The concept is to give behavioral requests that are specific and clear. The EPT can determine what those requests need to be.

Another possibility for Valentines is having actual work teams both write as well as read them. |

Time	Content/Process	Logistics
	re-form at their functional group table in fifteen minutes	logistics can be handing out assignments to tell functional groups where to meet to understand their valentines and make plans for change.
	Back home planning assignment:	
	■ "Go pick up the valentines addressed to your group and pass them around for everyone to read.	
	■ Choose a facilitator to help the group work through the four stages of responses necessary to make this work.	
2:25 (10)	1. *Read and Ventilate.* Talk about your astonishment that people could ask you about these "dumb" things. *'Don't they know anything about what we do?'*	
2:35 (15)	2. *Read and Listen* Pass the sheets around the table again and allow yourselves to "hear" what people are really saying. Remember these valentines represent people's "truths." They cared enough to tell you the truth. Don't deny their truth! You don't have to obey but it is important to allow it to get in. Facilitator—if people at your table are arguing with the "truth" still, send them back to Step I and ventilate some more. Then you can return to Step II. By then, they should be able to listen.	
2:50 (60)	3. *Identify Common Themes* There will be similar messages across many of the valentine forms. Notice that and be prepared to tell the community that you heard them.	
3:50 (5)	4. *Say What You Will Do Differently* Based on these common themes, the system wide action plans that the community developed, and your own knowledge and beliefs, identify things that your function will do differently ("You can count on us!") in the next six months to begin to move the organization towards its preferred future.	

CHAPTER 5: DESIGN POSSIBILITY: A GENERIC THREE-DAY EVENT PLAN

Time		
3:55 (30)	**5. Communicate** Decide how you are going to communicate the results of these three days to people in the organization who were not here. Choose a reporter, who will be prepared to give both a written and oral (three-minute) presentation of what your group heard and what you will do in the future. Have the reporter stand underneath your header to give the report. *Reports of commitments from representatives of functional groups.*	Logistics must make sure there are mikes available for spokespersons to use. Logistics will also be responsible for picking up the written versions of the commitments in order to have them typed. Make sure the name of the group is on the sheet they wrote. *Sometimes a consultant will need to facilitate a functional group because of its size. Use your small group facilitating skills to figure out how to help them hear the feedback, respond to the feedback, and make commitments they will all agree to and carry out.*
4:25 (15)	**Wrap up from leadership** Leadership needs to close the event by saying: ■ How he or she is feeling about the work the group has done together. ■ What he or she thinks should be the organization's next steps and what people in the organization can count on the leader(s) for.	
4:40 (20)	Do a call out of thanks to the logistics team and the event planning team.	
5:00	**Evaluation and Close** Have the group fill out evaluation forms. Some recommended evaluation questions are: ■ What were the most significant outcomes of these three days for you? ■ On a scale of 1 to 10, how confident are you that you will carry out your commitments to each other? 1————5————10 Not a chance Watch our Dust! ■ Why did you mark it where you did?	Logistics will have placed the evaluation forms in the In-boxes on each table.

Time	Content/Process	Logistics
	• What does the organization need to do to maintain momentum?	
	Adjourn Invite the EPT and the leadership team to join you in reading the final evaluations and talking about next steps. Get someone to summarize the evaluations and get the summary out to the participants along with the final back home commitments.	Logistics will stand at the door and receive evaluations as people leave.

Chapter 6
Alternative Designs: Possibilities for
Specific Whole-Scale Interventions

Over the years of its work, Dannemiller Tyson Associates has used Whole-Scale methodology in industries large and small, with community groups, with smaller groups such as Boards of Directors, and in not-for-profit organizations. The company has also worked in numerous other countries. Whole-Scale philosophy and methodology is robust and works equally well for any of these situations—indeed for any organization-wide change process you may have the opportunity to facilitate.

Included in this chapter are designs the company actually used with clients that represent the broad variety of organizational situations for which the methodology is appropriate. Included are the following:

- A Community Seeking to Intervene in Escalating Violence (Page 150)
- A Bank Redesigning a Major Global Process and Restructuring the Associated Organizations (Page 159)
- A Non-Profit Board of Directors (Page 178)
- A high-tech Company in the United Kingdom Needing Alignment and Strategic Planning (Page 183)
- A Fast-Growing Supplier for the Auto Industry Seeking to Develop New Strategy and Align New Acquisitions Around that Strategy (Page 200)
- A Training and Education Organization in the U.S. Government Redesigning Itself to Align with Customers' Missions and Operate as a Self-Funded Business (Page 211)
- A Metropolitan Police Department Needing to Build a Common Picture of Its New Strategic Direction (Page 225)
- A Strategic Reunion (Page 235)

Use these designs to deepen your understanding of how to apply Whole-Scale methods in different situations. While you won't want to copy the designs verbatim, the one most like the situation in which you are working could give you and the Event Planning Team ideas.

City of X: A Community Example

Situation and Convening Issue:
In the City of X, government officials, community organizations, and citizens had identified the need for a community driven plan to deal with the issue of escalating violence. Based on per capita numbers, the City of X was listed as one of the top five cities in the United States for violent crime. Initially the Mayor's Office asked a number of interested individuals and organizations (neighborhood associations, civic associations, advocacy groups, and professions) to work together to generate a common purpose, outcomes, and roadmap for creating involvement and ownership of all citizens in the community in whatever it took to reduce the rate of violent crime. Aligning the various community constituents proved to be a long and difficult process. Several high-profile murders finally pushed everyone towards alignment around the need to involve everyone in creating a community of which they could be proud.

Roadmap: Event Purpose and Its Role in the Overall Process
The meeting that is detailed next was identified as the launch event in a proposed process where citizens, law enforcement, and government would come together to clearly identify the problem and together create the alternatives. The whole community was invited to a launch event meeting to identify a vision and goals for a safe community and the actions and framework needed to achieve that vision. The **purpose** of the meeting in City X was "to come together as City Xers to plan and create a safe community of which we could all be proud."
Approximately 350 people attended the launch event (75 teenagers from the community attended). The local news media captured the outputs from that meeting and broadcast the results (goals and action plans) to the whole city on the evening news. During the meeting a continuation plan was proposed, tweaked, and agreed upon.

Interim Results:
Volunteers (who came forward and signed up during the October, 1998 event) met throughout 1999 and moved forward with the actions agreed upon in the launch event. A local grassroots organization stepped up to sponsor the continuation efforts and help move the steering committee forward. They (along with the Mayor's Office) identified the need for a reunion meeting to take some of the lessons learned through the efforts of the volunteer action groups and use them to generate plans, which would impact neighborhoods and districts.

Reunion Event and Continuation Plans:
A reunion event (not listed here) was conducted in November, 1999. Approximately 150 people attended the reunion event, which was again open to the entire community. Action plans for specific districts and neighborhoods were detailed and shared with the whole community. The grassroots organization will continue to oversee all follow-up activities along with a local non-profit organization, which obtained a grant to connect all of the continuation activities. Throughout 1999, law enforcement and state epidemiologists have been capturing and measuring progress toward identified goals. Violent crime rates are lower in 1999. Another reunion event is planned for January, 2001.

STRATEGY DEVELOPMENT IMPLEMENTATION ROADMAP (Whole-Scale Change for Strategy Development)

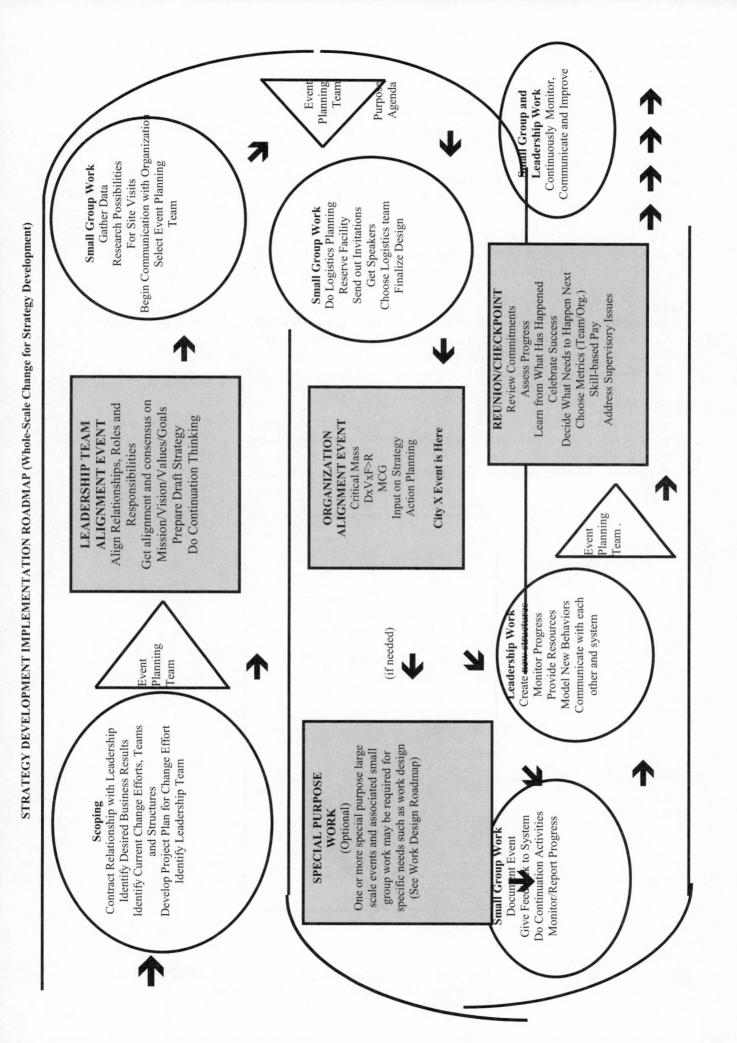

CHAPTER 6: ALTERNATIVE DESIGNS: POSSIBILITIES FOR SPECIFIC WHOLE-SCALE INTERVENTIONS

NO PLACE FOR VIOLENCE
A Conference to Plan and Create a Safe Community … Together

Wednesday, October 21, 1998
8:00 AM – 3:30 PM

Purpose: To come together as City Xers to plan and work together in order to create a safe community of which all city residents can be proud.

Expected Outcomes:
- Increase awareness of the full spectrum of violence in this community and how it affects everyone
- Create a common vision of what a less violent City X would look like
- Devise and commit to specific actions that promote positive alternatives to violent behavior
- Identify next steps to take so that everyone leaves the meeting with a clear idea of "What I can do."

Security Notes:
- Because this meeting specifically deals with violence and is advertised as such – security at the meeting is important. We need to deal with security issues early on (no one attends without being pre-registered, etc.)
- Security will be available on staging day to talk about security issues

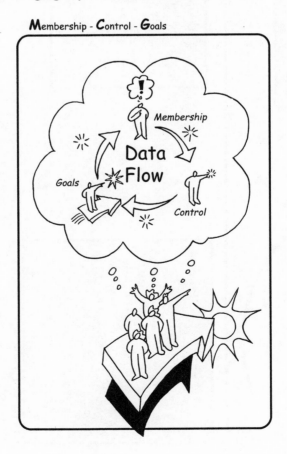

CHAPTER 6: ALTERNATIVE DESIGNS: POSSIBILITIES FOR
SPECIFIC WHOLE-SCALE INTERVENTIONS

Time	Content/Process	Logistics

October 20, 1998

Staging Day

9:00 AM   Consultants meet with Logistics team to set up the room.

Noon   Consultants meet – go over agenda and define roles

3:00 PM   Additional logistics arrive and are briefed

October 21

Time	Content/Process	Logistics
6:30 a.m.	Start coffee pot and help exhibitors to set up	The Logistics Team will have already prepared the items and will use this time to make sure all is ready to go ▪ Handouts (on different colored paper if possible) ▪ Post-it notes (large size), masking tape, pencils, dots, ▪ Start-up handouts for the tables: Table Roles and Rules of Brainstorming, One Page Agenda, and "Telling My Story" (in the In-Box.) ▪ Flipcharts/easels around the room (one per table and three on podium). ▪ Markers, tape, and first assignment (in the In-Box) ▪ Max-mix seating plans with directions on a flipchart outside the door. Registration packets include table assignment (write table # on nametag) ▪ A grid of tables + random table list. ▪ Sound system. ▪ List of phone and restroom locations. "Message board" or other means of getting emergency messages to participants. Number the tables Include the table # at which each participant is to sit in the registration packet Have something people can walk
7:30 a.m.	*Coffee and Registration* ▪ Provide registration tables (one for pre-registrants; one for on-site registration) ▪ Invite exhibitors of current	

Time	Content/Process	Logistics
	programs/organizations that deal with violence or violence prevention around the room • Planned Exhibitors • Grass root groups • 100 Black Men • Police (Community Policing and Neighborhood Watch YWCA/Battered Women/Stop Rape	around with for breakfast—so they can visit the exhibits (in order to learn more about current City X organizations/efforts
8:15 a.m. (10)	*Welcome and Opening Remarks* (Advertise 8:00 start but plan on starting at 8:15 to allow for late arrival) Mayor's office speaker should do the following: • Say what this meeting means to her • Say how she hopes everyone will work together today • Say what she hopes this meeting will accomplish • Note that this meeting is just the start of a process that the group will talk about later in the meeting • Let the group know that she can support the work only if there is follow-up and follow-through • Introduce the facilitators, from inside and outside the city itself.	President of the YWCA will : • Welcome everyone • Note sponsors • Introduce Mayor's office speaker Consider having a prepared bulleted reminder list for the Mayor's office speaker
8:35 a.m. (10)	*Purpose, Outcomes, Agenda* • Note that the EPT developed the agenda over a year ago and based it on data gathered by telephone interviews • Describe the purpose and anticipated outcomes • Explain why people are seated at max-mix tables • Walk through the agenda and explain the reason for each portion of it • Note bathroom locations, where messages will be, etc. Talk about norms for the meeting: • Listen to understand • Share air time • Respect differences • Be part of the solution	KATHY Refer the group to the one-page handout—with agenda on one side, norms on the other

Time	Content/Process	Logistics
8:35 AM (55)	**Telling Our Stories: Getting connected around our diverse experiences with violence**	JIM
(5)	*Framing*: "Each person take one minute to prepare to introduce yourself to the rest of your table group by thinking quietly about the answers to the following questions: 1. Who are you? What do you feel is important for everyone at your table to know about you? 2. What do you believe that violence has cost you personally? 3. What do you need to get out of today that will make you feel that the time has been well spent? Now, using the questions above as a framework take three minutes to introduce yourself to the rest of your table group.	Handout on Cue – Roles of Facilitator, Recorder, Reporter on tables
(25)	*At your table:* Choose a recorder to write on the flip chart and record: ▪ What was common at your tables?	
(10)	▪ In your conversation, what were the significant differences (if there were any)? ▪ A summary of what your table needs to get out of today (outcomes)." Call outs around the room. "I'm going to go by quadrants of the room."	
(15)		Logistics records for the callout up front. Post around the room during the break
9:30 AM (15)	**Break**	

Time	Content/Process	Logistics
9:45 AM (45)	**Perspectives on the Current State of Violence in City X:** *Framing for the Moderator:* ***A community perspective*** Speakers each have no longer then three minutes to make their point. (45 minutes for this panel) ▪ Security officer with Local Bank ▪ Social Psychologist with State Department of Health ▪ Teenager with history of armed violence ▪ Parent of murdered child ▪ Grassroots organizer ▪ Neighborhood organizer ***An enforcement perspective*** Speakers each have no longer than three minutes to make their point. ▪ Police Captain ▪ Sheriff ▪ District Attorney ▪ School System – Security officer	DON introduces Moderator Plan to meet Moderator prior to event to talk about the panel presentation (panel knows that time is limited – coach the panel the day of event on how the panel will operate and what the important points to make are)
10:30 AM (25) (15) (10)	**Table Discussion:** "Now turn back to your table and have a discussion answering the following three questions: 1. What did I hear? 2. What's my reaction? 3. How does what I heard change my perception of violence in our community?" Value Added Callouts (answers to last question) – may not need callouts – can ask two tables to combine and share insights with each other	DON Logistics records up front

Time	Content/Process	Logistics
10:55 PM (25)	**What's Working In City X: Strategies for Success:** (Moving success stories to this position provides examples and inspiration of what actions people in the community can take – participants will hear this now to set the stage for action brainstorming in the next agenda item) 1. Reverend with Grassroots organization 2. Mr. S - Neighborhood Security Dads 3. Mr. R – Federation of Civic Associations 4. Probation Officer	JIM

Time	Content/Process	Logistics
11:20 AM (10)	**Straw Community Goals Presentation** Framing: Now that we have heard about our current state of violence in our community and some success stories, we would like to offer three goals or themes that we heard you can all identify with. The way we identified these is …… 1. Everyone takes a personal responsibility to promote a safe City X 2. Our institutions are actively committed to non-violence. 3. Neighborhoods are safe.	YWCA PUBLIC POLICY REPRESENTATIVE ***Read with passion*** Write Straw Goals on flipcharts or banners to put up at this time
11:30 AM (30)	**Creating OUR Preferred Future:** *Framing:* "We would now like you to tell us what it would look like if you were successful in this community in ….. (each of the goals listed above). Individually – writing on the post-it notes – respond to the following statement: *Assignment:* It is October of 1999. You are pleased and proud of how effectively you have achieved the goals you identified.–What do you specifically see happening that tells you that you have been successful? What are people saying and doing that lets you know you have reached these goals? Use one post-it note for each activity or action you would expect to see. Please label the post-its with the goal number. Logistics will be coming by your tables to collect your post-its." "An example of what you might write would be ….."	RON Handout on cue Logistics: Hang three sheets of flipchart paper (banners) one for each goal. Take post-it notes when they are completed and evenly distribute on flipchart paper. Distribute post-its such that there is at least one flip chart for each table to work on later in the session. Output: flip charts with post-it notes affixed describing preferred future activities, actions, behaviors
12:00 Noon (40)	**Lunch** Participants have 40 minutes to take a break, go through buffet line and return to their seats	BUFFET PLANNED. Value is that no one stands in line longer than five minutes waiting for food. Need to have six lines for food.

Time	Content/Process	Logistics
12:40 PM (60)	**Creating Our Preferred Future Continued:** 1. Each table takes one or more sheets of flipchart paper with post-it notes attached and sorts them by similar themes 2. Each table will write a brief phrase or sentence that captures the preferred future that theme is identifying. (EXAMPLE – there are after school activities or care available to every child who needs it; everyone polices the neighborhood, ETC.) 3. Recorder puts each theme at the top of a flip chart and the people at the table brainstorm recommended steps or actions to take in the next six months to achieve that theme or preferred future. 4. The group picks the top four at their table to post for everyone to see.	RON Distribute flip charts with post-its affixed such that each table has an equal number of flip charts Logistics collects flip charts from each table (they can be turned into Expected Results statements by the continuation group) and posts on walls Output: flip charts from each table with themes at the top and brainstormed action items below
1:40 PM (15)	**Choosing What We Will Do (Vote on action items))** "Everyone gets three green dots – Use them to vote for any of the actions identified under the themes. Your vote means "we must take this action or step to achieve this theme" Everyone gets three red dots which mean, "No way should we do this. You don't have to use all of your dots!"	KATHY Output: flip charts with themes at top and dots on action items Logistics works with volunteers during the break to compile votes!
1:55 PM (15)	**Break**	

Time	Content/Process	Logistics
2:10 PM (20)	**Reporting Out on Choices**	Process: compile highest vote getters for both "we must" and "no way". Capture the "we must" items on flip charts so they can be distributed to the tables in next agenda item <u>Logistics</u> output: Flip charts with "we must" action items
2:30 PM (25) (5) (10) (2) (10)	**Ensuring Success:** *Framing:* "In order to ensure that everyone understands what you must expect of each other as you work toward creating a community which everyone is proud of, we would like you to turn back to your table and *Assignment:* 1. Choose a facilitator, recorder and reporter 2. Take 10 minutes to brainstorm at your table: "From our perspective, what part do we believe each of the stakeholder groups represented at our table (activist, retiree, police officer, preacher, etc.) needs to do to ensure that the actions we have suggested are successful? After 10 minutes give the next instruction: 3. Individually (not aloud), look at the list your table created from the perspective of where you fit. You may fit in several categories. Which of the items listed can you personally commit to?" After a couple of minutes give the last instruction: 4. "As a table, take at least 10 minutes to share your commitments with each other."	KATHY Handout on cue Output: flip charts from each table with the role each stakeholder group plays in performing the action items. Each individual places an asterisk (*) next to the item he or she is willing to personally commit to
2:55 PM (10)	**Next Steps- Our Continuation Process** Discuss continuation strategy and present draft charter for the continuation committee. "Right now we are saying that you are going to form	Speaker *Note:* *"A major role of the steering group is to charter the action groups – these*

Time	Content/Process	Logistics
	a virtual steering (volunteers) to provide oversight and continue the work you have done today on goals, themes and actions/steps. This group will also plan the next whole community meeting – next year's follow-up meeting. One possible next step is chartering at a first steering committee meeting (which you should hold within the next month). Ongoing communication ideas. How are you going to publicize what you have done? How are you going to spread the word to the rest of City X who did not attend this meeting? How will you make best use of the media?	*charters help the steering group get clear about the results needed and also gets the action group off to a fast start.*
3:05 PM (15)	**Next Steps- Our Continuation Process Continued (Nominations/Volunteers For The Steering Committee):** Each of the groups/functions identified on the draft continuation piece (hopefully they will map with the "we must" action items) need volunteers who would be willing to meet and decide together how action item(s) can happen. You also need one person to agree to host the first meeting of that action group – not be the chairperson!	KATHY Flipcharts with "we must" high votes up front with space for names and phone numbers. Flipchart for steering committee members up front also. Handout of charter draft for first meeting with draft agenda and volunteer facilitator (WHO DOES THIS AND WHEN?)

Time	Content/Process	Logistics
3:20 PM (10)	**Evaluations and Close** ■ How did today go for you? ➤ Highs? ➤ Lows? ■ On a scale of one to ten, how confident are you that we will carry out our commitments to each other, and create a community which we can all be proud of? ■ No Way – No How …Just Watch Us Do it! ■ Why did you mark it where you did? ■ What do you need to do from here to sustain your momentum?	KATHY Evaluation sheet in the In-Box YWCA will close the meeting and thank everyone for coming

A Bank
Redesigning a Major Global Process &
Restructuring the Associated Organizations

Situation and Convening Issue:

The Bank commissioned the Business Process Reengineering Team (BPE Team) to redesign the commercial lending process. This process in its original form involved 22 different departments in seven different cities. They described it as, at best, slow and difficult to service, inefficient, and costly to manage. With the introduction of a new information system (LSII), the bank was able to take advantage of the new software capabilities and information technology infrastructure to recreate the business process and overlay a new organization design.

The BPE Team began work approximately four months before it decided to call in Dannemiller Tyson Associates to support their efforts. During these four months the BPE Team had mapped the old process; talked to staff and customers about their wants, needs and ideas; benchmarked other successful information technology introductions; and met frequently with the Steering Committee (made up of senior leaders from across the bank).

As they moved from collecting data to creating a process, they became concerned about the following things:

- Creating the best design
- Gaining commitment and support from the 700 or so impacted staff
- Overcoming the fact that each city and function might only understand and see the process from their limited view
- "Selling" the eventual solution to the Steering Committee and staff

To address these concerns, the BPE Team decided they needed a high-involvement strategy for process and organization design. This strategy would enable them to involve a critical mass of employees and managers from across the system in some aspect of the redesign process. Each of the events they designed in collaboration with DTA facilitators consisted approximately 20% of those impacted. Each event had some overlapping participation. Each event involved 175-200 staff and in each approximately 1/3 of the participants had attended a previous meeting.

The event described here was the first of the three DTA supported. The Bank called these large group sessions Facilitated Design Sessions (FDS). Between these meetings, the BPE Team conducted small group interactive sessions to keep the broader population informed and involved.

Time	Content/Process	Logistics

Roadmap: Event Purpose And Its Role In The Overall Process

The purpose is of this first FDS was "to develop a viable new business process which delivers efficient, effective client-focused service for the continually changing environment: and together be committed to gaining organizational consensus to implement the new design." This meeting served as both the launch of involvement and the meeting that created the new business process for loan servicing.

The meeting began the first evening with dinner and a simulation. The simulation (created by the Event Planning Team) was intended to (1) teach people the high-level current situation; (2) ground everyone in the need to change (make the case for a new process); and (3) begin to implement changes consistent with the new process.

Brief results and Continuation Plan

This session resulted in a new business process that consolidated the work of several organizations in different cities. Specifically, these were:

- Twenty-two departments consolidated to three
- Seven cities consolidated to two
- Process cycle time reduced by 50%
- Span of control for managers reduced from 1:10 to 1:80 personnel

The continuation plan for this particular effort consisted of a series of Town hall meetings at each of the sites and through communications letters and bulletin boards across the organization. Town hall meetings communicated the work from Facilitated Design Sessions and tapped all employees' ideas as input to each next step. Follow-ups occurred during the Organization Design session (FDS II) and the Implementation meeting (FDS III), each of which included a different microcosm of staff.

Time	Content/Process	Logistics

A Bank
First Facilitated Design Session to Design New
Business Process Model

Session Purpose: "to develop a viable new business process which delivers efficient, effective client-focused service for the continually changing environment: and together be committed to gaining organizational consensus to implement the new design."

Day 1

Time	Content/Process	Logistics
7:30 am.	**Coffee, Rolls, etc.**	<ul><li>One flipchart per table & two up front</li><li>Blank name tags and markers on tables</li><li>Max mix seating chart at door</li><li>Open Forum questions on tent cards on tables</li><li>Handouts in order:<ul><li>Agenda/purpose</li><li>Role of facilitator, recorder, reporter</li></ul></li></ul>
8:00 (10 min.)	**Welcome/Purpose** *Project Manager does the following:*<ul><li>Presents expectations for the two days</li><li>Shares the ODS/LS2/BPE Umbrella Overview</li><li>Asks people to be candid</li><li>Explains the importance of the meeting to the bank</li><li>Tells how the bank got to this point: "Why we are sitting in this room"</li><li>Tells what has happened over the past year</li><li>Sets a positive and enthusiastic tone</li><li>Again, reiterates newness, difference, and cutting edge of this meeting</li><li>Introduces consultants/facilitators</li></ul>	<ul><li>Rules of brainstorming</li><li>First assignment</li></ul> Assign seating assigned in max-mix tables. Leadership participants are also in max-mix.

Time	Content/Process	Logistics

| (15 min.) | **Purpose and Agenda for the 2 days**

"Before I go over the agenda for these two days, I'd like to share how this forum came together.

Like Larry said in his address last night, most reengineering efforts fail. They don't fail because of bad designs; they fail because their organizations never accept them. They never accept them because an isolated reengineering team can't engage the hearts and minds of a critical mass of the system." | TONI |

| | ▪ "This project's reengineering team, and the project managers and coaches that support it were determined that *this project would not be conceived in isolation.*

▪ Instead, they brought together a microcosm of people from the system that's being redesigned. A microcosm of people that you see in this room today.

▪ This microcosm, the FDS Planning Team, came together for two days to listen, to connect, and to imagine. Together they mapped out the steps you will take to create a new process.

▪ If you open your folders they prepared for you to the top page, you'll see the purpose and agenda they created. Look at it as your invitation to go on a journey.--a journey in which you transform your own system. You make this transformation happen by opening yourselves to becoming 'one heart and one brain' during this two days.

▪ The Planning and Event Planning Teams for this first Facilitated Design Session established the Purpose Statement:

To develop a viable new business process which delivers efficient, effective client-focused service for the continually changing environment: and together be committed to gaining organizational consensus to implement our new design. | |

CHAPTER 6: ALTERNATIVE DESIGNS: POSSIBILITIES FOR SPECIFIC WHOLE-SCALE INTERVENTIONS

Time	Content/Process	Logistics

Agenda for the session:

Day 1
- Introductions and getting connected -- discover collective experience and wisdom at your table
- Force field: What drives and restrains change?-- Build a common data base about the critical factors that can make or break this change
- Origination, Distribution, & Servicing update, followed by Q&A -- What the LS2 and BPE teams have learned; where the projects stand
- Lunch
- Preferred future for Servicing your vision --To create breakthrough change we need the pull of our own compelling vision; the push of problem-solving just won't get us there.
- Process requirements: criteria for designing the new process
- Evaluation: How are we doing?

Day 2
- Continental Breakfast at 7:30
- 8:00 Reports on:
  - Evaluation results
  - Your choices of process requirements
- Process Models
  - BPE Team Options
  - Your ideas
- 1st Process Model Fishbowl Exercise to pull together your ideas
- Lunch
- 2nd Process Model Fishbowl Exercise to pull together your ideas
- Quick Hits and Next Steps: How to move ahead *starting now!*
- Conclusion and Evaluations: How did we do?

Introduction/Logistics Notes
- "This is *your* meeting. To give it your best efforts:
  - Take care of yourself – First break will occur at about 10:15. If you need to use the restroom or stretch before then, do it -- (*Provide restroom and smoking directions.*)

  - Remember when you leave that your table loses a unique perspective. Your absence diminishes your group.

  - Avoid getting your attention diverted. When you get up to stretch or use the facilities, don't get into voice mail. It has a way of sucking your attention out of here. Your table needs you here in body and mind, not worried about issues on the home front.

  - We'll have box lunches here both today and tomorrow.

Fill in restroom and smoking directions

Time	Content/Process	Logistics
	Don't plan on leaving during lunch because you'll have only 30 to 45 minutes to spend on lunch. • We'll end today between 4:00 and 5:00, tomorrow at around 5:00	

	• Now I am going to introduce the people who brought us to this point and planned this Facilitated Design Session. Will each contributor please stand as I mention your name so others can get to know you?
	   ➢ Business Process Engineering Team
	   ➢ Facilitated Design Session Planning Team
	   ➢ Alice Z. from Agency Management Services
		Check out names and areas from which contributors have come. Make sure you know how to pronounce peoples' names.

	• Finally I'd like to introduce one of my co-facilitators: • Colleagues with extensive experience in using large stakeholders meetings, such as this, to redesign work and organizations: Paul T. from the consulting firm of Dannemiller Tyson Associates and Craig M. from Flynn, McGee. • Paul will explain how these sessions work and guide you in getting connected within your table groups."	

CHAPTER 6: ALTERNATIVE DESIGNS: POSSIBILITIES FOR SPECIFIC WHOLE-SCALE INTERVENTIONS

Time	Content/Process	Logistics
8:25 (30)	**Meeting Processes and Team Building** *Framing: First you'll hear about the makeup of your table group and processes we'll use at this meeting. Next you'll do an assignment that will help your table group to get connected. And become a more-effective team. To do this assignment, we need to really listen to each other.* Paul explains: ▪ Max-mix seating ▪ Meeting processes: ♦ Voting ♦ Brainstorming ♦ Question & Answer ♦ Ground Rules for observers. ♦ Purpose of FDS and our expectations of them as participants.	PAUL
(5 min.) (25 min.)	Assignment 1. "Take two minutes to think about your responses to the following. ▪ What's your name; what do you do at the bank? ▪ What one movie or TV show reminds you most of working at the bank? Why? ▪ As you think about your work at the bank, describe the best day you ever had and why? ▪ Describe the worst day you have ever had and why? ▪ If you could change one thing at the bank, what would it be and why? ▪ Based upon all of the above, what do you think this group needs to accomplish in these two days to make them worthwhile for you? ▪ What are the two or three most important discussion ground rules we need to follow in order to work effectively together? 2. Choose a facilitator, someone who will keep you on time. 3. Take three minutes maximum per person to share answers within your table group."	Assignments in packets ▪ Review handout with roles of facilitator, recorder, and reporter ▪ Pick someone who is wearing a watch with a secondhand ▪ Remind participants to listen for understanding

Time	Content/Process	Logistics
8:55 (10 min.)	"After sharing answers: 1. At your table agree on and record: • Common themes • Significant Differences • Expectations • Ground Rules: Identify 2 to 3 norms that group must observe to have a successful meeting. Select a reporter to call out your outcomes."	Two recorders up front with flip charts and markers. Don't call on duplicates.
9:05 (15 min.)	2. Reassemble the whole group. Take and record call outs. 1. Common Themes 2. Significant Differences 3. Expectations 4. Ground Rules	**(WE HAD THIS GROUP IDENTIFY TABLE NORMS, SOMETHING WE DO NOT ALWAYS DO. THE PLANNING TEAM TOLD US THAT THIS GROUP WAS NOT GOOD AT MEETINGS AND CERTAINLY NOT GOOD AT STAYING ON TRACK DURING THEM)**
9:20 (10 min.)	**Structure of Content/Advance Organizer** Paul explains the conceptual framework and sequence of FDS. • $D \times V \times F > R$ Dissatisfaction Vision First steps Resistance	(DVF provided a backdrop for the call outs. Many fit into one of the three elements, a fact predicted by the event planning team) *After* Paul's explanation Hand out some kind of advance organizer graphic for $D \times V \times F > R$.

| 9:30 (45) | **Force Field Analysis**

A Force Field Analysis is a snapshot of what drives change and what gets in the way of it. The purpose for doing it is to discover the forces that impact the ODS Servicing Process. This activity will give you a common database from which to form a new process. You'll also use this information when you design new process models tomorrow.

Assignment

1. "Choose a facilitator (someone who will help the group truly brainstorm) and a recorder." | TONI

(We talked about using some other diagnostic framework and the force field seemed to be the most acceptable culturally for identifying the dissatisfaction)

Cue logistics to distribute handout. |

Time	Content/Process	Logistics

Walkthrough:

Rules of Brainstorming
- Do not discuss ideas (generate, don't evaluate)
- Do not judge ideas (good or bad)
- It is okay to repeat ideas
- Piggybacking off someone else's ideas is fine.
- Wait for silence to end; the greatest creativity follows.
- The more ideas the better.

2. "Think about all of the forces at work in the Bank with your Clients and brainstorm:
   A. What are all of the things that are going on in the Bank right now that are really driving us to change the ODS Servicing Process?
   B. What are all of the things that are going on right now that could hold us back from achieving this goal?

3. Now, go back and agree on the forces (both driving and restraining) your table believes are the key ones -- key means really significant and impactful. Circle the two to three key driving forces and the two to three key restraining forces

   Create a flipchart that highlights your table's view of the driving and restraining forces. The line that separates the driving and restraining forces represents the ODS Servicing Process.

4. Post your table's summary on the wall.

When you're finished you may take a break. We'll reconvene at 10:35.

Logistics (for above section): Remind reporters to huddle up. Agree upon cues.

Time	Content/Process	Logistics
10:15 (20 min.)	**Break**	Design and Planning Team pairs huddle over break and summarize common themes from tables. Get mikes to people at the wall.
10:35 (10 min.)	**Report out** *Toni* introduces report outs: (team members at wall displays will give these) - Driving forces: Gabriella Rinaldi and Alan Kobritz - Restraining forces: Don Moses and Shannon Collins Toni transitions to *Paul* to facilitate ODS project updates.	TONI
10:45	**ODS Project Update Presentations**	PAUL

Time	Content/Process	Logistics
(60 min)	The purpose of these presentations is to give you an overview of the: ■ Technology that will enable a new servicing process (from LS2 Team) ■ Groundwork and where the organization is now in reengineering the new process (from the BPE Team) ■ Current process (from the BPE Team) These presentations will give a high level overview; they will **not** go into details." Introduce *Karen P.* to explain what's happening with LS2	
(20)	**LS2 Presentation** *Karen* explains: ■ The kinds of things the bank will be able to do. ■ The enormous challenges, costs and complexity that will be impacting all of us over the next X years. ■ What the LS2 Team sees happening in customer service and how it could influence both client and providers as they do their work. ■ Overview of what LS2 is. Karen relays to *Chris R.* and *Nancy M.*	KAREN P. CHRIS R. & NANCY M.

Time	Content/Process	Logistics

(20)	**BPE Team's Presentation**
	They explain:
	
	▪ The expectations of the design effort
	▪ Their charter, givens, and constraints
	▪ The BPE Process
	  ♦ What will happen over the next few months?
	  ♦ What has happened to date?
		Handouts at break

(20)	They relay to *Alice G.* and *Gordy H.* who walk through an overview of the current process.	ALICE G & GORDY H
11:45 (45 min.) (15) (30)	**Open Forum**: *Paul* introduces the task and moderates the Q&A session *"The purpose of this forum is to become clear on the BPE Team's perspectives and direction, **not** to give feedback or edit."* 1. Have table groups read role descriptions and select: ▪ *Facilitator*: To keep discussion on time and on track ▪ *Recorder*: To capture key points in participants' own words ▪ *Reporter/question asker*: To call out table questions. 2. Have tables take 15 min. to discuss the following questions: ▪ What did we hear? ▪ What are our reactions? ▪ What questions of understanding do want to ask (of whom)? 3. Have each table take turns asking one question. Continue to take questions from alternating tables until time is up (20 min.) or all questions have been asked. 4. Save last 10 min. for "burning questions."	PAUL Let the audience know who will be on the panel. (LS2 Speaker, BPE Team) Have the table grid on the podium

12:30 (45)	**Lunch**	Handout assignment during lunch

Time	Content/Process	Logistics
1:15 (40) (10 min.)	**Preferred Future** Introduce Bob G. with advice on how to approach coming up with a preferred future. "The purpose of this section is to create our own vision of our preferred future. To create breakthrough change we need to do more than simply patch up the current system. This is your chance to imagine how a whole new way of working would look and feel. Some examples we've heard include: ▪ One process or system for everyone ▪ Problems resolved at their source in five minutes or less ▪ People work at home "in their jammies." ▪ No duplicate data entry"	TONI BOB G (Group vice-president) (We had Bob do the intro here because the planning team thought it would be more empowering to hear this assignment from him, more than from any other person.)
(30 min.)	**Assignment:** "It's October, 1998, three years from now. We have been incredibly successful at having recreated our ODS Servicing Process. We are pleased and proud that we have achieved our goals and have positioned ourselves as exceptional servicing providers for Origination and Distribution. As a result all of all our efforts, our clients love us and our employees are happy! 1. Close your eyes and imagine yourself, three years from now. What do you see happening that tells you that we have truly changed? ▪ How is the process operating? ▪ What are people doing? ▪ How about client experiences? What are they doing? 2. As a table, brainstorm round robin (go around the table in one direction until everyone has passed) listing on a flipchart what really important things you see that we have achieved. 3. Record recommended ideas on flip charts, ***leaving a 4" margin on the left for voting*** as shown. 4. Post each piece of flipchart on the wall. As you finish a page of flipchart, logistics will hang it. Think about: ▪ What do you tell your peers and colleagues? ▪ What's making the Bank of America truly unique and high performing? After most sheets are posted say: ▪ "Make sure all of your sheets are posted. ▪ Now you'll get a chance to indicate your preferences	Show two-column flipchart page with the word "Vote" as a heading for the left, 4"-wide column; and the words "Vision #, Recommendation" as a heading for the right column. Provide crayons or dots for people to use to vote.

CHAPTER 6: ALTERNATIVE DESIGNS: POSSIBILITIES FOR SPECIFIC WHOLE-SCALE INTERVENTIONS

Time	Content/Process	Logistics
	▪ Over the next break, read through the preferred futures you've posted, and put a checkmark (or dot) by the ones that you believe are essential. Indicate the voting tool (crayons or dots). ▪ Vote for as many as you think are essential and critical. ▪ We'll meet back here in 20 min. at (____).	

Time	Content/Process	Logistics
1:55 (20 min.)	**Vote and break**	Design /Planning Team Pair selects big vote-getters.
2:15 (10 min.)	**Report out of top vote-getters** Introduce *Design /Planning Team Pair* to report top vote getters: ▪ Kim and Al ▪ Mitch and Conchita Transition to Craig McGee, facilitator, who will guide you in thinking through process requirements—the design criteria the process must meet.	
2:25 (55 min.)	**Process Requirements** *To design a new process, we need to figure out the criteria that this new process must meet. The purpose of this section is to identify those criteria, or process requirements.*	CRAIG Handout Process Requirements Assignment. Give each table two to three index cards, each with a different design principle on it.
2:25 (10 min.)	**BPE Team's View** Craig shares the team's Process Requirements: ▪ What they are ▪ Why they are important ▪ How they will be used tomorrow	
2:35 (45 min.)	**Participants' Views** **Assignment:** 1. "Choose a facilitator and a recorder. 2. As a table, discuss the requirement examples provided. 3. Decide, from your table's perspective, if they are important and need to be a part of the final redesign criteria.	Provide different colored dots for "must haves" and "no ways."

Time	Content/Process	Logistics
	4. Recommend five to seven key, critical additions to the list the Event Planning Team has proposed. 5. Post them.	
	After most tables have posted their sheets, say: ▪ "Make sure all of your sheets are posted. ▪ Now you'll get a chance to indicate which of the posted process requirements you like, and which you can't live with. ▪ Over the next break, read through the posted process requirements and vote for your five favorites or "must have's" and five that you can't live with or "no way's". Indicate the voting tool (crayons or dots). ▪ We'll meet back here in 25 min. at (_____)." Craig then explains what will be done overnight.	
3:20 (25 min.)	**Vote and break**	

3:45
(10 min.)
	Evaluation
	
	The purpose of this segment is to find out whether the group is on course. The facilitators and the EPT will make necessary mid-course corrections based on your feedback.
	
	Assignment:
	
	"Take a few minutes to write:
	1. Highs for the day?
	  2. Lows for the day?
	  3. What, if anything, was critically missing from the day for you?
	  4. Recommendations to the Planning Team for tomorrow, to ensure that these two days have been worthwhile for you.
		PAUL
		
		Handout on cue. Give people any reading ("Straw Dog" models).

Time	Content/Process	Logistics
3:55 (5 min.)	**Close** ▪ Straw Dogs group reviews any assignment for tonight ▪ Adjourn ▪ Planning and Event Planning Team meet with consultants to read evaluations and review the plan for tomorrow. ▪ Event Planning Team (EPT) members summarize the evaluations and prepare feedback for participants. ▪ Event Planning Team compares priority Process Requirements, reconciles them and prepares final Process Requirements list of 10 to 12 items.	Make sure to relay final Process Requirements to logistics and graphic artists.

Time	Content/Process	Logistics

Day 2

Time	Content/Process	Logistics
7:30 am.	**Coffee, Rolls, etc.**	▪ Provide name Tags with table numbers on them. ▪ Extra copies of Day 2 FDS Agenda (for those who misplaced the agenda we passed out yesterday) ▪ Max-mix seating chart at the door
8:00 (15 min.)	**Evaluation feedback and agenda review** *The purpose of this section is to get an understanding of what the group has accomplished so far, how the group thinks it is doing, and overview what the group has to accomplish today before 5pm.* *Irene and Mitch* present evaluation feedback 1. Present common evaluations themes and read representative comments from Day 1. 2. Explain how those comments will or will not be addressed in day 2. *Gabriella* presents Agenda and Purpose for day 2. She reviews the FDS Purpose: Develop a viable new business process which delivers efficient, effective client-focused service for the continually changing environment: and together be committed to gaining organizational consensus to implement our new design. "Today we'll focus on putting together our Process Models and planning next steps.	Seating is the same as yesterday. IRENE & MITCH GABRIELLA (**Note:** Should a BPE Team Member do the Purpose and Agenda for Day 2 or do facilitators do this?)

CHAPTER 6: ALTERNATIVE DESIGNS: POSSIBILITIES FOR SPECIFIC WHOLE-SCALE INTERVENTIONS

Time	Content/Process	Logistics

	Here is the agenda for Day 2.
	   1.) Report out: What you told us about Process Requirements.
	   2.) Process models:
	      ▪ The BPE team's view
	      ▪ Your view
	   3.) Lunch and incorporating models (your models will be brought together in two rounds of fishbowl exercises with a lunch in between, at approximately 12:45)
	   4.) Moving forward:
	      ▪ Quick Hits
	      ▪ Next Steps and Communications Plan
	   5.) Summary conclusions and evaluation"
	
	Introduce *Gordy and Kim* to do Process Requirements Report Outs	

8:15
(45 min.)
 	
(10 min.)
 	
(15 min.)
 	
(20 min.)
	Process Requirements Report Out
	
	The purpose of this section is for you to hear the Process Requirements you'll use today to develop a new process model. Last night the BPE Team worked long and hard to incorporate your input into this finalized set of Process Requirements.
	
	Gordy and Kim share turnaround:
	  ▪ This is what we heard
	  ▪ This is how we redrafted your inputs and votes
	
	Tables huddle:
	  ▪ Did they get it?
	  ▪ Are we 70% comfortable, and 100% committed that for now these are the Process Requirements we hope to design to?
	  ▪ If not, what must be added or changed?
	
	Facilitator facilitates discussion to reach consensus.
		CRAIG FACILITATES;
		GORDY & KIM REPORT
		
		Handout Process Requirements (results of turnaround) on cue
		Graphic display of Process Requirements

Time	Content/Process	Logistics

9:00 (90 min.)	**Models and Options for Process Redesign: BPE Team Drafts**
	
	Purpose of this section is to provide you with options and ideas about how you might redesign this process. For the next 90 minutes, you'll study these choices. After that you'll have the rest of the morning to build on them, pick out favorite components, or create models of your own.
	
	Assignment:
	1. "You'll notice that the back and sides of the room are set up in four display areas.
	    ▪ Three of these areas have radical new process models that the BPE Team has come up with.
	        ➢ One model focuses on maximizing speed. Nancy and Alice will explain this one. (*Ask BPE Team Representatives to raise their hands.*)
	
	        ➢ One model focuses on eliminating redundancy and waste. Gabriella and Irene will explain this one. (*Ask BPE Team Representatives to raise their hands.*)
	
	        ➢ One model focuses on "doing only that which the client sees" and maximizing client flexibility. Don and Denise will explain this one
		TONI
		
		Handouts and displays of "Straw Dog" New Process Models and Ideas from Process Understanding Feedback Meetings (sessions held by the BPE Team to get inputs from the entire organization, prior to this meeting).
		
		Make sure BPE Team Representatives are stationed at the models they're representing *before* starting explanations.

	▪ The fourth area has ideas:
	        ➢ From inputs provided during the Process Understanding Feedback Meetings Chris and Kim will explain these.
	        ➢ From the reengineering literature BPE Coach will explain these (*Ask BPE Team Representatives and Coach to raise their hands.*)	

Time	Content/Process	Logistics

| | 2. When I tell you to Tables:
▪ 1, 2 and 8, go to Display #1
▪ 3,4, and 5 go to Display #2
▪ 6, 7, and 11 go to Display #3
▪ 9,10 go to Display #4
▪ Then you'll have 20 minutes at each station:
▪ For each of the process-model stations you'll spend the:
   ➢ 1st 10 minutes listening to explanations
   ➢ 2nd 10 minutes asking questions for clarification.

▪ For the ideas station:
▪ At the Process Understanding Feedback Ideas Section you'll hear some pointers on how to scan all the ideas displayed.
   ➢ At the Reengineering Literature Ideas Station you'll hear quick explanations of recommendations from experts in reengineering.
*Guides: Make sure to leave enough time for questions **at all stations**!*

3. At each station, take notes about what you like and don't like and why.

4. Don't move from station to station until I cue you to do so.

▪ Direct tables to stations so that there's a relatively even distribution of participants around the room.
▪ Notify participants at 17 and 20 minute intervals | |
| 10:30
(15 min.) | **Break** | Assignment out during break:Models and Options: Table View |

Time	Content/Process	Logistics

| 10:45
(60 min.) | **Models and Options: Table View**

The purpose of this section is to reach agreement within your table groups about the ideas or model components that you want to incorporate into a process model. After you reach agreement, you will either adapt an existing model, or design one of your own, or simply pick the components that you think the process needs to have! | TONI |

Assignment:

"Choose a facilitator and a recorder.

1. Utilizing the Process Requirements, our Preferred Futures and your own beliefs:
   - Discuss what you like and/or don't like about each of the model options presented by the Event Planning Team.
   - What aspects/elements of each model meet the criteria?

3. Based upon that conversation, select the options or elements that you believe most closely fit the Process Requirements that we have agreed to.

4. Recommend:
   A. An option (with you table's enhancements) that best meets the Process Requirements.
   or
   B. The aspects/elements of the models that best meet the Process Requirements
   or
   C. If none of these seems right, draft a completely new option. Identify the elements and Process Requirements that show why this model may be better.

   5. Prepare a flipchart with your table recommendations and be prepared to post them on the wall.
6. Finally, select two representatives from your table (two people with passion about your table's work) to sit in a fishbowl with representatives from other tables.

Note: A fishbowl is a forum that consists of an inner and outer circle of participants. The inner circle works together to do a task, while the outer circle observes and, in this

Time	Content/Process	Logistics
	assignment, tries to influence the inner circle to make sure critical stakeholder concerns and interests are addressed.

They will reconcile and create one process model.
You'll hand off your recommendations to your representatives | |
| | Give tables a 15 min. warning.

Transition to Craig who will guide groups in pulling together the models created by table groups. | |
| 11:45 (60 min.) | **Process Models: Fishbowl I**

The purpose of this fishbowl is to do a 1st iteration of pulling together into one the Process Models created by your table groups.

The representatives you've selected will go to a representative's table and work on pulling together the models.

The rest of you will be assigned stakeholder roles to play (interests to represent). You will agree upon the things that need to be in the Process Model that emerge from the representatives' table. You exercise your influence to make sure those ideas and interests are built into the Process Model.

Assignment for representatives:

1. "Choose a facilitator and recorder.

2. Share your table's options and elements with the representatives from the other tables. Compare notes:
    ▪ Highlight commonalties
    ▪ Note differences

3. Based upon your sharing and comparing:
Create one model option that *captures as many of the components and elements of each table's ideas as possible.* Be as inclusive as possible without jeopardizing the Process Requirements and your view.
Remember to **be radical** and think about the Purpose Statement for these two days! | CRAIG

(Some members of the tables become the employees, representing their interests in the new process; others become the customer, assuring their needs were met; and finally, another group of people from the table become the company, representing the business interests of the organization. Two people from each table became table representatives, sharing their model with the other table and representing the table's views.

This arrangement ensures that everyone remains engaged and to ensure that the solution has the broadest possible view.) |
| | **Purpose Statement:**

Develop a viable new business process, which delivers efficient, effective client-focused service for the continually changing environment: and together be committed to gaining organizational | |

Time	Content/Process	Logistics
	consensus to implement our new design. 4. Flipchart the model and key elements. 5. Select three representatives from your fishbowl (again, people with passion about your table's work) to share your table's ideas with representatives from the other three fishbowls."	

	Assignment for stakeholders:
	
	1. "Choose a facilitator and a "communicator" (this person will represent your table at the open chair of the fishbowl if necessary).
	
	2. Your table has been assigned one of three Stakeholder Views for this exercise. (See the "Role Description" for your assignment.)
	
	3. Using the Process Requirements and your own beliefs, discuss what is really important to the Stakeholder Group you now represent.
	
	4. Based upon that conversation, be prepared to provide inputs to your table's representatives to fishbowl group. You may do this in any of three ways. You may:
	  ▪ Sit in at the open chair
	  ▪ Send memos on the cards you've been provided
	  ▪ Ask one of your table's representatives to come back to your table for a "meeting."
	
	5. Your job is to make sure that whatever model the fishbowl develops is in the best interests of the stakeholder group you represent:
	  ▪ If they are doing good work, just encourage them.
	  ▪ If they are in need of help, offer it through one of the three means listed above."
	
	Give tables a 15 min. warning.
	Let participants know when we'll reconvene after lunch.
		Again, there are three stakeholder groups, each with a Role Description that highlights the issues and concerns of that group. The data for the role sheets comes from the BPE team's interviews with each of these groups.
		
		  ♦ Customers
		  ♦ Employees
		  ♦ The Company (representing the issues and concerns of Senior Leaders in the organization)
		
		Tell representative group and advocacy groups to huddle together so they can compare notes and be a good advocacy group

12:45 (45)	**Lunch**	
1:30 (60 min.)	**Process Models: Fishbowl II** *The purpose of this fishbowl is to do a final iteration that pulls together the Process Models created by the Representative Tables.* ▪ *The "inner circle" group will WORK on pulling together the models they represent.*	CRAIG We call this a double feature. Approximately 30 people will leave the room and complete the

CHAPTER 6: ALTERNATIVE DESIGNS: POSSIBILITIES FOR
SPECIFIC WHOLE-SCALE INTERVENTIONS

Time	Content/Process	Logistics

	▪ The "middle circle" group will be assigned stakeholder roles to play (the same stakeholder roles described in the last round). They will agree upon the things that need to be in the Final Process Model. ▪ The remaining tables will work on generating ideas for "Quick Hits," that is, things we can do right away to move closer to our new process and new way of working.	assignment below for representatives and stakeholders. The rest of the participants will remain in the main room and work on the next steps, in this case called "quick hits." You will find that assignment below with the 1:30 start time as well.

	Assignment for representatives:
	1. "Choose a facilitator and recorder.
	
	2. Share your table's options and elements with the representatives from the other tables. Compare notes:
	   ▪ Highlight commonalties
	   ▪ Note differences
	
	3. Based upon your sharing and comparing:
	   ▪ Create one model option that *captures as many of the components and elements of each table's ideas as possible*. Be as inclusive as possible without jeopardizing the Process Requirements and your view.
	   ▪ Remember; be ***radical*** and think about the Purpose Statement for these 2 days!
	
	Purpose Statement:
	Develop a viable new business process which delivers efficient, effective client-focused service for the continually changing environment: and together be committed to gaining organizational consensus to implement our new design.
	
	4. Flipchart the model and key elements.
	
	5. Identify the key issues (real hot potatoes that must be addressed in order to implement your proposal).
	
	6. Prepare a 5 to 10 minute presentation for the rest of the room. Walk them through the new model and how it meets the requirements we have agreed to.
	
	7. Select a spokesperson(s) to share the final model."
		This assignment is essentially the same as the previous one. This is intentional to ensure that each iteration is the same and that people are always being asked to do the same thing as they build to a consensus.

	Assignment for stakeholders: 1. Choose a facilitator and a "communicator" (this person will represent your table at the open chair of the fishbowl if necessary).	

2. Your table has been assigned one of three Stakeholder Views for this exercise. (See the "Role Description" for your assignment.)

3. Utilizing the Process Requirements and your own beliefs discuss what is really important to the Stakeholder Group you now represent.

4. Based upon that conversation, be prepared to provide inputs to your table's representatives to fishbowl group. You may do this in any of three ways. You may:
   - Sit in at the open chair
   - Send memos on the cards you've been provided
   - Ask one of your table's representatives to come back to your table for a "meeting."

5. Your job is to make sure that whatever model the fishbowl develops is in the best interests of the stakeholder group you represent:
   - If they are doing good work, just encourage them.
   - If they are in need of help, offer it through one of the three means listed above."

CHAPTER 6: ALTERNATIVE DESIGNS: POSSIBILITIES FOR
SPECIFIC WHOLE-SCALE INTERVENTIONS

Time	Content/Process	Logistics

1:30 (60)	**Assignment for "Quick Hits" Tables**
	
	1. "Choose a facilitator, recorder and spokesperson.
	
	2. Brainstorm/discuss priority actions that we can take (individually and/or collectively) based on the following criteria:
	  ▪ They are doable within 30 days
	  ▪ They are within our control
	  ▪ They impose minimum disruption and cost
	  ▪ They add maximum value to customers
	
	3. Pick from the brainstormed list three to five actions we can take in the next 30-40 days to ensure that change takes place in the bank.
	
	4. Flipchart the quick hit recommendations, identifying what the organization needs to do and which function needs to do it.
	
	Be prepared at _____ to give a headline (two-minute report) to the whole group describing the key quick hits that your table arrived at."
	
	Give tables a 15 min. warning.
	
	Let participants know when to reconvene after break.	

2:30 (15) **Note:** Agenda says 3:00.	**Break**	Next Steps assignment out
2:45 (30 min.)	**Report Outs** 1st Fishbowl group. 2nd Each "Quick Hit" Table gets two minutes to report the top two to three quick hit opportunities they identified.	PAUL Cue up Steering Committee to listen and think of how they will respond.

Time	Content/Process	Logistics
3:15 (45 min.) (10 min.) (35 min.)	**Next Steps** *The purpose of this section is to see where the organization is in the overall design process, see what comes next, and plan how to carry the message forward.* Introduce two BPE Team members who will to explain where the organization is and what comes next. They share: • Where the organization is in the Design Process • What happens within the next month • What the rest of the design is for creating the new process • How participants will be selected for the next conferences. Transition to *Toni* who introduces "Next Steps Assignment" **Assignment:** 1. "Choose a facilitator and a recorder. 2. Discuss the following questions: • What should we communicate out to people to keep them informed? • How should we communicate the results of this meeting and how could the people here help? 3. Create an agenda and speaking points that you can use to report the results of this FDS to your home areas." Give table groups a 10-minute warning. Transition to Steering Committee response.	Distribute handouts that list FDS I Feedback Sessions. Post sign-up sheets for Quick Hits in the back of the room. **Note:** When do participants actually sign up? I don't see this in the current agenda? Shouldn't they sign up for next steps as well as quick hits? TONI ?

Time	Content/Process	Logistics
4:00 (10 min.)	**Closing Comments by Steering Committee** *Toni* provides an introduction. *The purpose of this section is to get feedback from the Steering Committee, the leaders who are charged with overseeing the ODS Projects.* Introduce Steering Committee, point out SC Members who will be responding to report-outs *Steering Committee Members named at this moment* Steering Committee Representatives: ▪ Tell how they are feeling about these two days. ▪ Thank everyone for participating.	STEERING COMMITTEE MEMBERS
4:10 (10 min.)	**Evaluation and Close** *The purpose of this segment is to find out how well our first facilitated Design Session has worked. The consultants and the Planning Team will use your feedback in planning the next one. The items to which you're responding are based on the things on which the Planning Team wanted your input.* **Assignment:** 1. On a scale of 1 to 10, how committed are you to making the new high-level design a reality? Why did you circle the number you circled? 2. On a scale of 1 to 10, how important do you believe it is to change the current process? Why did you circle the number you circled? 3. In your opinion, what are the two or three most important things we've accomplished in this First Facilitated Design Session?	PAUL Cue logistics to pass out the evaluation sheets

Time	Content/Process	Logistics
4:20 (05)	**Adjourn** ▪ Planning and Event Planning Team meet with consultants to read evaluations. ▪ Paul provides "heads up" to Event Planning Team (and Steering Committee???) about what's important to keep in mind going forward. Consultants and Event Planning Team agree on time to meet tomorrow to debrief, give feedback, and plan "to do" items for feedback to the system and to prepare for next FDS Planning Meeting.	

CHAPTER 6: ALTERNATIVE DESIGNS: POSSIBILITIES FOR SPECIFIC WHOLE-SCALE INTERVENTIONS

Non-Profit Board of Directors

Situation And Convening Issue
A non-profit organization was established to serve as a catalyst and strategic advisor of business, education, health, philanthropy and government to make the state a world leader in using information technology in ways that better its citizens' lives. The Board seeks to become aligned with the organization's vision, strategy and forward movement.

Event Purpose
To align the Board around the organization's vision, strategy and forward movement.

Role Of This Event In The Overall Process
This was the second retreat of the Board and the first for many of the 16 board members. Board members come from across the spectrum of the state and include education, business, health and government. This was the first opportunity for all of them to come together and set strategy and directions for the organization.

Brief Results And Continuation Plan
- Higher commitment and more active board participation
- Greater communication within the team
- Clearly understood strategy and direction for the team
- Continuation plan is to begin to work on a financial model that will sustain the work of the organization and to set priorities that support the organization's mission and strategic plan.

STRATEGY DEVELOPMENT IMPLEMENTATION ROADMAP (Whole-Scale Change for Strategy Development)

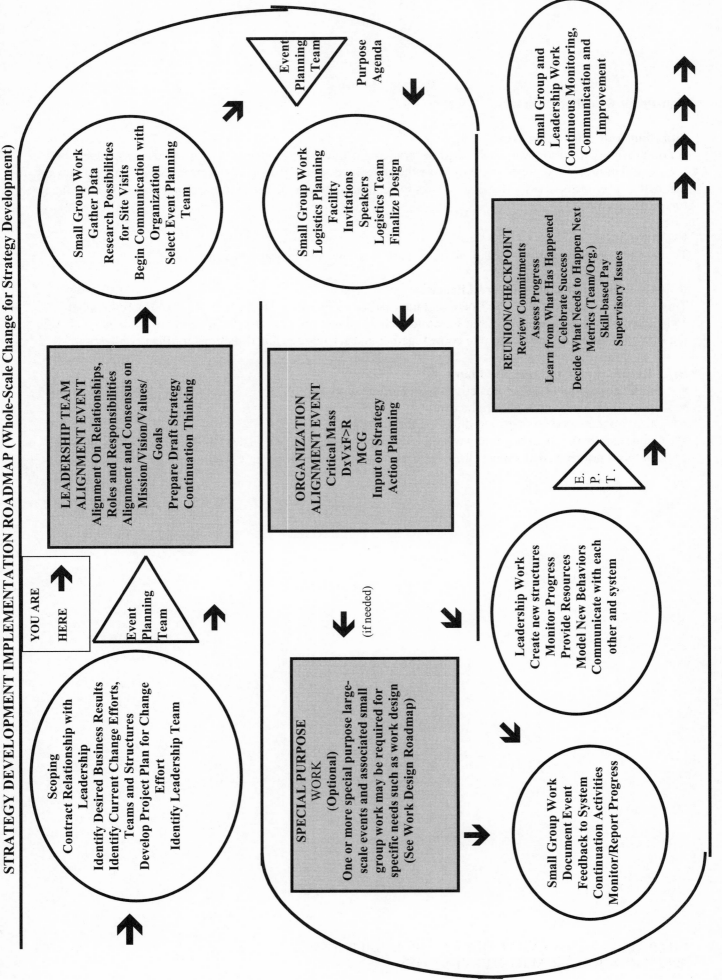

CHAPTER 6: ALTERNATIVE DESIGNS: POSSIBILITIES FOR
SPECIFIC WHOLE-SCALE INTERVENTIONS

Time	Content/Process	Logistics

Board Meeting
Final design

Purpose: To get the board aligned around the organization's vision, strategy and forward movement.

Day 1

Time	Content/Process	Logistics
		Logistics: Provide nametags, three flipcharts/stands, markers, and masking tape. Chart agenda (note documents)
8:30am (10)	**Welcome** Chairman of the Board and President of the organization Five minutes each<ul><li>Tell what he or she hopes to get out of the day</li><li>Set an open and relaxed tone for the day</li><li>Introduce facilitators</li></ul>	***Purpose – to welcome folks and set the tone for the day***
8:40 (10)	**Agenda, logistics and norms** Bring the agenda to life	Agenda on chart paper *Purpose – to take the mystery out of the day and agree on norms for working together*
8:50 (45) (25)	**Getting Connected** Have two max-mix groups of eight. Pose the following questions: 1. How is IT impacting your business? 2. What do you hope this organization will accomplish? 3. What excites, frustrates, and intrigues you about the organization? 4. What do you need to get out of this meeting personally? 5. How comfortable are you with IT? 6. What outcomes do you need from today? Give participants two minutes of "I" time. Choose a facilitator to keep time	**Handout** of questions with table roles and rules of brainstorming on the back *Purpose – to begin to build the team, to get folks connected around the work and their curiosity about each other*
(15)	Then have them take three minutes each to introduce themselves to others at the table	
(10)	Have them identify	

Time	Content/Process	Logistics
	▪ Common themes ▪ Significant differences ▪ Outcomes for the day. **Report out**	Refer to table roles

Time	Content/Process	Logistics
9:45 (10)	**BREAK**	
9:55 (65) (15)	**View from the Chair & President** Chairman of the Board & the President have seven7 minutes each. **Talking Points** ▪ What have you been up to? ▪ What's the role you want the board to play? ▪ Given the mission what is your vision for cyberstate.org? ▪ From your view what are the key priorities for the organization?	*Purpose – to give Chairman and the President a chance to hit the highlights and then give board members the opportunity to probe deeper for greater understanding.* Talking point questions on flipchart.
(10)	**Open Forum** ▪ What did we hear? ▪ What were our reactions? ▪ What questions of understanding do you have? For whom?	
(30)	Q & A	

Time	Content/Process	Logistics
11:00 (180)	**Strategy – What's our Common Vision and What are the Key Priorities and LUNCH** 1. Decide at your table if you need to take individual time to read through the document. 2. Given the mission, does the vision statement work for you, i.e., what do you like about it or what needs to change in order for it to capture your commitment and energy? **Report out** of the highlights of each table's conversation and its recommended vision statement. Work the room to **consensus**.	Refer them to the documents on "Setting the Course" and "Recommendations of the State Information Technology Commission." Bring extra copies of the FedEx Put mission and vision statements on chart paper Purpose – to build consensus and commitment to our vision of success, which builds the foundation for action.
1:55 (15)	**BREAK**	
2:10 (70) (30) (10) (20) (10)	**Revisiting Priorities** Assignment: "At your tables discuss and agree on the following: 1. In light of our mission and vision statements are these the right priorities or are there others that need to be added in order for us to fulfill the mission and achieve our vision?" **Report out and consensus** Return to your table to work and agree on 2. What are the things that need to be done in the next year? 3. Are these the right measures of success? If not, what are your recommendations? **Report out and consensus**	*Purpose – to build consensus and commitment to the action the board and organization will pursue.*
3:20 (15)	**Board Governance** President ▪ Using a Digital Board Room ▪ Approving the Consent Agenda ▪ Electing new Board member	

Time	Content/Process	Logistics
3:35 (15)	**Sustainability** On going communications: • With each other • From the President • Next steps, i.e., next board meeting is September 15th	
3:50 (5)	**Closing Remarks** Chairman of the Board and President • What happens after today? • How are you feeling about the day	
3:55	**Evaluations and Close** 1. What did you want from the day? 2. What did you get? 3. How confident are you that the work we did today will move cyberstate.org forward in meaningful ways? 1----------2-----------3-----------4----------5 not confident extremely confident 4. Why did you mark it where you did?	**Handout** *Purpose – to give participants an opportunity to reflect and comment on the process and outcomes of the day's work.*
4:00 PM	**Stay to Read Evaluations** Chairman, President and facilitators stay and read evaluations.	*Purpose – to review the day from the perspective of the participants*

The Star Model

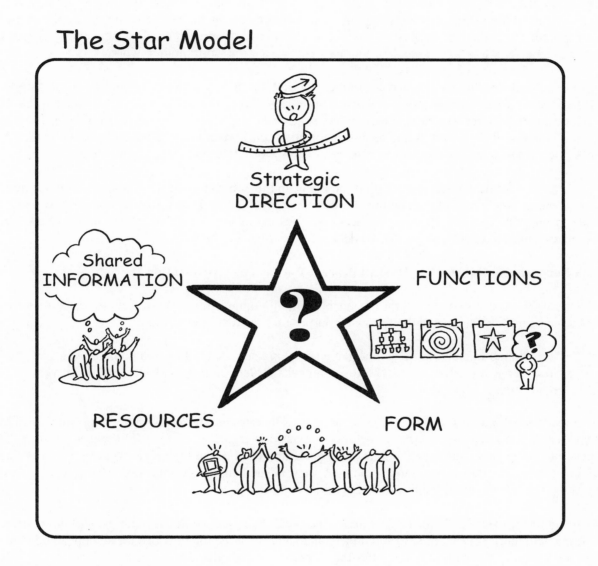

The Situation and Convening Issue:

Over the course of the past year HT organization had been struggling in a very competitive environment. Its global business had slowed and margins were eroding at about a 25% rate, per quarter. The business had been restructured and the new leadership team had been struggling to develop a strategic plan for a worldwide amalgamation of businesses, none of which seemed to have much in common historically.

The leadership team, aided by an outside Strategic Planning organization, had finally come together to develop the strategic intent of this partnership between groups and had begun to formulate a business proposition that would require much greater integration and coordination across the groups in the division. As the plan began to take shape, the consequences across the business and the implications for how the leaders and their organizations would have to behave became clear. This new clarity caused the leaders to look for a way to engage their top managers across the world in their work.

With the help of the Internal Human Resources VP and an internal OD consultant, the leadership team had the idea of a large group meeting that would engage the top three levels of the organization. The decision to hold the meeting outside the United States was intentional. The leadership team recognized that to be more global as leaders and as an organization, they were going to have to overcome their US-centric focus. The team invited leaders from around the world to England in July of 1999.

The convening business issue was to align the plans and the behaviors of the top of the organization, in order to move quickly in implementing the new strategy. The underlying issue was: how do you get people from different cultures and different businesses within the organization to put aside these differences and pull together to create and deploy a world-beater plan?

Event Purpose and Role In The Overall Process Within The Organization

A Planning Team, comprised of eight managers from all components and three countries, and two non-management employees, created the following purpose for this two-day meeting.

> "To catapult ourselves into a cohesive leadership team, committed to a common strategy in order to mobilize all of HT to dominate the data storage and information market opportunity. (Just do it.)"

The intention behind this meeting was to bring together traditionally disparate, highly independent, groups within the Division, in order to achieve the new synergies concerted effort makes possible. The leaders had completed what they thought was a good first draft of the high-level strategy. They believed that in order to create energy and momentum they needed to involve the rest of the top leaders in translating that strategy into implications and initial actions.

As a result of the meeting (1) the leadership from around the world would agree on the high-level strategy (or Strategic Intent); (2) everyone would understand and accept the implications for all concerned; and (3) the group would approve plans to complete the strategy and implement it.

Results and Continuation Plan

Within one month several teams of managers and staff began translating the agreed upon Strategic Intent into a real Strategic Plan. Other teams began to work on the implications (for technology, structure, communications, etc.). The session mobilized people across the globe to work together and develop integrated approaches to markets and customers.

Communication (*"In order to mobilize all…"*) was an important part of the meeting purpose created by the planning team, spirited by the two non-management participants. At the leadership meeting, managers identified communication strategies and key messages for key stakeholders. Immediately following the leadership meeting, managers conducted interactive employee communication sessions, utilizing video clips from the leadership meeting, to convey the energy, commitment, and key messages about strategic direction. In addition, managers communicated key messages about their strategic direction to customers, other company groups and outside partners.

The organization held a follow-up meeting approximately six months later to review progress resulting from the plans and agreements people had made at the previous session. They had made significant progress in positioning the organization for the future. As we go to print, tangible business results are not yet available.

STRATEGY DEVELOPMENT IMPLEMENTATION ROADMAP (Whole-Scale Change for Strategy Development)

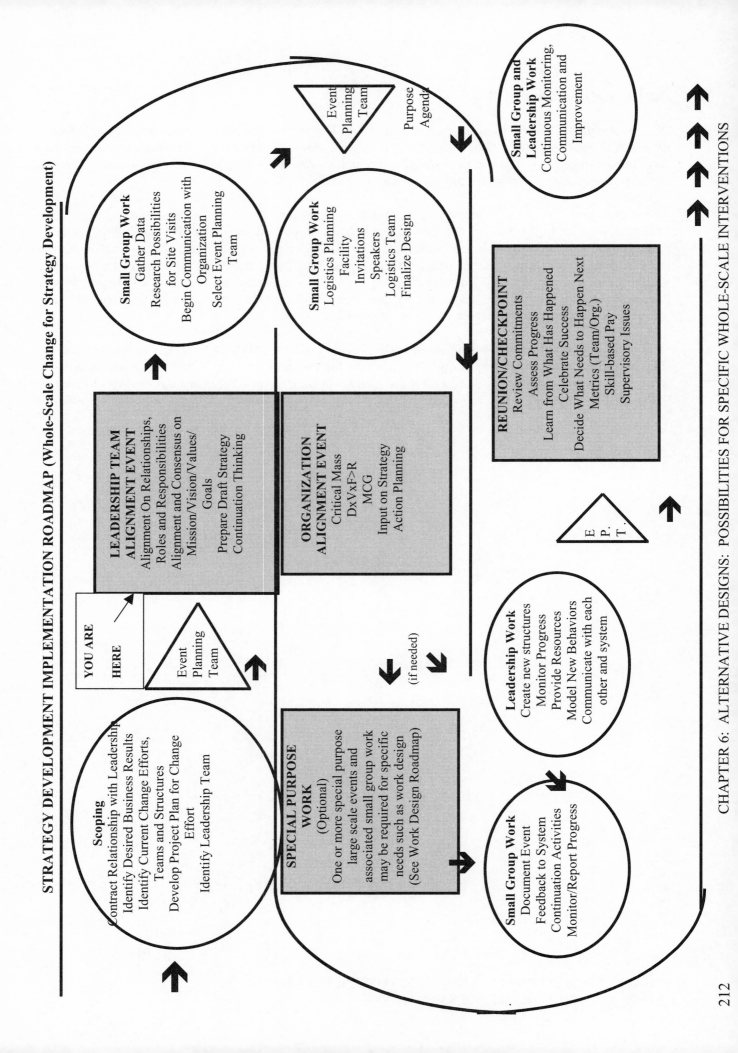

CHAPTER 6: ALTERNATIVE DESIGNS: POSSIBILITIES FOR SPECIFIC WHOLE-SCALE INTERVENTIONS

Time	Content/Process	Logistics

"A High Tech Company"
First Annual Senior Leadership Meeting
July, 1999

STAGING DAY – Tuesday, July 1999

	Content/Process	Logistics
	Purpose of Staging Day: ▪ To get everything set up and ready to go! ▪ To make sure presenters are ready ▪ To ensure that the Planning Team & Leadership Team & Facilitators are connected and ready to go	Logistics Team is clear on roles & goals, agenda flow, for the two days

	AGENDA	
9:00 am	**Logistics Team Meets** Paul, Sylvia, Nancy, Debbie, Kathy meet with Logistics Team to: ▪ Build the group as a team: Introduce people, get clear on Logistics role and people's expectations of each other ▪ Walk through the meeting agenda design to understand the flow and identify key logistics actions	**Consulting team and internal resources huddle** ▪ Have a list of logistics team members for everyone on the team ▪ Have a copy of agenda design for each logistics team member & HT Staff
About 10:00am	Kathy, Nancy & Debbie & Logistics Team begin to work to: ▪ Identify specific roles ▪ Set up a Logistics "command center" ▪ Make handouts for each place setting ▪ Put in-basket on each table ▪ Set flipchart easels around periphery ▪ Set up "registration table" set up with name ▪ Lay out tags ▪ Set up and test microphones ▪ Sort and label Day 1 and 2 handouts ▪ Make headers ▪ Train microphone people on Open Forum process and how to operate cordless, handheld microphones ▪ Train one person overall on working a/v system ▪ Make the Open Forum Grid and post on podium	**Possible Logistics Roles:** ▪ Audio system ▪ Handouts ▪ Microphone people (4) ▪ Laptop computer, documentation ▪ Climate Control ▪ Breaks & Lunches ▪ Speaker Assistant ▪ Flip Chart Notes Scribe

		Check supplies ▪ Two to three rolls of 1" masking tape ▪ 3x5 post-it notes: 1/2 pad for each person ▪ Crayons for voting

Time	Content/Process	Logistics
		▪ Dots for voting ▪ Flair-type pen, if available, for each person to write on post-it notes – otherwise, a pen or pencil for each person
2:00 PM	**Paul and Sylvia Huddle with the HT Staff** ▪ Get acquainted ▪ Review any presentations that they will do ▪ Review any handouts, etc they will use. ▪ Coach them and any others for the meeting Meet as a Planning Team to: ▪ Hear what's happening in the organization ▪ Tweak anything we need to ▪ Review everything and be ready	
4:00 PM	▪ Tag up with anybody we need to (presenters, leadership team…)	A Logistics supply kit is handy, with things like ▪ Three pairs of scissors, ▪ Stapler & staples, ▪ Paper clips, ▪ Rubber bands, ▪ Approximately 20 business-size envelopes, ▪ Scotch tape…
5:30 PM	**Adjourn & Get a Good Night's Sleep!!**	

CHAPTER 6: ALTERNATIVE DESIGNS: POSSIBILITIES FOR
SPECIFIC WHOLE-SCALE INTERVENTIONS

Time	Content/Process	Logistics

"High Tech Company"
First Annual Senior Managers Meeting
July, 1999

***Purpose*:**	To catapult ourselves into a cohesive leadership team, committed to a common strategy in order to mobilize all of ISG to dominate the data storage and information market opportunity. (Just do it.)

Tuesday
Pre-meeting Reception and Dinner

Time	Content/Process	Logistics
3:30 PM	**Transportation from St. Pierre Hotel to Reception**	
4:00 PM (90)	**Reception at Plant Site** – *HT Room, Bldg. 2*	*Luggage Storage for those arriving late from European cities*
5:45	**Transportation from Reception to Hotel**	
7:00	**Drinks available at Hotel –**	Arrange dinner seating to encourage mixing: Each table is a different number; each person draws a number from a bowl as they walk into the room
7:30	**Dinner at Hotel**	
(10)	**Before Dinner:** **Welcome by Division General Manger** • Says thanks for coming • Looks forward to a very successful meeting • Hopes to look back at this meeting as the beginning of a breakthrough era for HT • Introduces HT Staff (call up to front) • Introduces new faces: Paul, Sylvia, and Kathy T. from DTA and Mark L., from other consulting company we are working with • Acknowledges business accomplishment- great results)	Logistics, distribute a handout of morning pre-meeting activities and sign up sheets

Time	Content/Process	Logistics
(10)	**Welcome by Site General Manager, who:** ▪ Appreciates people being here ▪ Appreciates the various cultures and acknowledges that it's the first time meeting here…for the purpose of truly putting participants in a more global mindset! ▪ Remind people about Dave 's retirement presentation by Robert during dinner **Logistics for tomorrow – by Paul or Sylvia** ▪ Sign up for fun activities during dinner ▪ Have Debby discuss activities	
8:00 PM	**Adjourn to dinner and rest of the evening**	

Time	Content/Process	Logistics

"High Tech Company"
First Annual Senior Leadership Meeting
July, 1999

Purpose:	To catapult ourselves into a cohesive leadership team, committed to a common strategy in order to mobilize all of HT to dominate the data storage and information market opportunity. (Just do it.)

Wednesday, July 1999

Time	Content/Process	Logistics
7:00–9:00 am	**Breakfast available at Hotel**	<ul><li>Pre-reading</li><li>Catapult toys</li><li>Logo, T-shirts</li></ul>
8:00 am	**Beverages Available & General Milling Around**	Logistics:<ul><li>Name tags with table number on each for max-mix seating</li><li>Handouts at each place setting:</li><li>One-page Purpose & Agenda</li><li>Role of Facilitator, Recorder, Reporter & Rules of Brainstorming,</li><li>Table Introductions Assignment</li><li>DVF mode</li></ul>
9:00 am (10)	**Welcome – Division General Manager** <ul><li>Mike describes his hopes for this meeting</li><li>He shares his personal vision of this leadership group (FMT group)</li><li>He explains the importance of being present and participating fully in the meeting</li><li>He also emphasizes the importance of commitment and support of this leadership group to successfully implement HT strategy</li><li>He reframes the Group as an Information Storage and Management company</li><li>He points out that HT must be more than the sum of its divisions if it achieves the growth it is capable of</li><li>He introduce SWAT and Event Planning Teams and the Logistics team</li><li>He introduce the next speaker to provide the purpose of this meeting</li></ul>	**SWAT TEAM** Read out and acknowledge list of names **EVENT PLANNING TEAM** Read out and acknowledge list of names **LOGISTICS TEAM** Consists of six people from the US and UK. Read out and acknowledge list of

Time	Content/Process	Logistics
		names
9:10 am (10)	**Purpose- HT Staff Member : *Don*** To *catapult* us into a *cohesive leadership team, committed* to a common strategy in order to *mobilize all* of ISG to *dominate* the *data storage and information management opportunity*. ▪ *Catapult:* we are not operating as a cohesive leadership team now, and we will have to move very quickly to re-conceive ourselves in this way if we are going to meet the challenge – the meeting is intended to generate the thrust required to overcome the traditional division-focused perspective that has characterized HT's efforts in the past. ▪ *Cohesive leadership team:* we work together across divisions to create a force in the marketplace that is greater than the sum of our individual divisional efforts and that is based on a sense of shared purpose and accountability	Handout(s) with Purpose & Agenda
9:20 am (10)	▪ *Committed:* we are not looking for compliance here but rather to a high level of belief in and focus on a collective strategy that we all believe will allow us to win in the marketplace ▪ *Mobilize all:* we own the responsibility of getting everyone in HT committed to and aligned with the strategy ▪ *Dominate:* we want to be the market leader in the segments in which we choose to play • Data storage and information management opportunity: *the whole enchilada* **Agenda & Logistics – DTA Consultant** ▪ Give background on DTA ▪ Walk through agenda ▪ Describe purpose of max-mix table seating (microcosm) ▪ Talk about logistics – facility, telephone norms, regular breaks (manage your own needs), what else?	

Time	Content/Process	Logistics
9:30 am (55)	**Personal Introductions** *Activity Purpose:* Get to know each other; get data out (flip charts, handouts?) where people are regarding the meeting, the meeting purpose, strategy, group structure Vs division; Breaking the Ice; beginning to get out the "D" Remind people to "Listen to see the world"	Note: They did not like the idea of "Telling Our Stories" Logistics: Assignment on handout and in packets
(25)	*Table Assignment:* "Choose a Facilitator at your table to keep time. Take two minutes to think about your answers to the following questions and then each person take three minutes to share your answers at your table: ▪ Name, background, what you do ▪ What's the word on the street about the strategy work? Where are you personally? ▪ What are your hopes, your fears about this meeting? ▪ What's your reaction to the purpose of the meeting? What are the outcomes of this meeting that would make it worthwhile for you Discuss and record on a flip chart what you heard at your table:	
(10)	▪ Common Themes ▪ Significant Differences ▪ Your table's outcomes for these two days" Do a room-wide call out of common themes, significant differences and each table's desired outcomes	Have four recorders up front, each with an easel to capture the call outs
(15)	Walk through D x V x F > R model as a framework for two days	Handout of DVF is in packets
(5)		
10:25 am (15)	**Break**	Call out outcomes typed and ready to give back at lunch

Time	Content/Process	Logistics

10:40 am (75)	**Building a Strategic Database**	*Logistics:* **VIDEO**
	Activity Purpose: To determine what tells the organization to think bigger and to create the compelling future opportunity the organization needs—what the competition is doing, where storage is going:	
(3)	*Framing:* Link to purpose and overview process of first presenter who will "hit key points" and then allow time for tables to generate questions to probe deeper. Caution participants to listen to see the world this presenter sees.	
(50)	**Introduce Speaker: "Gill R."** **Presentation** *One Presenter @ 30 minutes* ▪ Noted International Author ("The Digital Estate" & "Net Future")	Gill R. needs bio of the presenter

(25)	**Questions from tables** (Last five minutes for burning unasked questions.)	Two hand-held mikes

CHAPTER 6: ALTERNATIVE DESIGNS: POSSIBILITIES FOR SPECIFIC WHOLE-SCALE INTERVENTIONS

Time	Content/Process	Logistics
11:55 AM	**Lunch**	Handout that tells where people should go to participate in what they signed up for.
	Outside Activity: Choose from a variety For example: -Swimming -Golf -Chepstow Town Shopping -Tinturn Abbey - Tethered Balloon Ride - Tennis	

Time	Content/Process	Logistics
1:55 PM (90)	**Building a Strategic Database II** *Activity Purpose: To continue to see what tells the organization to think bigger. To go on a learning journey to listen to the thinking underlying the strategy.*	*Logistics, Need a breakout area for each station.*
(5)	*Framing: Link to purpose to continue to build database and describe whole process of stations and then table discussions.*	**Internal Consultants work with presenters for standardized presentations, wall displays, and handouts**
(55)	**"Expanding our Views" Assignment:** *HT Staff: "L, G, and R"* ▪ Provide three "stations," with two people as "station master" at each station to present data. ▪ Pair SWAT Team member and HT Staff member at each station. (Coach presenters: don't soft-pedal; hit them in the head with the data) ▪ Post one staff member at each station to discuss and answer questions on how the data affected him or her. SWAT team member will provide the data; Staff person should focus on the impact on his or her thinking. ▪ Allow 16 minutes at each station—10 minutes to present; six minutes for Q&A ▪ Run three rounds so each person visits each station (two minutes between rounds to move) ▪ Provide handout of data from each station After visiting each station, return to original table seating for discussion." **Stations:** *A.* **Marketing size / Customer needs** *B.* **Competitive Landscape** *C.* **Trends in Industry**	*One-page handout of data from each station, stapled together. Cover page lists each station & its location*

	Content/Process	Logistics
	Table Discussions (back in Max-Mix Seating) Activity Purpose: *To relate all you've heard this morning and just now to what it could mean for you as individuals, as divisions, and as a group; opportunity to translate what you've heard into implications for you, for us; still working on "D" – dissatisfaction with status quo; be ready to listen to the strategy.*	Handout of discussion assignment in in-basket when participants return from the gallery walk

CHAPTER 6: ALTERNATIVE DESIGNS: POSSIBILITIES FOR SPECIFIC WHOLE-SCALE INTERVENTIONS

(25)	**Table Assignment**: • "Select a facilitator, and recorder. • What did you hear this morning and just now that really struck you? What did you learn? • What opportunities/threats do you see for HT? • What do you think we have to do to take advantage of the opportunities? To address the threats? • Select a reporter for room wide call outs.	
(5)	**Call outs: "Who has something in, something unique, important point?"**	Have hand-held microphones available

3:25 (15)	**Break**	**VIDEO Ready**

(15)	**Table Discussion**: • "What did we hear? • What are our reactions? • What questions of understanding do we want to ask?…of whom? Choose a facilitator, recorder, and question-asker".	Handout Tell them that the entire HT Staff will be on panel to receive questions

(40)	**Q&A with Panel of Group Staff:** Put the rest of staff up front in chairs (Last five minutes for burning unasked questions.)	Microphones available Seven Barstools
(10)	T-shirt presentation (by Planning Team members)	Six Chairs up front - facing front

Time	Content/Process	Logistics
5:45 (55) (5) (35) (15)	**First Impressions** *Activity Purpose: To help participants process the strategy in order to move forward. To begin to see the opportunities. To build commitment to this strategy, that it makes sense and gets the organization headed in the right direction.* *Framing: The road to commitment begins with understanding. As you look at the road to commitment, where are you?* **Table Discussion:** "Each person take a few minutes to think about: ▪ What's exciting about this strategy? ▪ What scares me about it? ▪ What opportunities, possibilities does it give us? Then discuss as a table." *Room-wide call-outs, where are we?*	Max-mix tables Road to Commitment Model Handout of the assignment on cue

6:40 PM	**Evaluation**
	▪ How did today go for you?
	Highs?
	Lows?
	▪ Given what you've heard today, how strong is your belief that HT can win with this strategy? (mark the scale)
	    1----2----3----4----5----6----7----8----9----10
	Not a chance Still need We can
	                  convincing do it !
	▪ Why did you mark it the way you did?
	
	▪ Advice for tomorrow?
		Handout of Evaluation on cue

6:30 6:45-7:45 7:30 PM 8:00-11:00 PM	**Adjourn** **Event Planning Team and Staff stay to read evaluations and tweak tomorrow's agenda as indicated.** ***Bus leaves for Dinner*** ***Dinner/Evening Activity*** Medieval feast/castle. No jeans	

Time	Content/Process	Logistics

Thursday

Time	Content/Process	Logistics
8:30 AM (15)	**Feedback on Evaluations/Agenda** *Activity Purpose: Everyone owning the meeting purpose and process and results of the agenda* ▪ Give brief recap of evaluation results ▪ Review agenda for Day 2 including any changes made over night	Sit at original Max Mix Tables

Time	Content/Process	Logistics
8:45 (50)	**Implications of this Strategy for Our Group**	**Bins:**
(05)	*Activity Purpose: To demonstrate commitment by thinking through implications to make this strategy happen.* Present and explain bin topics. -Nine max-mix tables volunteer for topics.	A. Critical HT relationships within the Company B. Capabilities and organizational alternatives: organization's ability to do certain things and possible structures to realize these things
(45)	*Assignment:* "For the topic that your table is assigned 1. Brainstorm and record on a flip chart What do we need to Keep? Drop? Create? 2. Clarify the meaning of each brainstorm item 3. Choose recommendations on each category: keep, drop, create 4. Prepare a self- explanatory flipchart of these recommendations of what to keep, drop and create 5. Choose a reporter who will describe your table's work to the breakout group when we return from Break. This person will also stay and work with the breakout. 6. Post your work."	C. What does leadership look like? (Leadership team – those in this room.) D. Beliefs - norms, values, attitudes, assumptions, operating principles E. Business models (How we earn money) F. Partnerships/ alliances G. Go to market strategies – How we reach customers H. Key business and business support processes – (defined set) I. Metrics, Rewards, Compensation system

		Logistics: Handout of bins with table assignments *After they do the work, collect the work of the Leadership Team group.* **Type their work and make copies to hand out to everyone over lunch**
9:35 (25)	**Break Assignment:** – "Roam and read the work on all 'bins' to decide which bin topic you want to work on after Break. (Do not sign up for leadership bin)"	

10:00 (135) (05)	**Group-Wide Planning** *Activity Purpose:* *To bring together people with an interest in each topic to identify and plan the actions needed to move the strategy forward, addressing the key issues in each topic area.* *Added framing: Decide how to handle the three boxes in the strategy. In the end, pick the two or three key actions that your group believes must be taken quickly, coming out of this meeting.* *Moving:*	Logistics: Hand out "Activity Maps" and assignment with breakout locations on reverse.
(10)	Individuals decide which Bin-group they will work in. Move to Bin breakout areas. At the Bin breakout area, Bin representative briefs everyone on the recommendations. **(Do not do "Leadership" bin)**	

Time	Content/Process	Logistics
(75)	*Breakout work* "Assignment ▪ Pick a facilitator, recorder, reporter ▪ Agree what the organization needs to drop, and what it needs to create ▪ For each "Dropped" item, list the major actions that need to happen to drop the item ▪ Separate these actions into those that need to happen over the next six months and those that need to happen longer term ▪ For those that need to happen over the next six months develop a plan using the following format:	Logistics: Put post-it note pads in in-boxes—One half pad per person. Put clean flip chart page next under Bin headers.

Name of "Dropped"	Who takes the lead	Who needs to be involved	Action Item	By When

| | For each "Create" item, list the major actions that need to happen to create the item.
▪ Separate these actions into those that need to happen over the next six months and those that need to happen longer term.
▪ For those that need to happen over the next six months develop a plan using the following format
▪ : | |

Name of "Create"	Who takes the lead	Who needs to be involved	Action Item	By When

▪ Post your work under the appropriate Bin header
▪ Identify someone in your group to stay and answer questions."

Time	Content/Process	Logistics

| | (30) After all groups have posted their work, grab a post-it note pad and circulates. Read the work and give ideas and acknowledgments. Focus on the two or three other implications that you are most concerned about. Stick post-it notes on the black flip chart page next to the group's work" (15) "Sub groups now re-huddle and look at the feedback and then decide what are the two three key next steps your group recommends the organization take coming out of this meeting." | **A sign-up sheet for people interested in being part of the action teams after this session** |

| 12:15 (60) | **Lunch** | Logistics: Put handout of the Leadership Team work form the morning into the In Box. |

| 1:15 PM (105) | **Leadership Team Role** *Activity Purpose: Clear about role and ready to lead implementation* (10) Report from the table that worked on the Leadership Team Bin in the morning. (40) *Assignment:* "Each max mix table discuss and answer: <ul><li>What does this organization need to start doing, stop doing, and keep doing as a team to effectively lead the implementation of the HT Strategy?</li><li>What is our role as individuals leading the implementation of the HT Strategy?</li><li>What do we need the HT Staff to do to help lead the implementation of the HT Strategy?"</li></ul> (10) Each table identifies three key points that they think are most important for strategic leadership. Collect and combine where appropriate | Return to max-mix Seating   Handout assignment   . |

Time	Content/Process	Logistics

(20)	"Post, read and vote on the answers. Use three green and three red dots max for each question.
	    Green dot – We have to do this
	    Red dot – I cannot support this idea"
	
	Tabulate votes; report the items that got the most green dots. Use these as a starting point to work to consensus of the whole.
		Give each person nine green dots and nine red dots

(20)	Ask for any disagreement with items receiving most votes. Work to consensus of the whole on each question. Consensus means people can at least say, "I 70% agree with the intention and am 100% committed to supporting it."	
(5)	End with closing comments from **Mike** on what the organization has agreed to. He should: ▪ Summarize the agreements ▪ Hold the group—and himself--accountable for following through on them	

3:00 PM (15)	**Break**	Handout – put in box at break
3:15 PM (15)	**Next Steps – HT Staff Member** *Activity Purpose: To sustain people's commitment to the strategy and belief that this meeting will result in action; and to demonstrate HT Staff's commitment to implementing this strategy.* **Presentation:** ▪ Clear set of next steps to move this strategy forward; and what's the structure to implement this strategy (content / process). ▪ HT's thinking to move fast. Commit to when the organization is going to have a transition plan (timetable). **Larry – Describe next steps with handout** **Mike – Make a brief comment about the organization's commitment to the effort**	

Time	Content/Process	Logistics
3:30 PM (45)	**Communications** *Activity Purpose: Plan consistent communication; ensure stakeholders get the information they need (from a high level, cross cutting standpoint).*	Recorders up-front. *Handout*
(20)	**Table Discussion***:* "What are the key messages that the organization needs to communicate to each of the following groups about the HT Strategy and the work this group has done here: ▪ HT employees? ▪ Customers? ▪ Other company x groups / or outside partners?"	
(25)	**Call out**: Choose one table for each group and ask if there is any additional input? Make sure everyone agrees who from the room will communicate these key messages company-wide and back home in Divisions.	
4:15 PM (10)	**Wrap-up: Mike** ▪ Offer *thank you's* to everyone: Logistics Team, Event Planning Team, SWAT Team, Participants	
4:25 PM	**Evaluation** ▪ "What were the most significant outcomes of this meeting for you? ▪ On a scale from 1-10, what are the chances that HT will successfully implement its strategy? (Mark the scale) Not a Snowball's chance anything will change Nothing can stop us!!!!! 1 — 2 —3 — 4— 5 — 6 — 7 — 8 —-9 — 10 ▪ Why did you mark it where you did? ▪ Any other comments?"	Hand out evaluations on cue Logistics team collect the evaluations as people leave the room
4:35 PM	**Adjourn** **Event Planning Team and HT Staff stay to read evaluations**	Late Tea (box food) available for people as they leave.

Manufacturing Company A, Inc.
Growing a Culture while Growing a Company

Situation and Convening Issue

Manufacturing Company A came into existence in early 1994 after investors purchased the Original Corporation in mid-1993. In late 1994, the CEO became the formal leader of the "foundation" company of two locations—at which 400 colleagues produced S83 million of structural metal stampings for the automotive industry.

Manufacturing Company A's strategy was to grow by balancing internal and external growth. Management expected new programs awards to provide a growth rate of between 10-15% per year. They expected a similar growth to occur as they acquired other companies, thus bringing new products, processes, and customers to the organization. By mid 1998, after Manufacturing Company A had acquired six additional companies, sales were in excess of $ 1.75 billion. Almost 9000 colleagues worked at 32 locations. The stock, priced at $11.50 per share in the initial IPO in 1995, was over $52.00 per share in early June 1999. *Fortune Magazine* cited the company as one of that year's 50 fastest growing companies in the United States.

The overall approach to integrating new acquisitions into Manufacturing Company A was to bring as many people as possible in this "new" organization into alignment with the company's overall strategic plan and culture and to do it quickly. The company president used the Whole-Scale process to help develop the company's strategy and values and to align the new acquisitions around that strategy and those values. In 1994, the organization held four large-group events, the first, two days long and the others each one day. The purpose of the first event was to begin to develop the company strategy and culture. At the end of those four events, about sixty leaders in the company had come to consensus on the company Mission, Vision, Values, and three-year Goals and had developed and implemented a short-term transition plan.

Beginning in 1995 and ending in 1998, the company held one-day "reunions" about every six months. Each reunion included up to 300 salaried and hourly colleagues from across the company. The purpose of these was to strengthen the culture and to align more colleagues around the strategy. In each year these sessions were used to deepen the knowledge, understanding and practice of a key part of the culture, for example, in 1995 Empowerment; in 1996 Leadership; and in 1997 Commitment.

In 1997, the leaders realized that the company had grown too big for the reunions to have the impact needed to continue the fast track of culture building and strategy alignment. They needed a different approach. Management believed that a key to the organization's success was the fact that it was a values-based company. Thus, in the fall of 1997 all business unit leaders, mentors and the leadership team met to begin a whole-system change effort to build commitment throughout the organization to being a values-based company. Another session followed in February 1998 that brought together 225 participants—including the same leadership group plus all of the business unit leadership teams. The purpose of this session was to speed the move to values-based leadership throughout the organization. Each business unit leadership team, mentor and the leadership team left the session with immediate action steps and a process for implementing values-based leadership at a faster pace.

A great part of the success of these sessions has been the work of Event Planning Teams. Each Event Planning Team session includes both hourly and salaried representatives from each location. The Event Planning Team met for two one-day sessions: the first about two weeks prior to the actual Whole-Scale event, and then another one week before the event. The result has been lively, Whole-Scale sessions with creative designs in which the Event Planning Team has ownership.

In late May 1998, the Event Planning Team from the February event met and discussed the progress that they had seen in the business units since the February session. Energy and enthusiasm for the continued implementation of values-based leadership was very high, and each business unit represented on the Event Planning Team was actively working to affect the culture in the unit.

Another important ingredient of the fast-track change seen by Manufacturing Company A has been the continued development of the leadership team, the executive level leaders of the corporation. In addition to monthly meetings and weekly telephone conferences, the team has held at least two retreats each year in which team members take a candid look at their performance, especially as leaders of the culture in the organization.

Many of the business units have used Whole-Scale events as part of their leadership processes. In 1995-96, one business unit held several Whole-Scale meetings to develop its strategy and use that strategy to drive the annual budget. Throughout 1997 business units held one-day strategic planning sessions to set direction for their unit. Beginning in 1998, business units began using large-group events as part of their approach to implementing values-based leadership.

In addition, the company has used large-group meetings for a variety of issues that require organization-wide thinking or action; for example, launching new organization-wide processes, such as the Manufacturing Company's production system. Through a series of large-group meetings, all colleagues in the organization were able to gain working knowledge and understanding of the Manufacturing Company's Vision, Mission, Values and Goals within one year.

As the organization grew, the number of leaders grew as well, and it became clear that many of them needed to expand their thinking outside their business units. In 1998, the Manufacturing Company began to hold quarterly "Strategic Thinking" sessions for all of the approximately 80 top leaders in the organization. These sessions formed a forum for members of this group to get a better understanding of issues that affect the strategy of the organization, hear each other's thinking on short and long term strategic plans and get to know one another better. The thinking and ideas discussed in these sessions have helped strengthen and broaden the business plans of the individual units.

The large-group approach worked well as the format of strategic planning meetings of the Board of Trustees in 1998 and 1999. A typical comment of the Board members about this approach was "This was a much more interactive type of meeting than we are used to having, and we got a lot done."

In summary, the Whole-Scale approach has been a key component of the processes Manufacturing Company A has used to keep the company on a fast track of growth and prosperity.

Roadmap

The three event designs included cover the Leadership Team alignment and an initial launch event for the new organization.

MERGERS/ACQUISITION ROADMAP

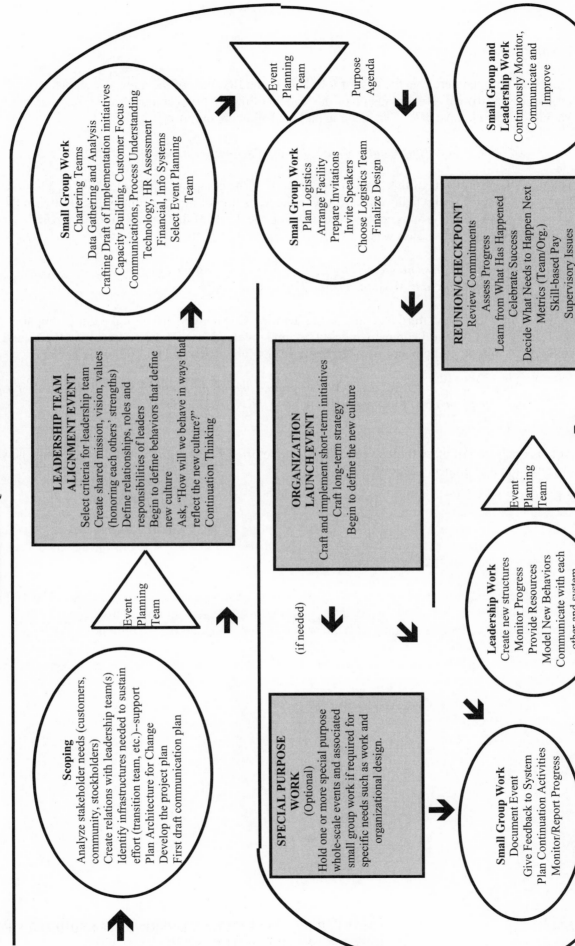

CHAPTER 6: ALTERNATIVE DESIGNS: POSSIBILITIES FOR SPECIFIC WHOLE-SCALE INTERVENTIONS

Event Purpose

The event outlined here was the first of four held in the first year of the company's existence. This first session was a two-day event made up of the leaders of the first two companies coming together to form Manufacturing Company A. The meeting had the following purpose:

> *To build relationships and start developing our long-term business strategy.*

The main work products of this session were a draft of the company's Mission, Vision, Values and Goals and four topics that the group believed were key to the transition of the two companies. Between the first and second sessions, small groups continued to develop the drafts of these parts of the company's strategy. The purpose of the second session was

> *To continue the strategic planning process by assessing our progress*
> *and completing our Mission, Vision, Values and Goals.*

Between the second and third meeting, Manufacturing Company had acquired a third company. Members of the leadership of the third company quickly became involved in working on transition topics and company strategy. About 60 participants attended the third session, which had the following purpose

> *To continue to integrate our three companies and to launch business planning at the business units*
> *that complements the strategy that we have developed together*

At the conclusion of these three events, the Manufacturing Company was ready to launch its new strategy with organizational alignment sessions.

Time	Content/Process	Logistics

Manufacturing Organization
Setting Strategy: Session 1
April 21-22, 1994

Purpose: To build relationships and start developing our long-term business strategy.

Time	Content/Process	Logistics
8:00 AM	**Room Setup/Staging**	▪ Four Max-mix tables of six ▪ Easels at each table with masking tape and markers. ▪ Name tags with table numbers ▪ Coffee and continental breakfast set up.

Time	Content/Process	Logistics
8:15 AM	**Continental Breakfast**	
9:00 AM (10)	**Welcome** The CEO explains the following: ▪ Why this organization is having this meeting now ▪ That this is the continuation of a process ▪ The work that has led up to this meeting ▪ How participants were chosen to be in this session. ▪ What he hopes the organization can get out of this meeting The CEO introduces Roland	CEO ROLAND

Time	Content/Process	Logistics
9:10 (10)	**Purpose, Agenda, Logistics**	**Handout Purpose, Agenda**

Time	Content/Process	Logistics

9:20 (55)　(25)	**Table Introductions** "Each person take three minutes to think about answers to these questions: ▪ Name, location, major responsibilities ▪ How long with Initial Organization 1 or Organization 2? ▪ What excites me about the future of Manufacturing Organization? ▪ What scares me about the future of Manufacturing Organization? ▪ What do I need to get from this meeting to make it worthwhile? Select a facilitator to keep time Each person gets a maximum of three minutes to 'tell your story' using these questions."	Assignment on handout Explain max-mix seating "Listen to see the world through each others' eyes"
(10)	Have each table summarize: A.　Common Themes　　　　　　　Differences B.　Specific outcomes from this meeting	
(20)	Report outs from tables	

| 10:15
(15) | **Break** | |

Time		Content/Process	Logistics
10:30 (80)	(35)	**Stakeholder Analysis I** Ask the Chairman to take 30 minutes maximum to address the following questions: ▪ What is the main reason that you wanted to establish the "Platform" for Manufacturing Organization? ▪ What are your long-term goals for Manufacturing Organization? ▪ What do you expect from Manufacturing Organization over the next two years? ▪ What do you believe are the key challenges and opportunities for Manufacturing Organization?	CHAIRMAN

	(15)	**Open Forum** Tables take 15 minutes to discuss the following questions: ▪ What did we hear? ▪ What are our reactions? ▪ What are our questions of understanding?	
	(30)	**Q&A**	

11:40 (45)		**Lunch**	

Time	Content/Process	Logistics

| 12:25
(80)   (35)

(15)

(30) | **Stakeholder Analysis :**
Ask each speaker to give at most a 10-minute presentation, using the following questions as a guide:

- What are the major challenges facing your company over the next two-three years?
- How is your company planning to meet those challenges?
- What do you expect from Manufacturing Organization as one of your suppliers?
- What do you need from Manufacturing Organization in this transition of integrating Organization 2?

Open Forum
Tables discuss the following questions:
- What did we hear?
- What are our reactions?
- What are our questions of understanding?

Q&A | CUSTOMERS 1, 2, & 3

Manufacturing Organization wants this process of integrating Organization 2 into Manufacturing Organization to be "seamless" to the customer.

Note that the customers are speaking at separate times because the Manufacturing Organization was afraid that if the customers were together they would not tell the truth.

The tables have an open forum after each speaker; and one Q & A session after all the speakers have finished. |

| 4:05
(85)   (20)

(15) | **View from CEO's Bridge**

Have the CEO use 20 minutes maximum to address the following questions:

- Why did you take this job?
- What excites you and what scares you about it?
- What are your long-term goals for Manufacturing Organization?
- What do you expect from Manufacturing Organization over the next two years?
- What do you believe are the key challenges and opportunities for Manufacturing Organization?

Open Forum
Tables take 15 minutes to discuss the following questions:
- What did we hear?
- What are our reactions?
- What are our questions of understanding? | CEO |

Time	Content/Process	Logistics
(40)	**Q&A**	

Time	Content/Process	Logistics
5:25 PM	**Evaluation**	
5:30 PM	**Dinner**	
6:30 PM	**Celebrating Diversity – Myers Briggs Personality Types**	
8:00 PM	**Adjourn**	

Time	Content/Process	Logistics

DAY 2

Time	Content/Process	Logistics
7:30 AM	**Continental Breakfast**	
8:00 AM (10)	**Feedback On Evaluations, Agenda**	
8:10 (100) (15) (55) (15) (45)	**Looking at Where We Are: Part I** *Framing:* *Strategic Planning Model* *Working definition of Mission, Vision and Values.* Have each table read the Mission, Vision, and Values for the two organizations. For each, list : - Similarities - Differences **Post and Read Assignment** "Using the data that you have generated and what you believe, draft the Mission, Vision, Values for the Manufacturing Organization Post these, and then spend some time reading what others have posted." Working as a whole group, develop a draft, if possible, for each of the Mission, Vision, Values. Identify issues in each that a subgroup made up of representatives from each of the two organizations can address. This group will meet outside this meeting and address the issues and prepare a draft for review at the first "Reunion."	Combining the Mission, Vision and Values from the two organizations Handout at the break. - Original company's Mission, Vision, Values - Organization 2's Mission, Vision, Values - Strategic Planning Model
10:15 (15)	**Break**	

CHAPTER 6: ALTERNATIVE DESIGNS: POSSIBILITIES FOR SPECIFIC WHOLE-SCALE INTERVENTIONS

Time	Content/Process	Logistics

10:30	**Looking at Where We Are: Part II**	**LOGISTICS**
(65) (5)	*Framing: You need to identify the key transition issues that the organization needs to address over the next three to six months. A key issue is an opportunity that you have or an issue that you must address to make this a smooth transition.*	
(20)	**Assignment**	
(20) (20)	<ul><li>"Each table brainstorm all of the key issues that you can think of.</li><li>Choose the five most important from that list.</li><li>Post your five for everyone to read</li><li>Each table leaves one person behind to answer questions about any of the issues on the list.</li><li>Everyone gets five votes – two * - "if we don't do this we will fail"; - and three ✓'s – "these are very important as well."</li><li>Tabulate the votes</li><li>The CEO and his key staff will make the final decisions over lunch."</li></ul>	

| 11:45 (60) | **Lunch** | |

Time	Content/Process	Logistics
12:45 PM (45) (5) (20)	**Drafting Strategic Goals** - Revisit the Strategic Planning Model. Emphasize the definition of goals. - Describe "preferred futuring," where it originated and why it is useful to develop goals. **Assignment:** It is two years from today and you are pleased and proud of how well Manufacturing Organization is performing. What do you see that makes this so? - Each person write one idea per post-it note. - Write as many ideas as you can – be specific. 'Satisfied customers' is too vague. 'Customers tell us that we are easier to do business with than ever,' is more specific and helpful. - Post these on a flip chart sheet. - Each table take a page of flip chart paper with the post-its on it. - Sort the notes into three to five themes. - For each theme write a draft goal statement. - Each table read their draft goal statements. - Identify those that are common themes. - A subgroup will work on these after this session."	Everyone gets one-half packet of 3x5 inch post-it notes and a black felt tip pen. Logistics walk around and pick up the post-its and stick them on flip chart sheets.
3:00 (15)	**Break** On the way to the break, participants need to sign up for one of the work groups for the following: - Mission, Vision, Values - Transition topics: - Goals	Post sign-up sheets, one for each work group area.

Time	Content/Process	Logistics
3:15 (25)	**Back Home Planning** "Re-form into working groups. In your group discuss: ▪ What have we learned here that impacts our work? ▪ What are we going to do differently to take advantage of what we have learned? What do we need to communicate to whom about what we have done here?	Handout assignment
3:40 (15)	**Next Steps** The CEO leads the group to determine next steps, helping them discuss the following question: "What are we going to do to continue the work that we have started on the Strategy and the Transition Issues" Participants and CEO decide that: ▪ Teams will meet ▪ The organization will have a "Reunion of this group" on June 3 to continue the work the group has started here.	CEO
3:55 (05)	**Evaluation**	Evaluation Handout
4:00 PM	**Adjourn**	

A Training and Education Organization in the U.S. Government
Designing the New Organization

Situation and Convening Issue:

In 1997, an agency of the U.S. Government asked its Office of Training and Education (OTE) to move to a Working Capital Fund operation. This meant that essentially the Office would become a for-profit business, operating with the agency as its primary customer and the government community as a secondary set of customers. The move to this new form of organization required new budgets, marketing plans, a real understanding of the customer's needs and a complete business plan to be submitted to and approved by the appropriate agency staff.

The internal change team made up of the senior leaders of OTE and an internal consulting team charged with developing the business plan realized that the key to success in this shift was the staff. Moving to a Working Capital Fund not only required a different way of doing business, but demanded a transformation in the culture of this office as well.

To be successful OTE had to (1) redesign many of its business processes; (2) engage with and understand the customers' requirements (now and two to three years out); (3) change the organization structure, many of the managerial jobs and most of the support organization's roles and responsibilities; and (4) involve everyone in the decisions that would transform the culture.

During October 1997 the internal change team devised their plan. The critical issues were (1) getting middle management commitment; (2) engaging the entire staff; (3) transitioning a new leader for the organization; and (4) making it all happen and be ready to implement by the start of the new fiscal year.

The plan called for:

- Concurrent work being done for the management system and the Working Capital Fund Project Team
- A series of Whole-Scale events (called WOW's for "Whole Office Workshops") and small-scale events
- Task teams engaged in everything from interviewing customers to designing processes developing marketing plans

CHAPTER 6: ALTERNATIVE DESIGNS: POSSIBILITIES FOR
SPECIFIC WHOLE-SCALE INTERVENTIONS

Roadmap

The roadmap depicts the activities Dannemiller Tyson Associates engaged in with the client. You will see a series of Management Off-Sites (prior to each Whole Office Workshop), the four WOW's themselves and the interim task teamwork that contributed to the larger events. This chapter describes the WOW #3, the meeting in which the whole office chose the new organization design to take into the Working Capital system. WOW #3 followed WOW #2 in which the entire office determined the qualities and attributes they would like to see in the new organization, and the Management system off-site, where all of the managers (approximately 60) met to develop the structural options the whole system would choose from.

Immediately following this session, the next level of organization design (what we called Mezzo Design) began. Mezzo Design took the high level template agreed to in WOW #3 and determined the next levels of specificity (e.g., roles and responsibilities, hierarchy; integrating and coordinating mechanisms across the new groups, etc.).

Event Purpose and its role in the overall process

WOW #3's purpose was to " embrace a new organizational model with a shared commitment to make it happen!" This two-day meeting involved the entire workforce in selecting, from the three options created by managers, the new organization framework.

The work force also incorporated ideas from the other two models into the final. Over the course of two days 350 people from across the organization reached consensus on the new model and put in place plans to make it happen in the next four months!

This meeting was pivotal in several respects. First, those who wished to maintain the old way of doing things lobbied for the model most like today. Second, customers and leaders were concerned that the model chosen would not meet the longer-term needs of the Agency. Finally, many believed that the Director really had the answer predetermined and that in the end, he would not accept their choice. Ultimately 350 people choose the most forward thinking, customer aligned and creative solution from among the three choices available to them. People were able, with a common database about personal needs, customer needs and the longer term direction of the Agency, to select the least selfish and most enlightened solution.

Being apart of this, and seeing everyone come together for the greater good of the Office, provided the fuel to really propel everyone forward.

Brief Results and Continuation Plans

The most significant results were the following:

- Cost reduced 10%
- Significantly reduced levels of management and manager to staffing ratio without a single grievance
- The creation of two new organizations, positioned to better align with customers needs
- 30% of positions changed/recreated to create customer focus
- Increased freedom on the part of staff to band together to market and provide services to the customer
- The introduction of a sophisticated knowledge management system to provide real-time customer, business and office information to every staff member

The organization continues to use Whole-Scale processes as a way of working together. They engage microcosms to continue to refine roles and tasks. The organization has designed and facilitated its own reunion involving the whole office.

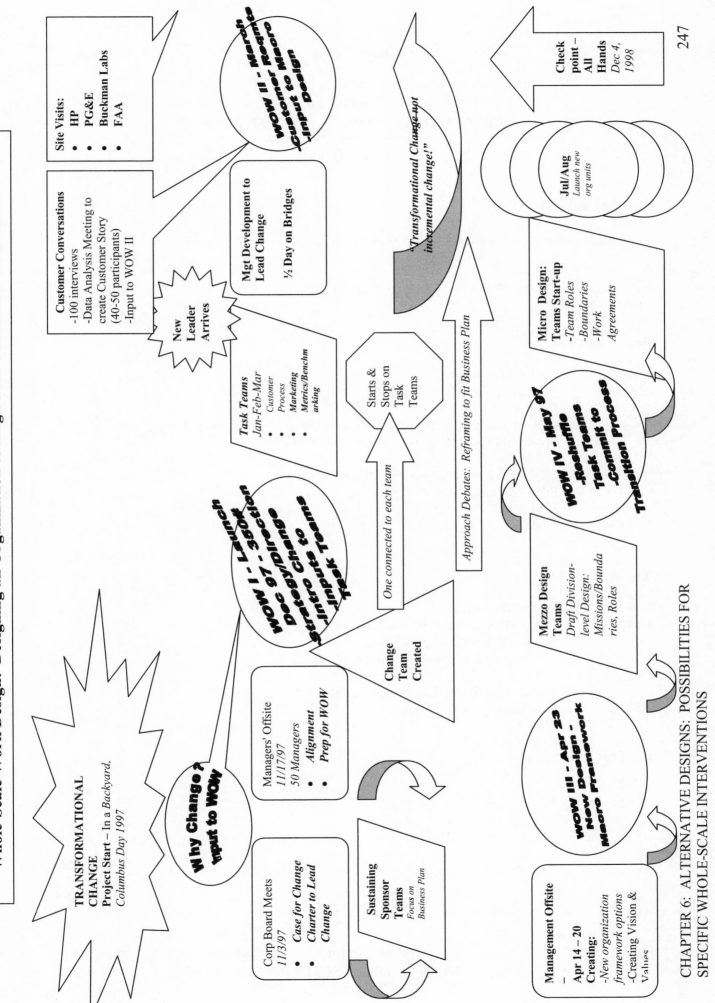

Whole-Scale Work Design: Designing an Organization to Align with Customers' Missions…

Site Visits:
- HP
- PG&E
- Buckman Labs
- FAA

Customer Conversations
-100 interviews
-Data Analysis Meeting to create Customer Story (40-50 participants)
-Input to WOW II

WOW II - March Customer to Macro Customer to Input Design

Check point – All Hands *Dec 4, 1998*

Mgt Development to Lead Change
½ Day on Bridges

New Leader Arrives

"Transformational Change not incremental change!"

Jul/Aug *Launch new org units*

Micro Design: Teams Start-up
-Team Roles
-Boundaries
-Work Agreements

TRANSFORMATIONAL CHANGE
Project Start – In a Backyard, *Columbus Day 1997*

Task Teams
Jan-Feb-Mar
- Customer
- Process
- Marketing
- Metrics/Benchmarking

Starts & Stops on Task Teams

Approach Debates: Reframing to fit Business Plan

WOW IV - May 97
-Reshuffle Task Teams to Commit to Transition Process

One connected to each team

Why Change? Input to WOW

Managers' Offsite
11/17/97
50 Managers
- Alignment
- Prep for WOW

WOW I - Launch Dec 97 - 350+ Strategy/Direction Change to -Intros Teams Task Teams -Inputs Teams

Change Team Created

Mezzo Design Teams
Draft Division-level Design: Missions/Boundaries, Roles

WOW III - Apr 23 - New Design - Macro Framework

Corp Board Meets
11/3/97
- Case for Change
- Charter to Lead Change

Sustaining Sponsor Teams
Focus on Business Plan

Management Offsite
– *Apr 14 – 20*
Creating:
-New organization framework options
-Creating Vision & Values

247

CHAPTER 6: ALTERNATIVE DESIGNS: POSSIBILITIES FOR SPECIFIC WHOLE-SCALE INTERVENTIONS

WOW #3
ENSURING OTE'S FUTURE IN A WCF ENVIRONMENT:
Designing the New Office
April 23 & 24

WOW #3 Purpose:

To embrace a new organizational model with a shared commitment to make it happen!

AGENDA

Day 1 – April 23

8:00 AM	Coffee Shop Open
8:30 AM	Purpose & Agenda
	Connecting at our Tables
	Getting grounded in the Macro Design: Presentations & Open Forum
	Possibility Panel: Presentations & Open Forum
	LUNCH
	Exploring 3 Models from the Macro Design
	Pros & Cons
	Evaluation
4:30 PM	Close

Day 2 – April 24

8:00 AM	Coffee Shop Open
8:30 AM	Feedback on Evaluations and Agenda for Today
	Assessing & Enriching the Models
	Agreeing on Our New Organizational Model
	LUNCH
	Taking Next Steps: Understanding the Work
	Contributing to Next Steps
	Wrap-Up
	Evaluation
4:30 PM	Close

WOW #3

ENSURING OTE'S FUTURE IN A WCF ENVIRONMENT:
Designing the New Office
April 23 & 24, 1998

STAGING DAY – April 22

April 22 9:30AM 'til finished	Staging	Room in General
	Everything set up and ready to go! Presenters ready Logistics Team - clear on roles & goals, agenda flow, for the day	▪ Max-mix seating--tables of eight ▪ Nametags on registration table, each name tag with table # on it. ▪ Microphones set up: four cordless, hand-held microphones; one at podium, two on panel table. ▪ Up-front: Riser with podium & panel table. Open Forum Grid --on podium

| | | ▪ One Flipchart easel available for each table, set up around periphery of room to start the day.

On each table:
▪ In-Basket
▪ Open Forum Tent Cards
▪ Marker pens

At each place setting:
▪ One-page handout of purpose/agenda
▪ Summary of WOW #2 evaluations
▪ Customer Story with graphic on cover
▪ Characteristics of new Office (WOW #1)

Other supplies:
▪ masking tape 1"
▪ 4x6 post-it notes |

CHAPTER 6: ALTERNATIVE DESIGNS: POSSIBILITIES FOR
SPECIFIC WHOLE-SCALE INTERVENTIONS.

249

WOW #3
ENSURING OTE'S FUTURE IN A WCF ENVIRONMENT:
Designing the New Office
April, 1998

WOW#3 Purpose:
To embrace a new organizational model with a shared commitment to make it happen!

DAY 1

Time	Content/Process	Logistics
8:00 AM (30)	**Coffee Available** Schmooze, have coffee Participants pick up name tag with table number on it	Name tags with seating on table outside room. Seating mixture at each table: ▪ Someone from macro design meeting ▪ Whole office representation ▪ Rotationals out and in sprinkled around ▪ Communications Group ▪ Champion Group
8:30 AM (15)	**Opening Remarks:** Eric will give the purpose & expectations for these two days. He will touch on the following ideas: ▪ Designing a new office is hard work ▪ The group is here to select the best choice & enhance it to make it work ▪ Who's here? The voice of the customer; plus one to two managers from the macro Event Planning Team at each table (they bring gifts, but nee to watch out—no lobbying, no control!) ▪ There will be a Town Hall Monday morning for those who can't attend to hear about the work this group will do these two days.	ERIC At each place setting: ▪ One-page handout of purpose/agenda ▪ Summary of WOW #2 evaluations ▪ Customer Story with graphic on cover ▪ Characteristics of new Office from December WOW (WOW #1)

	Feedback summary of evaluations from WOW#2 – *Agenda & Logistics:* • Describe the planning process for this meeting and who was involved. • Give the purpose & walk through the agenda for today • Describe logistics for the day (e.g., smoking, restrooms, telephones, security…anything else people need to know)	JAN FACILITATOR

8:45AM (15)	**Connecting at your Tables** At your table, each person take two minutes to introduce yourself and tell anything you want your table to know about you."	FACILITATOR This group had done so many getting connected and "telling our stories" assignments that the planning team told us to leave it very loose this time

9:00 AM (30) (05)	**Getting Grounded: Presentation** *Framing: Our assignment was to bring it down to three alternatives and we made no decisions until we had the whole office*	On tables, Twila's handouts: ▪ One-page agenda from macro-design ▪ Summary of advice to managers
(10)	**Presentations:** *Overview of Macro-Design work by management group* ▪ Big picture of five days ▪ Process/some of the tasks ▪ Key lessons about design the group took away ▪ 70% comfortable-100% committed/ decision criteria	TWILA
	Products we "produced": ▪ -What business we are in – Eric ▪ -Values we share – Eric (10 minutes) ▪ ▪ -Lines of Business - Manny ▪ Criteria by which we judge the structure: how we got them, how we used them	ERIC & MANNY Other handouts on cue when Eric gets up to speak: ▪ What business are we in ▪ OTE Statements of Values ▪ Lines of Business ▪ Criteria for Judging Design Alternatives
(20)	*Key messages:* We don't want you to lock in on these - Manny 1. These do not presume that we will do these in-house 2. We can't decide until we know what the customer	(Note: these handouts were put on Lotus Notes this week, prior to workshop and provided as pre-reading for people)

CHAPTER 6: ALTERNATIVE DESIGNS: POSSIBILITIES FOR
SPECIFIC WHOLE-SCALE INTERVENTIONS.

251

Time	Content/Process	Logistics
9:30 AM (45) (15)	wants 3. These are fluid 4. Business drivers will cause change *Criteria we used* **Open Forum** Tables discuss the following questions: ▪ What did you hear? ▪ What are your reactions? ▪ What questions of understanding & clarification do you have? For whom? Have each table choose a new facilitator, recorder and reporter/question asker Tell them all the presenters will be on the panel for Q&A	Three Open Forum Questions on Table-Tent on each table Open Forum Grid --on podium

	Content/Process	Logistics
(30)	**Q&A with presenters** Save last 10-15 minutes, move to "burning questions"	Three to four microphone people Ask tables to put table #'s upright, visible for microphone people

Time	Content/Process	Logistics
10:15 AM (15)	**Break**	▪ John greets presenters and brings them to consultants' table to connect. ▪ Huddle w/model presenters on who, where, logistics

10:30 AM (30)	**Panel of Possibilities: Presentations & Open Forum**
	
	Framing:
	▪ *Purpose: to get ideas,*
	▪ *Process: Listen to all, then Q&A*
	▪ *Who: (timekeeping agreement)*
	▪ *The three models you're going to hear after lunch incorporated many of the good ideas you're going to hear right now.*
	
	Presentations @ 6-10 minutes each:
	▪ Outside Speaker: Dept of the Interior
	▪ *Managerial Visits:*
	  ➢ Bruce K. (PG&E/HP)
	  ➢ Carol (Buckman Labs)
	  ➢ Mike D. – Procurement, Department of Interior, heads a power unit that essentially went out and found new business w/50% market outside Dept of Interior.
		Handout:
		Perhaps a mini agenda for presentations
		
		Handout of Site Visits
		
		Summary story w/handout
		
		For each company:
		▪ Background of company
		▪ Why changed
		▪ New model highlights
		▪ What they'd do differently
		▪ Lessons for our transformation, ideas applicable to us.

11:00 AM (15)	**Open Forum** Tables discuss the following questions: ▪ What did you hear? ▪ What are your reactions? ▪ What questions of understanding & clarification do you have? ...For whom? Tell them all the presenters will be on the panel for Q&A	
(45)	**Q&A with presenters** Save last 10-15 minutes, move to "burning questions"	Three to four microphone people ▪ Ask tables to put table #'s upright, visible for microphone people; ▪ Ask spokespersons to stand to ask table's question
NOON (60)	**Lunch**	On your own

Time	Content/Process	Logistics
1:00 PM (5)	**Exploring 3 Models from Macro Design** *Framing:* ▪ *Stick to the big picture* ▪ *If you get stuck in the weeds, put your questions on post-its* ▪ *The details are not a part of this; microdesign comes next*	Four tables go to model 1, Station A; four tables go to model 1, Station B. Participants get 35 minutes at that station to hear the highlights. (20 to hear the highlights, 15 to ask questions, document for themselves their own pros & cons, and capture down-stream questions.)
(10)	**General Presentation to Whole Room:** "Before you go off to hear about each of the models, to see how they are different and to learn about the unique features of each, there is some general information we want you to hear about what they have in common. ▪ Common Assumptions ▪ Common Features ▪ Process we're going to use now to hear about the three	JOAN & LISA
1:15 PM (10)	**Walk-throughs of Three Models** Walk-through the Process: ▪ Six stations around room for approximately 35 people at each station (e.g., two stations for each model). ➢ Customized Solutions Model ➢ Entrepreneurial Franchise Model ➢ Knowledge Network Model ▪ Four huddles of four tables; two huddles of three tables.	3x5 card on each table listing Rounds Header above each station, with model name Pros & Cons Handout: One sheet for each of the three models, titled for that model Post-it notes at each station for people to write downstream questions on.

(130) 2:30 PM (15)	At each model: (20) Presentation on that model (15) Participants ask questions of understanding; note on sheet what they see as the pros & cons of this model, put post-its on questions for future implementation. Build in a Break	
2:45 PM (35)	***Round III***	Once completed, everyone goes back to their assigned table

3:25 PM (60)	**Pros & Cons:** *Table Assignment:*	On tables: complete packets of all three models

CHAPTER 6: ALTERNATIVE DESIGNS: POSSIBILITIES FOR SPECIFIC WHOLE-SCALE INTERVENTIONS

	▪ "For each model, discuss your individual reactions to the three models, pros and cons. ▪ Then flipchart your tables' summary of the pros and cons to each model. ▪ Note that there are two people at each table who were at the macro-design who can help others to speak. ▪ Roll & save their pro/con flipchart sheets when they are finished. ▪ Think about the models and what you wrote overnight"	

4:25 PM	**Evaluation** ▪ With some enhancements from our table, I could be 70% comfortable and 100% committed to one of these options. Circle one 1 = Nothing could get me from here to there 3 = If the right one gets picked, I'd still be okay 5 = With some changes I could live with any one of these Why did you mark it the way you did? ▪ Given how the group worked together today, what are the ground-rules that I think are critical for our success tomorrow? ▪ What needs to happen tomorrow in order for you to leave feeling you accomplished your purpose **Close**	Handout on cue WOW 2 Event Planning Team & Integration Team stay to read evaluations
4:30 PM		Game Plan over Dinner.

CHAPTER 6: ALTERNATIVE DESIGNS: POSSIBILITIES FOR
SPECIFIC WHOLE-SCALE INTERVENTIONS.

255

Time	Content/Process	Logistics

DAY 2

8:30 AM	**Summary of Evaluations & Agenda for Today**	

8:40 AM (90) (15)	**Assessing & Enriching the Models:**
	
	Purpose: Building acceptance for all three options
	
	Room-wide:
	Eric roams among the tables with a microphone (Donahue-style) and asks people what they thought:
	• What ab*out each* model do you find attractive? And why?
	• For each of you, which model represents
	   ➢ Comfort?
	   ➢ Challenge?	

9:00 AM (45)	**Table Assignment:** "Given your criteria and your assessment yesterday afternoon, look at each model. Assume that each of these models has been chosen as the preferred model. Your job as a table is now to look at each model and answer the following question: What improvements would need to be incorporated into this model to get everyone at our table 70% comfortable, 100% committed to it?"	

CHAPTER 6: ALTERNATIVE DESIGNS: POSSIBILITIES FOR SPECIFIC WHOLE-SCALE INTERVENTIONS

10:10 AM (20)	**Agreeing on Our Organizational Model**	Put multiple voting sheets for each model, spread them apart so people are not crowded, and can get to the voting.
	Framing: Using the metaphor of "platform" for building a car), we are converging on the "platform"-- a platform on which to build the chassis.	
	Framing Points:	
	• There's been a lot of talk about "voting" (proxies, etc…) I want to disengage you from voting and have you think about choosing – a platform to build on.	
	• Both/and – You can choose one platform and add features from others	
	• Think about it as the future. You can transition; be where the hockey puck will be.	
	• Go back to the criteria and look at the models. Which	
	➢ Takes you to future	
	➢ Meets criteria	
	➢ Is the most versatile to enhance	
(20)	**Voting Assignment**	
	Break/Vote on One Model:	
	• "Now pick the model that in this moment is the closest to the right answer with the least amount of work.	
	• Each person gets one green dot.	
	• Put your green dot on the blank sheet of paper next to the model you say is the right answer in the moment.	
	• Which in this moment is the closest to what the right answer needs to be? This is the model that is closest to a score. This is the model about which you are thinking, 'It may take a little work, but I could see us doing this.' "	

CHAPTER 6: ALTERNATIVE DESIGNS: POSSIBILITIES FOR
SPECIFIC WHOLE-SCALE INTERVENTIONS.

257

Time	Content/Process	Logistics
10:30 AM (10)	**Coming to Consensus:** Is there a clear choice? Convergence? Tell the room how the dots counted (including last night's choosing) ■ Knowledge Network (Actual votes 77/7) ■ Customized Solutions (39/14) ■ Entrepreneurial (45/1) Ask, Is there anyone who can't move forward?"	A number of people who could not be there the second day completed their voting prior to leaving the night before.
10:45 AM (30)	**Enriching the Model:** "Now, at your table, go back to the model you've just chosen and look at all the improvements you nominated earlier. Nominate the two to three key improvements that you believe are essential to your success in this new organizational model. Write each nominated improvement on a separate post-it." *Note: we didn't do the following assignment since we already had convergence, but it was an option we planned for:* *Tables pair-up to discuss and nominate two to three improvements. Write each nominated improvement on a separate post-it. Pick a spokesperson for your table pair.*	4x6 Post-it notes for each table
11:15 AM (30) 11:50 AM (60)	**Affinity Diagram Improvements:** Call outs ■ Have one table calls out one improvement. ■ Ask, "How many other tables had a similar one?" ■ Repeat callout process until participants have no more improvements to suggest. **Lunch & Voting on Improvements:** Each person gets one blue dot. Put the blue dot on the improvement that is essential to incorporate into our chosen framework.	Flipcharts up-front labeled "Key Improvements" with eight inch left-hand margin for voting Logistics picks up all related post-its and puts on flipchart.

CHAPTER 6: ALTERNATIVE DESIGNS: POSSIBILITIES FOR SPECIFIC WHOLE-SCALE INTERVENTIONS

1:00 PM (10)	**Report out of Big Vote Getters**	
1:10 PM (10)	Describe Next Steps to Finalize Model: Six-member team (Three from original team who worked on this model, and three others) will work this afternoon to incorporate recommended improvements and report out to you at end of today for your 70-100 check	Self-select; then recruit

1:20 PM (20)	**Taking Next Steps: Understanding the Work**	ERIC AND BARRY
	Eric: Says thank you to everyone who has been on teams to date. Brings closure to and thanks the old teams.	***Teams*** ▪ Unit Design (three to four teams) ▪ HR ▪ Cost/Finance ▪ Internal Communications ▪ External Communications ▪ Marketing
	Barry: Describes the work that needs to happen between now and Memorial Day. Explains mezzo-level work, micro, and implementation.	
	Asks what the buckets of work are and how will they coordinate and integrate?	▪ Technology/ Knowledge Management ▪ Curriculum Development Process ▪ Product Development Process (and that may be a role in one of the models) ▪ Integration Group (chair of each team) to resolve cross-group issues,
	Tell people that today they will self-select to work on one of those teams to get them started.	
	Forming Work/teams: Eric (handout) ▪ Select team leadership (why new and who) ▪ Self-select into teams ▪ Take team charters (given drafts)	
	Tells everyone, "Be at all-hands Monday morning."	And do the Business Plan! Handout of Team Charters

CHAPTER 6: ALTERNATIVE DESIGNS: POSSIBILITIES FOR SPECIFIC WHOLE-SCALE INTERVENTIONS.

259

Time	Content/Process	Logistics
1:40 PM (90)	**Contributing to Next Steps** Tell participants, "Self-select to spend time today with the team you are most interested in." Describe the assignment. Be clear about signup for team membership. Be clear about the fact that when people link up with a group today, that does not assume automatic "membership" on the team. Membership is scoped, today's work is short term and tactical.	Identify Breakout areas/tables Team Headers posted at breakouts. Sign-up process for Teams Date of first meeting for each team.
(60)	*Team Assignment*: ▪ Review the charter ▪ Think the next 30 days. What's doable? ▪ Is the purpose clear? ▪ Are the deliverables understandable? Are they doable? ▪ What advice does this team need to help them work better?	Double Feature: The Model Finalization Team meets to incorporate improvements and prepare report out at end of day.
(30)	**Report outs**: Three minutes per team Includes Finalization Team	

3:10 PM (15)	**Finalization Team Reports-Out** 70/100 check point (get applause on)	

3:25 PM (15)	**Wrap-up Points:** ▪ *Uplifting* ▪ Nobody taking it lightly; everyone serious ▪ Benevolence ▪ Anxiety provoking ▪ Thank them (good work these two days) ▪ Nobody died in Lewis/Clark	ERIC Thank you's: Give Eric list of logistics people, including their organization

3:45 PM (5) 3:50 PM	**Evaluation** (same as at Macro design meeting) **Close** Event Planning Team, Change Management Team, New Integration Team members stay to read evaluations and discuss next steps.	Handout on cue

METRO POLICE DEPARTMENT

Situation/Convening Issue for Metro Police Department

The recently appointed Chief of the Metro Police Department brought together the command staff to build a common picture of the strategic direction of the department.
The new Chief was anxious to hear from his leadership team about the issues and challenges they faced on a daily basis that impacted their ability to provide optimal service to their community. It was important that each person felt safe enough to speak his or her individual truth and give honest feedback without fear of retribution. The Chief (who came up through the ranks of this same organization) was committed to developing a new culture of openness and trust to help move the department forward.

Event Purpose

The event planning team (EPT) believed the purpose of their first event was to combine their wisdom and experience as leaders and work as a team to create a Metro Police Department that they and the community could be proud of. In addition to their own departmental goals, the department needed to continually integrate the over-arching, city-wide goals (as defined by the Mayor) into their own strategy. For one and one-half days, they worked closely together to:

- Help the Chief see the world in which they lived daily,
- Better understand the pressures and challenges that the Chief was facing,
- Identify their most pressing operational issues and concerns, and
- Agree on what needed to happen to enable them to serve their community better.

Results/Sustaining the Momentum

The response to this first meeting was tremendously positive as participants expressed their appreciation for the opportunity to speak freely and openly, some for the first time in their many years of service with the department. Task teams took on the responsibility to continue working on the issues that event participants identified as priorities. Participants agreed on key messages and ways to report the results/outputs of this event and ways to stay connected as they moved forward. The Chief committed to periodic reunion meetings to keep the dialogue open with the command staff, monitor progress, and continue to involve his leadership team in shaping the future of their department.

CHAPTER 6: ALTERNATIVE DESIGNS: POSSIBILITIES FOR
SPECIFIC WHOLE-SCALE INTERVENTIONS.

261

Metro Police Department
Leadership Conference
Fall 1998

Purpose:

To combine our wisdom and experience as leaders and work as a team to create a Metro Police Department that the community and we can be proud of.

Desired Outcomes:

- Create a climate of openness and trust that facilitates on-going communication amongst the Command Staff.

- Develop a common definition of police service and community relations, and the implications for our work.

- Gain deeper understanding of our needs and our role in supporting this department.

7:30 AM **(30)**	**Breakfast**	▪ Names tags in alpha order on registration table. ▪ Eighty participants seated in max-mix; rounds of eight. ▪ One page agenda/purpose (table roles on reverse side) at each place. ▪ First assignment in in-boxes. ▪ Table numbers; tent card with open forum questions on each table. ▪ Mike grid taped to podium. ▪ Security check for Mayor's visit.
8:00 **(10)**	**Welcome** Chief of Police welcomes his command staff and turns mike over to Police Commander/EPT member.	CHIEF OF POLICE *Purpose: To communicate what the Chief expects from the event and set the tone for the two days.*
8:10 **(10)**	**Purpose/Agenda/Logistics/Norms** ▪ Commander/EPT member introduces rest of EPT members; presents purpose statement and discusses process for developing purpose, outcomes and agenda for the event. Turns mike over to facilitator. ▪ Facilitator reviews agenda/logistics/ norms (cell phones, responding to calls) and explain the purpose of max-mix seating.	COMMANDER/EPT MEMBER *Purpose: To clarify what the participants can expect in the next two days.* *Emphasize purpose again.*

Time	Content/Process	Logistics
8:20 **(40)** (20) (10) (10)	**Table Introductions: Building a Common Database** *Assignment:* "Take two minutes to prepare to introduce yourself to the rest of your table group by responding to the following: <ul><li>Name, assignment, background, how long have you worked for MPD?</li><li>What has MPD accomplished in the past year that made you feel especially proud?</li><li>What you have found to be most frustrating for MPD in the past year?</li><li>What you need to get out of the next two days?</li></ul> Each person has two minutes to share answers with the table group. Choose a facilitator to keep time." Summarize on flip chart paper: <ul><li>Common Themes</li><li>Significant Differences</li><li>Desired Outcomes</li></ul> Choose a recorder and spokesperson." **Call Outs**	*Purpose: To clarify what the participants can expect in the next two days.* Handouts in in-boxes. Assignment on flipchart. Logistics captures call outs on flipcharts in front of room. Post during Break.
9:00 **(15)**	**Stakeholder View: The Mayor's Vision for Metro** The mayor presents his vision for a "world class" city, role of MPD.	THE MAYOR *Purpose: To show his support for the MPD and this event and commit to partnering with MPD to create a safer Metro that everyone can be proud of.* [Note: Must be flexible here in case Mayor's arrival is delayed, etc.)
9:15 **(15)**	**Break**	Check panel set-up for leadership's presentation. Keep as informal as possible.
9:30 **(75)**	**View From the MPD Leadership's Bridge**	CHIEF, ASST. CHIEF, DEPUTY CHIEFS *Purpose: To hear the perspectives of top*

(30)	Presentation – Chief, Asst. Chief, Deputy Chiefs (5-7 mins. each) Frank discussion focused on: ▪ What we will build on from the past ▪ What we need to do differently ▪ Creating a climate of openness and trust.	*leadership and their vision for the department focusing on the upcoming calendar year.* *(This is the new Leadership's first opportunity to address the department in this type of forum.)* Chief to provide a macro perspective; Asst. Chief to discuss operational matters; Deputy Chief to represent the precincts; a different Deputy Chief to present bureau perspective. Refer participants to tent cards for Open Forum questions.
(15)	**Open Forum:** Tables discuss the following questions: ▪ What did we hear? ▪ What are our reactions? ▪ What questions of understanding do we have and of whom?	Mike grid taped to podium; logistics also has grids, and is ready with cordless mikes.
(30)	**Facilitated Q&A** (Save last 10 mins. for "burning" questions.)	

Time	Content/Process	Logistics
10:45 **(45)**	**Organizational Diagnosis: What Does the Survey Tell Us?**	*Purpose: Internal perspective - begin to look at how we presently operate and opportunities for improvement.*
(15)	Presentation of Survey Results	Handout of survey results on cue. (Survey results presented by public affairs firm as one data point for understanding how the organization presently operates.)
(20)	Choose a facilitator, recorder, and spokesperson. Tables discuss the following questions: ▪ What was surprising to you regarding the survey results? ▪ What insights did you gain from the survey results? Record responses on flipchart paper and prioritize for call outs.	Assignment on flipcharts.
(10)	**Call Outs (Value-Added)**	Logistics captures call outs up front. Post during lunch.
11:30 **(60)**	**Lunch**	
12:30 **(75)**	**What's Working/Not Working** Topics: ▪ Empowerment (Decision Making) ▪ Internal Processes ▪ Quality of Work Life ▪ Resource Allocation ▪ Career Development/Rewards and Recognition ▪ Paperwork	Handouts: Assignment (everyone); List of Topics (highlight one topic on each sheet in advance so that topics are evenly divided among the number of tables; randomly distribute one sheet to each table now).
(15)	*Assignment:* (Part I) 1. "Choose a facilitator, recorder, and spokesperson. 2. Agree on a working definition of your topic. 3. Brainstorm everything you can think of that's working/not working for your topic. (Remember this is a brainstorm, not a debate!)	Sample template on flipchart up front. Refer to rules of brainstorming. Logistics posts sheets under topic headers for voting. Spokespersons from tables with same topics count and report out top vote-getters to whole group.
(20)	*Roam/Read/Vote* Each person gets *three checkmarks per*	

CHAPTER 6: ALTERNATIVE DESIGNS: POSSIBILITIES FOR SPECIFIC WHOLE-SCALE INTERVENTIONS

	topic for those items you strongly agree are *working; three checkmarks per topic* for those items you strongly agree are *not working*!	*Purpose: To identify some "quick hitters" that would have an immediate impact on our daily operations and begin to boost morale throughout MPD.*
(10)	**Report Outs**	
(20)	*Verbal Assignment:* (Part II) 1. Reflecting on the top vote-getters for your topic, what ideas/recommendations can you propose to leadership to make a difference in this particular topic area (start/stop/continue)? **Identify at least one opportunity for a "quick hit", i.e. achievable and doable within the next 30-60 days.** Be as specific as possible. 2. Record your responses on flipchart paper. Please include your table number in case clarification is needed. Be prepared to report out your table's headlines including "quick hit" opportunity."	Revisit table roles. Logistics to collect data during Break. Have on hand for the evening turnaround session with leadership.
(10)	**Report Outs** (Headlines only!)	
1:45 (15)	**Break**	

Time	Content/Process	Logistics
2:00 **(115)**	**What is Goal-Based Governance System (GBGS) and What Does It Mean To Us?**	*Purpose: To gain shared understanding of the city's GBGS vision, mission, goals, measures, and targets, the specific implications for the police department, and how we must integrate MPD's goals with the overall goals of the city.*
(30)	**Presentation on GBGS** (including 15 min. tape from the Mayor on GBGS).	Handouts on cue.
	Tables discuss the following questions: ▪ What did we hear? ▪ What are our reactions? ▪ What questions of understanding do we have and for whom?	DEPUTY CHIEF Deputy Chief to focus on the plan for the next calendar year.
(15)	**Break**	Advise participants that Q&A will be held after next presentation.
(15)	**Presentation on MPD Reorganization Strategy**	ASSISTANT CHIEF Handouts on cue.
(15)	Tables discuss the following questions: ▪ What did we hear? ▪ What are our reactions? ▪ What questions of understanding do we have and for whom?	
(40)	**Facilitated Q&A with the entire Leadership Team–Chief, Asst. Chief, Deputy Chiefs)** (Save last 10 mins. for "burning questions.)	Logistics ready with cordless mikes.

CHAPTER 6: ALTERNATIVE DESIGNS: POSSIBILITIES FOR SPECIFIC WHOLE-SCALE INTERVENTIONS

3:55 (30)	**Feedback on Strategy** *Assignment* "Choose a facilitator, recorder, and spokesperson. In your table groups, discuss the following: • As we reflect on the GBGS and the reorganization strategy, what did we learn about our strategic direction? • What remains unclear to us? What's missing? • What would help us to move forward? • What is our advice to leadership? Record your responses on flipchart paper. Please include your table number in case clarification is needed."	*Purpose: To provide leadership with honest feedback on the strategic direction of the department.* Assignment on flipcharts. Data will be collected by logistics for use in turnaround session with leadership.
4:25 (15)	**Wrap-Up** Final thoughts from the Chief letting participants know he *will* participate in tonight's turnaround but will be unable to attend tomorrow. Assistant Chief and Deputy Chiefs will communicate the results of the turnaround session tomorrow.	CHIEF OF POLICE *Purpose: To express his on-going commitment to this open communication process and reiterate his support for implementing actions agreed upon during this event.*
4:40 (5)	**Evaluations** • Highs • Lows • Advice for tomorrow?	Handout on cue. Logistics to collect at the door.
4:45 pm	**Adjourn**	Invite the EPT to review evaluations and discuss next day's agenda. Leadership team convenes to prepare for the Day 2 "Response from Leadership."

DAY 2

Time	Content/Process	Logistics
7:30 am (30)	**Breakfast**	
8:00 (5)	**Evaluation Feedback/Agenda Review**	
8:05 (85) (40)	**Response From Leadership** Presentation: Reaction(s) to input from yesterday: ▪ Survey results; What's working/not working; feedback on strategy ▪ Here's what we changed in the strategy and why. ▪ Next steps for continuing the work, moving forward.	*Purpose: Demonstrate that yesterday's input was valued/heard.* LEADERSHIP PANEL—ASSISTANT CHIEF, DEPUTY CHIEFS **Important:** Remind participants that the Chief did participate in the turnaround and was directly involved in developing leadership's response.
(15) (20)	**Open Forum**: ▪ Table Discussion ▪ Q&A (Five mins. for "burning" questions.)	Mike grids. Logistics ready with mikes.
(10)	*Formation of Action Teams* Recruit volunteers "real time" and create action teams to continue working with leadership after this meeting to implement agreements.	Leadership proposes framework for action teams taking into consideration existing task forces and standing committees. Ask volunteers to report to the front of the room for coaching on next steps.
9:30 (15)	**Break**	

9:45 (45)	**Sustaining the Momentum**	*Purpose: To sustain our momentum by agreeing on key messages from this event and ways to bring the rest of MPD on board.*
(15)	*Assignment:* "Choose a facilitator, recorder, and spokesperson. In your table groups, discuss the following: ■ What are the key messages that we will take away from this event? (What will you tell someone that wasn't here?) Prepare a 1-min. headline report.	Assignment on flipcharts.
(10)	**Report Outs (Value-Added)**	Logistics ready with mikes. Logistics to collect data after report outs.
(15)	**Communication Processes** Room-wide brainstorm on processes for communicating meeting results/outputs (including existing forums).	Logistics to capture on flipcharts.
(5)	**Wrap-Up** Plans for transcribing and distributing outputs from this meeting.	
10:30 (60) (40)	**What is Ideal Police Service?** *Assignment:* ■ "Choose a facilitator, recorder and spokesperson. ■ At your table, brainstorm all of the elements of ideal police service and community relations. ■ Review the data and agree on the top two or three elements that are most critical. ■ Write a definition that includes these critical elements. Record on flipchart paper."	Purpose: To give participants an opportunity to explore different views regarding "police service" and community relations and establish a common definition (what it is and what it isn't). Bridge to afternoon's guest speaker. Handout on cue.

CHAPTER 6: ALTERNATIVE DESIGNS: POSSIBILITIES FOR SPECIFIC WHOLE-SCALE INTERVENTIONS.

271

Time	Content/Process	Logistics

(10)	Report Outs	Logistics ready with mikes.
(10)	Assignment: • In your table groups, discuss your reactions to the various definitions. • Determine recurring themes. • What did you hear that surprised you? • Based on what you've heard, what changes (if any) would you make to your earlier definition? • Record final version on flipchart paper; keep your sheet at your table.	Assignment on flipcharts. Logistics will collect flipchart papers at the end of the day.
11:30 **(60)**	**Lunch**	

| **12:30**

 (75)

 (15) | **Polishing Brass: Mastering Police Service and Securing Community Support**

 Part I.
 How to Stay Motivated Through the Difficult Times

 Break | GUEST SPEAKER

 Purpose: To stimulate thinking about ways to optimize police service by seeking more opportunities to demonstrate leadership in our daily work. |

| **2:00**
 (120) | Part II.
 Leadership's Challenge: Getting the Best From Detroit's Finest
 (Personality Type Indicators) | Purpose: Optimizing police service by getting the most from our team. |

| **4:00**
 (10) | **Closing Remarks** | ASSISTANT CHIEF |

| **4:10**
 (5) | **Evaluations**
 • What were the most significant outcomes of these two days for you? | Handout on cue. Logistics to collect at the door. |

CHAPTER 6: ALTERNATIVE DESIGNS: POSSIBILITIES FOR
                    SPECIFIC WHOLE-SCALE INTERVENTIONS

	<ul><li>On a scale of 1-10, how confident are you that we'll keep the commitments to action that we've made here today?</li><li>(Not a snowball's chance…watch our dust)</li><li>Why did you mark where you did?</li></ul>	
4:15 pm	**Adjourn**	Invite the Leadership and EPT to stay and read evaluations.

CHAPTER 6: ALTERNATIVE DESIGNS: POSSIBILITIES FOR
SPECIFIC WHOLE-SCALE INTERVENTIONS.

273

Time	Content/Process	Logistics

STRATEGIC REUNION DETAILED DESIGN
NEWCO

Purpose:

To check on the progress we've made in implementing the Action Plans from our Strategy Development Event.

Outcomes:

Our intended outcomes are:

- To assess progress against our Action Plans.
- To understand what we've learned from our Action Plan Implementation activities and results.
- To update our Action Plans as needed.

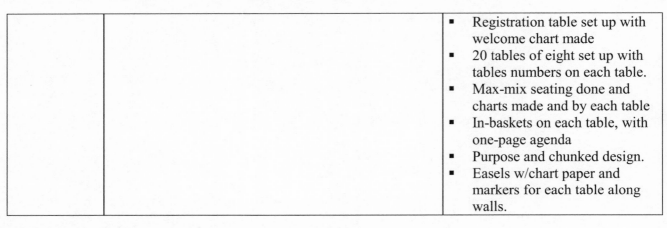

Time	Content/Process	Logistics
		▪ Registration table set up with welcome chart made ▪ 20 tables of eight set up with tables numbers on each table. ▪ Max-mix seating done and charts made and by each table ▪ In-baskets on each table, with one-page agenda ▪ Purpose and chunked design. ▪ Easels w/chart paper and markers for each table along walls.
7:30 AM (30)	**Continental Breakfast, Registration**	
8:00 AM (20)	**Welcome, Purpose, Agenda, Logistics** ▪ Newco President convenes meeting, welcoming participants and reading Purpose and Outcomes with passion. ▪ HR internal consultant covers agenda and logistics of meeting.	NEWCO PRESIDENT AND INTERNAL HR CONSULTANT.

CHAPTER 6: ALTERNATIVE DESIGNS: POSSIBILITIES FOR SPECIFIC WHOLE-SCALE INTERVENTIONS

9:20 AM (70) (05)	**Getting Reconnected** *Framing: Getting reconnected so we continue to build our common data base on how we're progressing on our Action Plans.* *Assignment:* "Choose a facilitator, recorder, and reporter. Take two minutes of "I" time to think about answers to the following questions: - What is your name and current role? If your role has changed, how? - What have you done in your work since the last reunion to make the Action Plan come to life? - What has frustrated you in your effort to make the Action Plan come to life since we developed it? - What did you learn from your activities in making the Action Plan come to life? - What are the particular challenges you are facing right now? - What do you need to get out of the morning in order to feel confident in your ability to help make the Action Plan come to life?	INTERNAL HR CONSULTANT
(40)	Now, each person take five minutes to share your responses with your tablemates. Choose a facilitator to keep time and a recorder and reporter.	
(10)	After you have shared responses, recorders take flip charts from easels and move easels out of the way. At your table, summarize common themes, differences and key outcomes. Reporters be prepared to call out your common themes, differences, and key outcomes." **Table Report Outs**.	Two logistics team members with flip charts up front to record callouts.
(15)		

Time	Content/Process	Logistics
9:25 AM (35) (05) (30)	**Action Plan Progress—Station Presentations** *Framing: Now we are going to take a deeper look at how we're doing as a basis for updating our Action Plans.* *Assignment:* "Divide your table to cover all eight Stations. Send a representative to each Station. Each representative's mission is to be a scout for the table to learn about: ■ Progress ■ Activities ■ Issues ■ Help needed Tables divide and conquer to cover all eight Stations. Collect info and come back prepared to report on Action Plan progress and issues."	INTERNAL HR CONSULTANT Set up eight Stations for the eight Action Plans: ■ Engineering ■ Operations ■ Finance ■ Contracts ■ Marketing ■ Information Systems ■ HR ■ Supplier Management Each station has a Station Master who gives a 15 minute presentation (based on one page—front and back side sheet) covering the Action Plan: ■ Objectives. ■ Key activities. ■ Results compared to objectives. ■ Issues and help needed to resolve them. Each person gets a handout of the one-page (front and back) presentation from each Station, but only goes to the Station assigned. Each station has a 15-minute Q&A session for understanding and clarification.
10:00 AM (15)	**Break**	

CHAPTER 6: ALTERNATIVE DESIGNS: POSSIBILITIES FOR SPECIFIC WHOLE-SCALE INTERVENTIONS

10:15 AM (50)	**Lessons Learned—How We're Doing**	INTERNAL HR CONSULTANT
(05)	*Framing: With the data collected, assess progress and lessons learned.*	
(30)	*Assignment:* "Choose a new facilitator, recorder, and reporter. At your tables, share what you each learned: • Progress • Issues • Help needed Prepare a flip chart that describes the most significant progress made, the most important issues, and the most critical help needed. Reporter prepare to call out."	
(15)	**Table Call Outs.**	
11:05 AM (95)	**Updating Our Action Plans.**	INTERNAL HR CONSULTANT Move to functional seating. Need breakout area handout for functional seating.
(05)	*Framing: With the data we've shared on progress and issues, let's update the Action Plans as part of action learning.*	
(65)	*Assignment:* • Move to your functional breakout areas. • Take your one-page sheet from each Station with you. • Based on all you know and have learned, make any necessary revisions to your Action Plans you need. • If you need help from another functional area, send a negotiator to that area and negotiate the help you need. • Prepare a three-minute report out on any changes you make to your Action Plan. including Objectives, Activities, and Help Needed **Functional Report Out**	
(25)		

CHAPTER 6: ALTERNATIVE DESIGNS: POSSIBILITIES FOR SPECIFIC WHOLE-SCALE INTERVENTIONS.

277

Time	Content/Process	Logistics
12:30 (05)	**Evaluation and Adjourn** Evaluation questions: ▪ What was the most important progress for you? ▪ What are the most significant issues for you? ▪ Based on the new Action Plans, how confident are you that the Strategy will work? ▪ 1—No way ▪ 10—it's in the bag ▪ Why did you answer the way you did?	INTERNAL HR CONSULTANT

CHAPTER 6: ALTERNATIVE DESIGNS: POSSIBILITIES FOR SPECIFIC WHOLE-SCALE INTERVENTIONS.

279

CHAPTER 6: ALTERNATIVE DESIGNS: POSSIBILITIES FOR
SPECIFIC WHOLE-SCALE INTERVENTIONS

Chapter 7
The Real Secrets of Whole-Scale

Those of you who have tried to follow someone's excellent recipe and then have had the product turn out to be something less than the chef produced, will know that the missing element is usually something that is so much part of what the chef believes, that he or she doesn't even think of it. We at Dannemiller Tyson Associates want to add some important pieces before you head out to actually utilize the very good tools of Whole-Scale. The real secret, that we do not want to forget to tell you, is in underlying principles and beliefs—about people, about empowerment, about integrity and trustworthiness—that shape everything we do. They are so important that the client will know, on some level, if you don't have them…and the recipe will produce a mediocre product. In our experience, our tools never truly fail…but mediocre is a failure we can't live with…and if you don't want to live with it either, compare your beliefs to the following.

We don't assume that we have a unique "corner" on good principles. You have plenty of your own. But we do know that the theories, processes and tools of Whole-Scale will only truly work if you believe these principles…*truly* believe them.

First, let us describe what the outcomes of this work need to be. Barry Camson, a senior consultant trained and experienced in Gestalt Therapy, process consultation and work design (STS) processes, describes it best. Barry visited us when we were working with a Ford Motor Company Plastics Plant some years ago. We had been dong the work for several months when he arrived, and the day of his arrival was the first day of a 250-person three-day launch event. Three DTA partners were facilitating the launch. Barry watched and noted what we did and wrote up a paragraph describing the outcomes, as follows:

> "This is a generative, transformative action. It is facilitated when people are fulfilling the need they have to have their voices heard and to belong to a community or society in which they believe. It starts with the existing perspectives and the individual truth that each person brings with them. It moves beyond that to a collective knowing – to a new ordering of old and new wisdom that comes from within and from outside the community. It expands what people know as individuals into a common database of what people know collectively. This knowing becomes the basis for their collective wisdom. What people know as a whole becomes their new truth. Generativity starts with each person's yearning and moves toward an image, an idea, a concept that serves to unite the yearnings of many diverse people and which has a universal appeal to it. Such an image appeals to the hearts as well as the minds of people. It is out of this generativity that new paths are forged which serve to integrate planning and action, policy and implementation."

Profound thoughts Barry uncovered—the real explanation, we believe, of the "magic" we keep uncovering in organizations. If you truly believe in the power and integrity described in that paragraph, take another step to look at another of Barry Camson's gifts to us.

Barry took notes during the three-day launch event he observed and sent them to us when he returned to Boston. His notes profoundly described everything we believed, and had worked out in our processes. Since that time, we have been using this brainstorm of principles as we teach people to do Whole-Scale work. They are true statements of the work we do with clients and why we do it.…in a large meeting, in a small meeting, in any part of the relationships we build and honor with our clients.

As you read these principle statements, look for one or two that are vitally important to you in your work with clients. These are so critical that you could never forget to live them. Then watch for statements that speak to what you truly believe, but you sometimes have a little trouble living. Get a colleague to read them also and identify the two types of statements. Take 20-30 minutes to share with each other what you have chosen and identify implications for the future:

WHOLE –SCALE PRINCIPLES

BARRY CAMSON, OBSERVER AND DOCUMENTOR

This work is about many things:

- Moving people from passivity to activity – the activity of mind, of action, of faith, of trust, of engagement of people with each other and their work.

  > e.g.   Representative participants are engaged in the planning and logistics process so as to move them from passivity to activity.

- A sincere, deep, abiding, unwavering, and non-faddish view of empowerment that runs to the core of one's being and is reflected in behaviors with other consultants, with the client and in how one works with the client. It is totally encompassing and pervasive.

- Personal commitment to contactfulness in any personal interaction, of expressing feelings and expectations, and a willingness to do so in as close to real time as the realities of the work allows. This results in an ability and willingness to facilitate and support the client in being similarly contactful with each other. Not doing the work as a consultant can result in blind spots with the client around the same issues.

- Tradition – a knowing, deep and abiding commitment to the roots of organization development as a democratic practice, which support the empowerment of people to achieve their full potential as individuals and as groups and to live in a humane way.

- Using the different technologies to carry out the intentionalities of democratic and empowering values rather than using the technologies in a detached or value-independent mode. It is about using the technologies in ways that continually track and respect where the organization is at any given moment in their path toward their desired future.

- Freeing up the flow of valid information within a client group and supporting that flow and helping people to develop and fully use the skills that will enable them to fully make use of the information.

- Living out of your heart.

- Sharing the wealth with the abiding faith that those who receive will do the same thus creating an ongoing, positive force for change.

- This work is about the assumption of responsibility by all. Participants operate in roles of facilitator, recorder, reporter. Ask everyone to take responsibility for creative thinking.

In doing Whole-Scale work, you will do the following things:

- Create a contactful environment. Contactfulness is built into the heart of the event. Enable people to make contact with each other. Facilitate points of contact among different views. Enable each person – leader, member, management, union – to articulate what he or she believes. Support each person in listening to the other's truth and not arguing with it.

  - From the very beginning, stress a different kind of listening—a neutral, non-judgmental kind of listening.

  - Support people in taking in and reflecting on what others have said.

    e.g., the open forum format of:
    - what we heard others say
    - what is our reaction to it
    - what questions of understanding do we have

    e.g., keep easels out of the way except when people are working on them so that nothing blocks contact, interaction.

    e.g., when asking questions of people up front in the open forum, put their name first.
  - Support a different kind of speaking as an alternative in which people take time to listen to themselves before speaking.

    e.g., facilitator suggests, "take a minute and go inside to reflect on your answers."

  - Also stress bringing the speaker's voice out into the room

    e.g., "telling our stories"

- Focus on the details of empowerment.

  - Help create an environment where people are willing to push-back and have comfort around that.

    e.g., ask participants if they got the answer they were looking for from the speaker. "Did he get it?" "Don't just say it was answered if it wasn't."

    e.g., "Don't let us beat you down" is an occasional reinforcing comment from the facilitator.

  - Create an environment that fosters a willingness, skills and a feeling of safety to speak out.

THE REAL SECRETS OF WHOLE-SCALE

- Create mini moments of truth.

    ➢ Ask people to speak out if their questions were not answered.

    ➢ Intervene to push leaders to answer tough questions.

        e.g., "Will you overrule the team's decision if you feel it was wrong?"

    ➢ Intervene to facilitate people getting to and speaking out of their courageous parts.

        e.g., "Do you believe him?" (in response to a leader's answer)

    ➢ Intervene to facilitate clean interactions.

    ➢ Intervene to paraphrase to help make points clear where there may be some confusion or to show where people agree.

- Create interaction based on a perspective of multiple realities. Help create an environment where each person realizes that they bring their own truth; that when dealing with each person's own truth, there is no right or wrong way.

    ➢ Help people become aware of how each hears the message differently. This reinforces awareness of multiple realities. It also enables people to begin to become aware of how their own filters, perspectives or need to be defensive impacts the message.

    ➢ Help people to attain some degree of neutrality regarding other peoples' truths. Help people to listen to see the world through each others' eyes.

        e.g., Leaders set out their truth, participants set out theirs.

- Operate with a maximum mix of viewpoints. Utilize microcosms of the whole – a holographic approach in Event Planning Team work, logistics team work and in some subgroupings used in the workshop.

- Create in the workshop a community operating from one brain and one heart. The community builds a common, interactive picture of their future arising from a common data base which is composed of the individual pictures of each member of the community. This leads to a common sense of caring amongst the members of the community.

- Derive everything in the workshop, in the change work of the organization, as well as its future operation from the vision and values. This is the major value and core of this process. The organization and consultant always tune into that and keep going back to it as the core of all current and future work.

Vision and values are powerful because they arise from full input of all members of the organization, the certainty of being heard, full opportunity for clarification, and consensus among everyone. The possibility of coercion is checked out.

- Help the organization have a common picture of where the organization wants to be and unite around some strategic direction—this becomes an important guide to the organization around choices.

- Bring data into the workshop forum from a variety of different sources and in a variety of different modes.

- Build competencies along the way, e.g. in listening, speaking, scribing, recording and in more subtle skills such as identifying themes.

- Use the dynamic huddle. "Stand, pull-up a few chairs." People end up standing, talking, huddling around their work. This results in keeping the room in motion, in ongoing momentum, activity. Instead of having groups sitting and working around tables all the time, a flow in the room is maintained by having people stay active.

- Enable the organization to diagnose itself and make meaning out of it.

    e.g., Sads, Mads and Glads look at what has worked, not worked in the organization.

    Hearing from competitors and best practices from site visits enables participants to diagnose what their own organization needs and could apply in moving to a desired future state.

- Help to build the organizational field. Provide input continually from different sources. The group field continues to be enhanced through discussions in different groups. Out of each of these groups emerges key questions which have the virtue of having the support or awareness of that group behind them. These questions are asked of people up front and perhaps of each other. The answers as well as the questions then move into the organization field from which new key questions, ideas, awareness arise on a large organizational level.

    e.g., Bring in input from a variety of outside sources using a variety of modes, e.g. customers, views of competitors, benchmarking ideas from other redesign sites through the research team.

    e.g., Facilitate creation of a larger and collective group field through the "Open Forum" which expressly looks at what people heard, what reactions and what questions of understanding they have.

- Create contact with outside information – from customers, from competitors, from benchmarked organizations. Activities in the workshop help facilitate this contact.

  e.g., Presentations by customers followed by an open forum. Role-play presentations of competitors followed by an open forum. Presentation by Event Planning Team after site visits followed by an open forum. Panel of Possibilities setting out what has worked, been problematic in other sites.

  Continually ask the implicit question: "what is the most important thing that has stood out for us that the organization could learn from?"

- Create the Event Planning Team/research team as a facilitating and catalyzing force for larger organizational involvement. Bring new people into this configuration from the organization and enable it to be used in different ways and in different configurations.

  Imagine a constantly changing, self-organizing entity moving through the heart of the larger organization, responding to different situations with different modes of self-organization as a model of the future and as a way of bringing light to and releasing energy in all different parts of the organization.

- Emphasize the importance of bringing yourself fully into the process as:

  ➢ Management leader

    e.g., leader shares a very personal vision. "I walk in and I see…."

    e.g., leader shares personal anecdotes of how she got where she was at the start of the work and how she moved to new places during the work.

  ➢ Union leader

    e.g., union leader sets out his high level of commitment and what the union is willing to do in the context of personal stories about himself. "My daddy once told me…."

  ➢ Members

    e.g., members are asked to tell their stories at an early part of the workshop.

    e.g., volunteerism to the extent used, asks the members to take an affirmative action to bring themselves more fully into the process – their volition married with their actions.

> Consultants

    e.g., the consultants constantly demonstrate and model that they are willing to be themselves and help the community gain some insight about this way of being.

- Demonstrate the value of transformational leadership. This is the process of speaking out, of allowing others the space for taking in what was said, the process of each enriching what the other has contributed. The act of taking in and enriching in return transforms the listener.

    e.g., the leader sets out his/her vision for the organization, the members take that in and enhance it with their own.

- End the work with specific, realistic and supported action plans with commitments made to take action on them. This enables moving from the desired future and supporting values – to intentionality and volition – and then to concrete behaviors. This is crucial in order to dispel the memories of past failures, to build credibility and to enable this work to have full operational value.

- As the consultant, be open to live your commitment to your client. Be open to that commitment engaging your heart, gut, intellect, and spirit and your values, personal vision, and enthusiasm. Be willing to be expressive about that commitment.

At the same time recognize that the client must decide to take responsibility for their individual change and for leading the organizational change. Consultant commitment to the client does not mean doing for the client.

Be prepared to live out of that commitment.

    e.g., "We'll come in that day for free if it will make the difference in bringing about the changes needed."

The commitment of consultant to the client at its ideal is based on unilateral love by the consultant for the client in which the consultant affirms the client for who he/she is. This results in pulling forth the essence of the client and a working relationship based on trust.

- Create a large group, total system dialogue.

  > Create conversations among small groups

  > Create conversations with sources bringing information into the room.

  > Create conversations among teams, sub-groups.

  > Create conversations between consultants and the client.

  > Create conversations among and within the large group.

- Have groups speak their commitment.

- Build teams at different levels of the organization.

       e.g.   Event Planning Team/research team
                      logistics team
                      individual, max-mix working groups
                      the overall organization

There is an undeniable power in having the whole organization in the room. It enables the organization to change in real time, both incrementally and in major paradigm shifts. It creates a common shared experience that the organization and all of its components can reference and operate out of in the future which will in time as it is enhanced take precedence over the old ways. The workshop becomes a river in which the many strands of the organization are immersed, risking a complex flow of chaotic elements until the threads of the new organization begin to emerge.

So, friendly Reader, there you have it -- just about everything we think we know at this moment. Let us know what you learn from what we've given you. We want to learn more! Good luck and thanks for hanging in with us…The Dannemiller Tyson Associates partners

ABOUT DANNEMILLER TYSON ASSOCIATES

For twenty years, Dannemiller Tyson Associates has pioneered large group processes that unleash true empowerment within organizations and communities, resulting in rapid, significant and lasting organizational change. We are passionate advocates for whole system. We, ourselves, are a virtual company, operating around the globe with one brain and one heart to help our clients be successful in their environment. Together with our clients, we focus on expanding the boundaries of whole-system approaches to change.

Our passion is to share with others the work we have created and what we continue to learn in our journey. In this book, we look at the way we make the change journey happen, to give you our tips on how to design Whole-Scale events as accelerators in that journey. In its companion book, *Whole-Scale Change: Unleashing the Magic in Organizations*, we cover the underlying theory, foundations, and history, taking you on the adventures which we have taken with organizations and communities around the world.

You can reach us, Dannemiller Tyson Associates, at www.dannemillertyson.com

ABOUT THE AUTHORS

JEFF BELANGER is an organization development practitioner. At the core of his work is attention to the system as a whole while focusing on specific organizational challenges. He specializes in coaching leadership teams for alignment and large-scale event design and facilitation.

ALBERT B. BLIXT came to whole system change work in the mid-1990's after multiple careers as a professor, attorney, art gallery owner and co-founder of a successful advertising agency. His practice focuses primarily on leadership development, strategic planning, culture change and team-based work redesign for business, government and non-profit clients. He enjoys the challenge of pushing the boundaries of the Whole-Scale™ approach to find new ways of engaging people in the change process. Al is the author of numerous articles on organizational change and other business subjects. He is the co-author of the 1996 book *Navigating In A Sea of Change* and a frequent public speaker. He holds a Juris Doctor degree from the University of Michigan.

KATHRYN CHURCH designs and facilitates group process including real time strategic change, strategic planning, team building, multiple party disputes, and workplace conflict. Kathy is particularly interested in dispute systems design, and is currently working with an organization of 850,000 employees, facilitating their dispute system design. Also she conducts on-site interventions to assist management, employees, and dislocated employees deal with the trauma of involuntary reduction-in-force (RIF), reorganizations, and workplace conflict. Ms. Church is qualified in the Myers-Briggs Type Indicator, and often uses "type" to enhance team performance or resolve workgroup conflict.

KATHLEEN D. DANNEMILLER is the founding partner in Dannemiller Tyson Associates and co-inventor of the Real Time Strategic Change and Real-Time Work Design (now called Whole-Scale). Kathie has been a passionate advocate of empowerment, systems theory and whole system change for more than 30 years. Kathie has been a consultant, coach and mentor to countless leaders, consultants and organizations as they build a better future. Kathie is recognized worldwide for her ability to move entire organizations forward with speed, depth and spirit. She believes there is no conversation that is above or beneath anyone and that everyone needs to have a voice, a real voice in shaping their future. She has been a political organizer at the national, state and local levels as well as a community organizer. She is a member of the National Training Laboratory and National Organization Development Network.

MARY EGGERS is a designer/facilitator of the Whole-Scale change process and of Developing Whole-Scale™ Change Competencies workshops. What excites her most is the opportunity to work in partnership to tap the spirit of individuals and organizations. This happens by involving everyone, empowering them to participate in meaningful ways and giving them a voice in creating and implementing the organizations preferred future. Mary has been in the field of organization development since 1985 and has experience in healthcare, education, government, information technology, not for profits and manufacturing. She has an MS in Organization Development from the American University/National Training Laboratories. She is a member of the National Organization Development Network, the Chesapeake Bay Organization Development Network, Women in Technology and the Strategic Leadership Forum Washington DC Chapter.

ALLEN B. GATES has extensive history as an executive leading and managing organizations using Whole-Scale change. Allen was a Ford Aerospace executive in the early 1980's when large scale, interactive change, the progenitor of Whole-Scale was invented by DTA. During the next 15 years, he led various change efforts, accomplishing dramatic and rapid results. He spent part of 1995 and 1996 as a DTA partner before returning to an executive role and returned as a DTA partner in late 1998. He worked for the US Navy at China Lake, CA as an engineer, line manager and program manager. After leaving China Lake, he worked in senior executive positions at Ford Aerospace, Computing Devices International, General Dynamics Information Systems, and was President, Kaiser Electronics. He holds BSME and MSME degrees from the University of Nevada, Reno, a PhD degree in Systems Engineering from Case-Western Reserve University (Navy Fellow) and and a SM in Mgt degree from MIT (Sloan Fellow).

LEIGH M. HENNEN is a seasoned professional with 28 years of broad experience in all aspects of Human Resource Management and Leadership, Organization Development, Strategic Planning, Whole Systems Change, and Employee and Marketing Communications. The first 26 years of Leigh's experience included management and executive roles in the Disk Drive Design and Manufacturing industry; the Aerospace Electronics Design, Manufacturing, and Systems Integration industry, and the Information Services industry. Leigh also had two years of experience as an independent Organization Development and Change Management Consultant prior to joining DTA as a partner. International experience includes a three-year expatriate assignment in the United Kingdom and a one-year assignment in Canada. Leigh's practice has primarily involved integration of Mergers and Acquisitions, Strategic Planning, Organizational Alignment, and Culture Change. Leigh is a member of the National Organization Development Network, the Society for Human Resource Management, the International Society for Human Resource Management, and the American Compensation Association.

SYLVIA JAMES has worked as an internal and external consultant for twenty-five years, pioneering Whole-Scale processes in aerospace in the early 80's. She works with communities and organizations to bring about a variety of whole system change efforts in high tech, service, manufacturing, government and education systems in North America and globally. She has extensive experience designing/facilitating large group interactive meetings involving over 1,000 participants for strategy, mergers, culture change, and organizational design. She has presented at conferences and led workshops on Whole-Scale processes in North America, Europe, the United Kingdom, and Australia. The past seven years she has specialized her practice in applying the Whole-Scale approach to organizational and work design, helping organizations to make rapid, sustained change in up to eleven core processes simultaneously, while creating a culture and structure to that enables results and agility. Sylvia's recent focus is creating one-brain, one-heart in virtual environments.

HENRY JOHNSON has been involved with OD technology, directly and indirectly for over twenty-five years, most recently focusing primarily on Whole-Scale™ change. He has spent the majority of his adult life in organizations that make a difference and sees his work with DTA as an extension of those efforts. His strengths are in Whole-Scale change technology related to organizational alignment, strategic planning, diversity training and culture change. He has a special interest in working with educational systems and transformation initiatives in urban areas. He is retired from the University of Michigan as Vice President Emeritus for Student Affairs and Community Relations, and has served as Trustee of the Ann Arbor Public Schools. Henry is a graduate of Morehouse College and Atlanta University. He holds certificates of postgraduate study from the Menninger Clinic, Topeka, Kansas, and from the Institute for Educational Management, Harvard University.

LORRI E. JOHNSON. Lorri's experience in the application of Whole-Scale methodology includes strategic planning, work redesign, and culture change. She has consulted in a wide range of industries such as automotive, manufacturing, health care, and information technology. Her interests include the use of Whole-Scale in government, community transformation, and the not-for-profit sector. In addition to the design/facilitation of large-scale interactive processes, her practice includes all phases of Whole-Scale ranging from leadership alignment through implementation. She is a faculty member of the Association for Quality and Participation/School for Managing and Leading Change. Lorri's background includes 14 years experience with Xerox Corporation and Bell & Howell in the areas of human resources, sales and marketing.

STAS' KAZMIERSKI spent 15 years as an internal consultant at Ford Motor Company creating high-performing teams, training/coaching team leaders and engineering program managers and redesigning Ford's product engineering process. He led the design of cross-functional, co-located vehicle platform teams for vehicle engineering and development. In the past nine years as an external consultant he has consulted in health care, manufacturing, mining and petroleum, energy, scientific research, universities, retail food, government and not-for-profit organizations. He holds a BS and MA in Education, and graduate work in chemistry and physics. His current interest is in creating strategically based, rapid, sustainable change in large organizations and helping to create organization and process designs that support humane workplaces.

RON KOLLER is an organization consultant, trainer and coach working unlock human potential at work. He specializes in working with front-line employees up to middle managers as they participate in whole system change. Ron consults with clients ranging from small business, construction companies, high tech, organized labor, aerospace, chemical, and automotive. Sports and entertainment are industries where his future work will take him.

ROLAND LOUP has been a consultant since 1986 using Whole-Scale change in high tech companies, healthcare, manufacturing, the service industry, government and academia. Roland also designs and leads courses in Whole-Scale change. Through his efforts in international training, consultation and coaching, he is working to ensure that the Whole-Scale approach is being used throughout the world. His consulting and courses have benefited organizations in the U.S., Canada, Europe, India and Australia. As a Whole-Scale practitioner he specializes in the architecture of system-wide change efforts, coaching individual leaders and leadership teams, and design and facilitation of large-group events. Over the past few years, he has begun applying the Whole-Scale approach to mergers and acquisitions. Roland is co-author of *Real Time Strategic Change: A Consultant Guide to Large-Scale Meetings*.

JIM McNEIL is a nationally recognized labor leader who brings a unique perspective and passion to the work of developing and improving labor/management relations. As a consultant and trainer, he specializes in organizational change. His background and hands-on experience with workplace change efforts and study of Organizational Development theory and practice provide a unique grasp of the issues that confront today's workers and employers. Jim is a retired three-term president of one of America's largest local unions. He has successfully negotiated numerous collective bargaining agreements with dozens of employers and was chairman of United Auto Worker's national negotiating committee at Ford in 1993 and 1996, where industry-wide patterns were developed.

PAUL D. TOLCHINSKY has been consulting to major companies in North America for the past twenty-five years. He has extensive experience in managing and facilitating large system change efforts; new plant design and start-ups; redesigning existing manufacturing facilities, particularly where unions are involved and has led numerous study missions to Japan. Paul's particular expertise is in the design of organizations, applying socio-technical principles and Whole-Scale Approaches to the process. He is internationally known as a pioneer in the development of Whole-Scale (Whole System) Approaches to change. The author of numerous articles, his work is featured in Large Group Interventions (Bunker and Alban, 1997) and Fusion Leadership, Daft and Lengel (1998). Dr. Tolchinsky is listed in Who's Who in Science and Technology and Who's Who in the Midwest. Dr. Tolchinsky received a BA in Business Administration from Bowling Green State University (1971 and a Ph.D. in Organization Behavior and Design from Purdue University (1978).